D1171370

Dickens and the 1830s

DICKENS
AND THE 1830s

KATHRYN CHITTICK

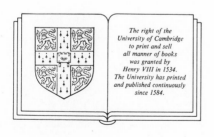

The right of the
University of Cambridge
to print and sell
all manner of books
was granted by
Henry VIII in 1534.
The University has printed
and published continuously
since 1584.

CAMBRIDGE UNIVERSITY PRESS

Cambridge

New York   Port Chester   Melbourne   Sydney

Published by the Press Syndicate of the University of Cambridge
The Pitt Building, Trumpington Street, Cambridge CB2 1RP
40 West 20th Street, New York, NY 10011, USA
10 Stamford Road, Oakleigh, Melbourne 3166, Australia

© Cambridge University Press 1990

First published 1990

Printed in Great Britain at the University Press, Cambridge

British Library cataloguing in publication data

Chittick, Kathryn
Dickens and the 1830s: Kathryn Chittick.
1. Fiction in English. Dickens, Charles, 1812–1870 –
Critical studies
I. Title
823'.8

Library of Congress cataloguing in publication data

Chittick, Kathryn, 1953–
Dickens and the 1830s / Kathryn Chittick.
    p.   cm.
Includes bibliographical references.
ISBN 0-521-38174-6
1. Dickens, Charles, 1812–1870. 2. Novelists, English – 19th
century – Biography. 3. Great Britain – History – William IV.
1830–1837 – Biography. I. Title.
PR4582.C48 1990
823'.8 – dc20
[B]   90-1404 CIP

ISBN 0 521 38174 6

WG

To
Garfield Dixon Chittick
(1927–1981)

"the sunk pillar"
        (Carlyle)

Contents

Preface   *page* ix
Acknowledgements   xii
Note on the text   xiv

1   1828–1833 The parliamentary reporter   1

2   Literature in 1833   18

3   1833–1836 The sketch writer   43

4   1836–1837 The qualifications of a novelist:
    Pickwick Papers and *Oliver Twist*   61

5   1837–1838 The editor of *Bentley's Miscellany*   92

6   1838 The writer of parts   114

7   1839–1840 The "Man of Feeling": *Nicholas
    Nickleby* and *Master Humphrey's Clock*   130

8   1839–1841 The historical novelist: *Jack
    Sheppard* and *Barnaby Rudge*   152

    Conclusion   178

    Notes   183
    Further reading   200
    Index   205

Preface

This study began as a historical account of the critical commentary that the work of Charles Dickens received during the early years of his writing career. My intention was not to compile statistical information about Dickens's readers or reputation but to consider his direction as an apprentice author in the context of London literary life during the 1830s. It was the profession of authorship that emerged as the dominant theme of my research, as I began to see that Dickens's transformation into a novelist during the years 1833 to 1841 was not the inevitable matter it is usually taken to be.

Dickens published his first sketch in December 1833; it was no more than the work of an anonymous and unpaid contributor to the old *Monthly Magazine*. Although he might be a professional newspaper-man, he was still an amateur in authorship. Eight years later, by December 1841, after nine books, three plays, and three magazines, Dickens, not yet thirty years old, worried that he might have written himself out. The work that was to have made his reputation as a respectable author, a three-volume historical novel in the mode of Sir Walter Scott, had been promised to his publisher in 1836; it did not appear until 1841 and went almost totally unnoticed. With the failure of that work, *Barnaby Rudge*, Dickens saw the literary profession he had projected for himself about to dwindle away: he could no longer rely on a mere change of binding to translate serial instalments into cloth volumes. All this was a matter of public knowledge and discussion in the periodical literature of the day.

In considering the development of Dickens during these years and how his writing changed the conventional generic expectations of the novel, one is in fact considering the literary criticism of the 1830s. After looking at one hundred and twenty magazines and newspaper titles — something like 25,000 daily issues, 12,000 weekly issues, 3,500 monthly issues, and 225 quarterly issues — I have seen over eight hundred reviews of Dickens's work for the years 1833–41. In attempting to understand the literary scene onto which he made his entrance, I have also looked at four hundred reviews of ancillary interest which treat of such topics as the status of the professional journalist, the nature of the contemporary novel, and the domination of literary life by Reform Bill politics. All these things had their part in what was seen by contemporary critics as the decline of the traditional canon of literature. It is a small but notable fact that Dickens was not reviewed under the heading of "Literature" when he began writing those works that are now classics of the English curriculum. This points to a historical difference between what the term meant for the early nineteenth century and what it means for us. During the 1830s, books of biography and literary criticism filled the newspaper columns under "Literature," while novels were found among the ephemeral notices; reviews of Dickens's books are generally to be looked for under the headings of "Magazine Day" and "Miscellaneous." Today, Dickens is a staple of literary studies, while it is considered mildly innovative to include biography in the curriculum and to argue that criticism is itself a type of fiction writing. In 1830, biography was unquestionably part of the literary canon, and criticism was far more respectable than the novel.

The definition of "Literature" is also crucial to the later chapters, as I follow Dickens's transition from reporter to author. I attempt to understand what the prospects facing Dickens were in 1833, when he had already won some acclaim as a reporter, and to show the direction given him by contemporary commentators, some of whom were known to him personally. The explosion of reviews during 1837–38 forms the most intense period of his early career, and it was the notice given *Oliver Twist* and *Nicholas Nickleby* that may be said to have propelled Dickens to the attention of the quarterly guardians of literature.

Yet, at the same time, Dickens seems to show a far more determined interest in becoming known as an editor. The preface written for *Nicholas Nickleby* at the close of its serial run, and the alacrity with which he took up plans for *Master Humphrey's Clock* when his editorship of *Bentley's Miscellany* ended, show Dickens's fondness for the editorial role. This aspect of his early writing cannot be overlooked: the preoccupation of Dickens with journalistic ventures helped change the generic nature of the novel. *Pickwick* was essentially a magazine consisting of only one article, and *Oliver Twist* merely political ephemera, before they came arbitrarily to be bound in cloth volumes and called novels.

However, Dickens's failure to become the editor of a popular magazine and to project himself as a historical novelist meant

Preface

that by 1841 he was forced to halt and consider where his future
direction as a writer was to lie. The Victorian novel has many
beginnings, and Dickens's insistence on remaining a Fleet Street
man is one of them. The discussion of how his works moved from
the "Magazine" columns to the "Literature" columns is both
a historical and a critical one.

Acknowledgements

It is a pleasure to acknowledge the help of all those who have made the experience of writing this book such an enjoyable one. K. J. Fielding introduced me to Dickens scholarship, and I benefited inestimably from early discussions with him. John Sutherland and Philip Collins were generous, too, in sharing their knowledge of Dickens and Victorian studies. And Roy Graham also encouraged me through the years with my thinking about this research. For guidance in the field of Victorian periodicals, I must, as always, thank Merrill Distad.

Most of my research has been done at the National Library of Scotland, where the staff met my requests with unfailing assiduity and humour, and I have fond memories of my summers there. The British Library at Bloomsbury was also important to my research, and I am grateful for access to that collection and to the collection of nineteenth-century newspapers at Colindale, which is unrivalled. The Harriet Irving Library at the University of New Brunswick, with its exceptional collection of Dickens material, proved an unexpectedly significant aid.

The Social Sciences and Humanities Research Council of Canada provided the main source of my financial support for these researches, and Queen's University and Trent University were generous with their limited research funds. And I should also like to acknowledge the assistance of Anthony Pugh and Anne Cameron at the University of New Brunswick in helping me to pursue this work.

I am grateful for the interest and support of my colleagues at Trent, including Orm Mitchell and Michael Treadwell. Zailig Pollock and Fred Tromly were generous with their personal time and scholarly advice, and Barb Mitchell gave me welcome last-minute assistance.

Susan Anderson caught many errors early on and produced an admirable typescript. Laurie Gehrling guided me patiently through the technical difficulties of word processing. And for continual help and support of the sort that can never adequately be acknowledged, I am grateful to Mary Chittick.

xii

Acknowledgements

Kevin Taylor at Cambridge University Press was a source of much cheerful encouragement throughout the process of producing this book, and I am pleased to acknowledge the importance of his assistance. My copyeditor, Mary Baffoni, proved to be both thoughtful and efficient in handling a mass of detail and weeding out mistakes.

Finally, I could not have produced this book without the help of Stephen Brown, who scrutinized every word of this script. The mistakes are all my own, but I have found it impossible to do without his imaginative suggestions and critical toughness.

The book is dedicated to the memory of my father, Garfield Dixon Chittick, whose gentle curiosity was unquenchable and who pursued his researches with persistence and complete self-abandonment.

Note on the text

To save on footnoting, most references to contemporary periodicals are given parenthetically after the passages quoted. For a complete list of the periodicals consulted as background research to this study, the reader is advised to see my *The Critical Reception of Charles Dickens 1833–1841* (New York: Garland, 1989). It includes approximately eight hundred reviews of Dickens's works for these years and another four hundred reviews of critical interest for the years 1814–41; the reviews are listed by chronological appearance, by periodical, and by the work of Dickens reviewed.

References to Dickens's works are to the original editions except where stated otherwise.

1

1828 – 1833 The parliamentary reporter

I

Literary critics have usually had little to say about the 1830s. The era between the Prince Regent and the Prince Consort is often thought of as an interregnum. The great men of the Romantic era, Byron, Napoleon, and Beau Brummell, had all died in exile, and William IV's reign (1830–37) seems but a brief prelude to the settling in of the domesticity of Victoria and Albert and *In Memoriam*. Still, the bohemian literary life of that decade took on something of a legendary nature for the young inhabitants of New Grub Street who came afterwards. A generation of writers of whom Dickens is only the most famous served their apprenticeship then. A number of them, including Dickens, left highly personal accounts of these formative years: *Pendennis, Godfrey Malvern, Ranthorpe,* and *David Copperfield.*

Thackeray's Arthur Pendennis represents the typical young literary idler who imagines that a bit of writing will support him until called to a proper profession such as the bar. He falls for the cheerful projections of an Irish newspaper man – clever Irishmen and scandalous sporting papers were a quintessential feature of Regency London – who tells him that a successful novelist can command £300 a volume. Thus, with the help of a few mediocre verses and an Irishman, Pendennis makes his début as a hack and gets some books to review. His future seems assured. He will take up his legal studies ("I shall take chambers ... and enter myself at an Inn of Court") and in the meantime take his place in the literary world ("I have little doubt my pen will support me, as it is doing with several Oxbridge men now in town").[1] Pendennis is perhaps complacent because, along with his verses and his reviews, he has also a tragedy, a comedy, and a novel in his trunk: there is therefore every reason to believe that this twenty-one year old will dazzle the London literary world. None the less, even his closest friend remains oddly sceptical of this hero's talent: "There are thousands of clever fellows in the world who could, if they would, turn verses, write articles, read books, and deliver a judgment upon them" (I, 327).

This satire on the vanities of authorship is one of the most constant features of a novel where the rhetoric about literature is steadily unromantic. The daily drudgery of the author's life is one ingredient of Thackeray's realism, and, by the second volume, it becomes apparent that a naive climb to fame could never be mistaken for this novel's definition of heroism. Pendennis's fine speeches about critical honesty and Grub Street's reform are put down to youthful conceit merely. When his own precious volume of verses is published, it is handed over by his editor to a critic named Bludyer: this dispassionate judge, "having cut up the volume to his heart's content, went and sold it at a bookstall, and purchased a pint of brandy with the proceeds of the volume" (I, 352). Pendennis's biographer does not seem to find this a harsh or inappropriate fate.

Still, it is acknowledged that Pendennis's hackwork for the *Pall Mall Gazette* is proficient of its kind, and for this he earns £4 4s a week; with freelance magazine work, his annual salary comes to £400 a year, a rather good sum for an unmarried man. Pendennis's eighteen-twentyish fashionable novel, *Walter Lorraine*, written while he is a young man at Oxford, also does well. But Thackeray's realistic novel of the 1840s preaches scepticism in the face of such success:

I shall not mention what was the sum of money which Mr. Arthur Pendennis finally received for the first edition of his novel of "Walter Lorraine," lest other young literary aspirants should expect to be as lucky as he was, and unprofessional persons forsake their own callings, whatever they may be, for the sake of supplying the world with novels, whereof there is already a sufficiency. Let no young people be misled and rush fatally into romance-writing ... (*Pendennis* II, 29)

What young writers might be apt to overlook is that *Walter Lorraine*'s publication owes more to the quality of its author's gloves than his talents. In selling Pendennis's novel to an interested publisher, his friend Warrington emphasizes that Pendennis is himself a member of the best London society. The publisher is a social climber who has no opinions on the novel itself and leaves the reading of it to paid hacks and to his wife; in calling on Pendennis, he happens to see various cards of the *haut monde* on the young man's table, and this fortunate accident clinches Pendennis's future. Pendennis's reputation by virtue of his manners, dress, and invitations is that of a man who can write at his leisure − "than which there cannot be a greater recommendation to a young literary aspirant" (I, 355). It is to the acceptance of his person that Pendennis owes the acceptance of his novel. Warrington may be just as trenchant in his criticism, and Captain Shandon may be a good deal more learned, but it is Pendennis who acquires the reputation both for gentlemanly frankness and for scholarship.

After a while, Warrington's social status is exploded by the revelation of a *déclassé* marriage, and Captain Shandon, like too many real literary men of the time, is relegated to prison.[2] Pendennis's friendship with him after this seems almost an act of condescension. For Pendennis comes (and it is this which marks him as the hero) into property. His uncle Major Pendennis says, "You are like the fellow in Sterne, sir – the Marquis who came to demand his sword again ... never forget you are a gentleman" (II, 230). Little more about Pendennis's daily routine as a writer is heard of after this. A landowner now, he looks forward to becoming an M.P. and a husband. Marriage earlier in the story would have meant not only financial hardship but also professional disgrace – *vide* Warrington, who must virtually put his wife away in order to carry on in literary society, and Shandon, whose wife is hardly to be seen outside the prison she must share with him. However, property safe in hand, Pendennis's moral career is capped by prudent marriage to a respectable woman who will not have her value impugned by taking up residence in Grub Street. The moral seems to be that writing for newspapers and leading the life of a literary hack constitute a form of wild oats, something forgivable only in bachelors.

This is the moral, too, of *Godfrey Malvern; or The Life of an Author* (1842) – a working-class *Pendennis* – by Thomas Miller (1807–74), a poet and author of some forty-five works. Miller was a basket-maker who came to London to set up a business, and having enclosed some of his verses in baskets sent to the Countess of Blessington, was noticed by the most fashionable part of literary society.[3] The hero of Miller's novel, Godfrey Malvern, is a poor country schoolteacher who writes some verses, and, having achieved a local fame, goes to London. He is fortunate enough to be given reviewing hackwork and to have verses accepted by an annual, one of the coffee-table books of pictures and verse that were in their heyday during the twenties and thirties. His verses are noticed by Lady Smileall (perhaps a compliment to the Countess), who invites him to one of her soirées, where his figure and face are striking enough for him to make a hit. With a reputation for being "intellectual" (he is tall), he thus falls into what Miller calls the

3

"'LITERARY RAT-TRAPS.'"[4] This is a facile kind of literary celebrity Victorian novelists are always warning their readers against, as if it were a particularly regular temptation of the era. Miller is as moralistic as Thackeray in showing how a young author may be falsely seduced by the hectic social blandishments of London into becoming one of its passing entertainments:

> There is a kind of neutral ground which talented authors will ever occupy; and although they may never become what the world calls "gentlemen," in the worldly sense of the word, still they will always be received and treated with respect, by those who move in the highest circles of fashionable society.
> (*Godfrey Malvern* I, 59)

Malvern's rural schoolmastering background is completely forgotten, and as a sort of natural reward for versemaking and poetic good looks, he becomes the lover of a dark-eyed young Brompton woman.

Unlike Pendennis, however, Malvern is already married. In the country scenes during the first third of the novel, he has wooed and won the squire's daughter. In London, Malvern attends his literary assemblies as a bachelor, as was the custom. Malvern's moral position is akin to that of Thackeray's Warrington, but he does not maintain the same integrity. Eventually, for all her tempestuous intellect, the dark-eyed young lady falls in love with the tall Malvern and becomes pregnant. All is made right at the end, however: the mistress conveniently dies in childbirth and Malvern goes back to his country wife. And like Pendennis, he turns out to be really a gentleman after all, for he is discovered to be the rightful heir to the squire's estate. The false mistress Literature is powerless to keep the hero from his rightful consort – Politics.

In his literary life, Malvern, like Pendennis, had taken to heart the advice offered by his first editor, that although "The political principles of a literary man have often a great influence in his works … an author ought not to belong to any party" (I, 108). But it is perhaps a sign of the fascination of political topics for this period that, even if both Malvern and Pendennis easily enough put politics to one side in their literary lives, in their prosperity they choose to stand as members of Parliament. The question of party is fudged in both cases: it is the issues embraced – the Poor Law and repeal of the Corn Law – which are given pride of place. Thus, it is boasted of Malvern, "he is not the man to say, 'Aye, or No,' at the bidding of any party-leader in the House" (II, 397). Pendennis also refuses to be a party man and tells Warrington, "There are no politics now; every man's politics, at least, are pretty much the same" (II, 309).

4

Later, he will describe himself as a Liberal Conservative, which is to say:

"I shall go pretty much with Government, and in advance of them upon some social questions which I have been getting up during the vacation; – don't grin, you old Cynic [this aside to Warrington], I *have* been getting up the Blue Books, and intend to come out rather strong on the Sanitary and Colonisation questions." *(Pendennis* II, 309)

The connection between literature and politics is crucial to any study of the 1830s. John O. Hayden in his introduction to *British Literary Magazines: The Romantic Age 1789–1836* is inclined to discount the importance of party politics in reviewing at this time, and this is suggested by the personal stances of Dickens and Thackeray, both of whom showed a distaste for party-mongering though not for politics. Hayden cites a discussion by De Quincey in 1835, for example, on the question of Coleridge's political affiliations. In his essay "Samuel Taylor Coleridge" published in *Tait's Edinburgh Magazine*, De Quincey argues that the terms *Whig* and *Tory* are being replaced by "Conservative" and "Reforming," and that the strength of institutionalized party interests is much overestimated.[5] *Whig* and *Tory* are merely two varieties of aristocratic feeling; Reformism is the popular sentiment of the day, allied to the growth of the fourth estate.

In defence of Coleridge's infamous Toryism, De Quincey further argues that, for the generation before Reform, Toryism had meant little more than support of the war against Napoleon, and Whiggism, withdrawal from Europe. It so happened that the Tories were in power when war was declared and hence became the party of nationalism and the defence of Europe against Napoleonic imperialism: "all distinctions of party were annihilated – Whig and Tory were merged and swallowed up in the transcendent duties of patriots" *(Tait's* NS 2 no. 13 Jan. 1835: 8). The parliamentary Whigs may have tried to maintain some sense of themselves as the Opposition, but opposition to the defence of liberty could only make for a sterile existence in the 1790s, and in so far as they might have insisted upon party distinctions, the Whigs extinguished themselves. Coleridge would not be the only example of a Tory tracing his pedigree back to Napoleon.

The Whigs were no stronger in 1830, for by then national sentiment was Reformist, and this merely shifted the emphasis slightly on to them as the other half of the coalition. Peel was astute enough to realize that though in opposition the Tories might still direct Government policy; when the reaction against the Whigs came in 1835, he had succeeded in distinguishing the "Conservatives" from the old patriot Tories. His triumph in 1841 was impatiently awaited from the mid-thirties.[6]

The Peelite statements of both Malvern and Pendennis are a faithful reflection of the prevailing sentiment after Reform had had its day: "The fiercest reformers grow calm, and are fain to put up with things as they are" (*Pendennis* II, 233). This brand of 1840s popular liberalism does not pass without satiric jibes from Warrington:

"We give lectures at the Clavering Institute, and shake hands with the intelligent mechanics. We think the franchise ought to be very considerably enlarged; at the same time we are free to accept office some day, when the House has listened to a few crack speeches from us, and the Administration perceives our merit." (*Pendennis* II, 310)

Not all novels of literary life in the 1830s end with the translation of an author into landowner and parliamentarian. George Henry Lewes's *Ranthorpe*, written in the year of *Godfrey Malvern*'s publication and published five years later (1847), depicts the author's life as an ambition for its own sake. The hero, Percy Ranthorpe, is an attorney's clerk at 10s a week who writes poetry and is impatient "to set himself fairly afloat upon the wide sea of literature."[7] The trouble is, as a publisher tells him, that poetry is no longer the rage that it was in the 1820s: " 'I couldn't sell "Childe Harold" if it were now first published' " (18). However, Ranthorpe is finally launched when a newspaper editor offers him a guinea a week to write regular theatrical reviews and occasional poetry criticism. The young critic's pride in his profession is supreme: "Every Sunday morning the paper lay upon his breakfast-table, and made him feel that he was 'somebody,' as he cut the leaves and eagerly read over his own contributions" (38). Alas, this pleasure palls after his Sunday appearances have become a matter of routine. He publishes a volume of poetry at his own expense, quits his job and starts work on a tragedy. He becomes a Literary Lion.

Lewes is agreed with Miller and Thackeray that lionism is not necessarily a sign of genius: "handsome young men, of gentlemanly bearing, and living in a certain style, are always gladly invited to parties" (60). However, the fawning approbation of Ranthorpe's person at fashionable parties gains him neither lasting affection nor glowing reviews. His second volume of poetry is panned, and his tragedy is treated as a farce. At this point, Ranthorpe escapes for two years to Germany, where he gives English lessons and devotes himself to private study.[8] The work of this interval enables him to produce a dramatic work of solid merit. Lewes is elliptical about exactly how Ranthorpe manages to get his drama staged — "the usual harassing preliminaries, which need not again be described" (285) — but his success this time is emphatic, and "Ranthorpe from that day took his place amongst the literary men of England" (285). This time he avoids the pitfalls of literary lionism and adheres to a quiet routine where the reward of an author's life is the creative life itself. Lewes's novel, which is a good deal shorter than *Malvern* or *Pendennis*, ends with domestic peace and professional activity: "The storms are below him. The poor attorney's clerk has become an honoured author" (350). Lewes does not seem to find it remarkable that this serenely famous man is only twenty-five years old.

Unlike Miller or Thackeray, Lewes is at pains to stress that authorship is an honourable profession. The literary activities of Godfrey Malvern and Arthur Pendennis fall out of view once their position in society is established by other means, and, in retrospect, their literary life is known only as a period of temptations and failures. The solitary pleasures, whatever they might be, remain undepicted. What becomes of lifelong bohemians such as Captain Shandon is not significant. In fact, the scholar and hack generally taken to be the original of Shandon, William Maginn, died bankrupt and consumptive in 1842 — the same year *Ranthorpe* was completed and *Malvern* published.

There is reason to believe that Lewes had the career of Dickens in mind when he wrote *Ranthorpe*. The editors of Dickens's letters remark that the novel "betrays Lewes's mingled admiration and half-jealousy of CD's 'genius' and success."[9] And reading Lewes's maxim that, even if one is "immortal amongst gerunds" at Cambridge, a knowledge of books is insufficient to compete with a knowledge of life, one cannot help but think of the young Boz, famous at twenty-four. Dickens did not come down from Oxbridge, a book of poems tucked carelessly under his arm, to dabble in law and literature. The practice of law was not for him something to be put off as long as possible with Pendennian idylls in Bohemia. He never had the leisure to write a *Walter Lorraine* — or any three-volume novel. Nor was newspaper work a casual pocket-money affair for Dickens, who took great pains to get taken on full-time at the *Morning Chronicle*. Not a scholar or a gentleman, nor ever likely to be, his great advantage over an Oxbridge wit was to be already in London and at work. In the early years he did show some jealousy of the institutionalized rewards of the life of the bar and the three-volume novel, but his own urgent need of a living resulted in his making professional authorship uniquely remunerative. Dickens read *Ran-thorpe*, and he expressed great pleasure at its moral to Lewes: "When Literary men shall begin to feel the honor and worth of their pursuit, as you would teach them to, Literature will be a happier calling" (*Letters* V, 191). Much as Dickens responded to *Pendennis* (and Thackeray noted the writing in *David Copperfield* as one sign that he was responsive), he and Thackeray were always to be at variance on the respectability of the literary profession.[10]

Dickens's novel of literary apprenticeship contains no fond accounts of the Bohemia frequented by Arthur Pendennis. David Copperfield approaches reporting with a blueprint for fame: "I had heard that many men distinguished in various pursuits had begun life by reporting the debates in Parliament."[11] In the MS, for "various pursuits," Dickens originally wrote "at the bar and in other pursuits," and, as we shall see, the combination of parliamentary reporting and legal studies was commonly taken as a route to success. When David looks back at this period later, he ascribes his "success" to "thorough-going, ardent, and sincere earnestness" (518). Where *Pendennis* dilates on the pleasures of good living, *David Copperfield* praises undivided attention to work: "Never to put one hand to anything, on which I could throw my whole self; and never to affect depreciation of my work, whatever it was; I find, now, to have been my golden rules" (518). The ascent into authorship is equally single-minded. David one day sends something to a magazine, and quite simply by the next he has a regular income. What takes Lewes or Thackeray a whole volume to relate occupies Dickens for no more than a paragraph. The praise of critics seems to have been anticipated, and David is self-collected enough not to have his head turned. Whatever temptations in the way of literary lionism he has to endure take no more than a paragraph to recount (588). The last extended treatment of the topic of his vocation is just another aside: "Having some foundation for believing, by this time, that nature and accident had made me an author, I pursued my vocation with confidence" (589).

The evidence provided by the letters of Dickens himself undercuts the idea that any author's relationship to his vocation is a straight-forward one. The word "accident" in David's description should not be overlooked. We may be reminded of it when reading a con-temporary discussion of professional authorship. In the *Morning Advertiser* of 19 April 1838, there is a letter to the editor which in the context of the copyright debate then going on talks about the inducements – or lack of them – to take up authorship as a living. The writer of the letter comments on how nearly it was, for instance, that Scott did not publish *Waverley,* because of the low status accorded to authors. Of the recent rise to fame of Charles Dickens, the letter comments, "He has got beyond his *accidents*[12] — that is all."

The letter goes on to stress how unlikely it was that *Sketches by Boz* or *Pickwick Papers* should ever have been published:

Some will believe that when an author displays himself to be a genius, and produces certain works — that these were inevitable — that he being a genius *must* have of necessity produced these very works. To an author this will at once appear an absurdity ... (*Morning Advertiser* 19 Apr. 1838)

Critics since 1838 have continued to commit this kind of absurdity; they continue to discuss the development of Dickens into Boz, man of letters, retrospectively — that is to say, as inevitable. What is offered here instead is an account of the uncertainties of the young reporter in the parliamentary press gallery of 1833 — when Dickens hardly knew whether or not he should turn out to be the hero of his own life.

II

In order to understand Dickens's movement into the realms of professional authorship, it is useful to look more narrowly at what the life of a parliamentary reporter would have been like during the 1830s. In the first years of the decade, Dickens's alternating ambitions were to get taken into the law or to become a full-time reporter on one of the prominent dailies. His training in shorthand was the first step to be taken in either case. Like David Copperfield, he had noticed that many distinguished careers had begun in the parliamentary press gallery. It is important to see how the circumstances of such a life then intersected with the emerging ambition to become a writer.

Dickens's career as a parliamentary reporter coincides with the years of most intense political excitement for the early nineteenth century. He became a freelance shorthand reporter in 1828, and, between the ages of sixteen and twenty-one (1828–33), witnessed the repeal of the Test Act, the end of George IV's reign, the passage of the first Reform Bill, and two general elections in two years. In 1833, when his first sketch appeared, he had been a shorthand reporter on the *Mirror of Parliament* for at least two years and on the *True Sun* for an overlapping period of five months (March–July 1832). He came into parliamentary reporting just as momentous changes for the better were taking place. Over the course of the late eighteenth and early nineteenth centuries, parliamentary reporters had to fight Parliament's objections, first, to "strangers" being admitted ("I espy strangers" signalled the closing of the gallery), to notes being taken, and, finally, to seats being specially provided for those taking notes. But by 1828, Macaulay was able to say that "The gallery in which the reporters sit, has become a fourth estate of the realm" ("Hallam's Constitutional History," *Edinburgh Review* 48 no. 95 Sept. 1828: 165), and he traced support for the reporting of parliamentary proceedings to growing public criticism of the British constitution. Parliament had used to be the public censor of the Crown and hence preferred to preserve some secrecy about its proceedings; by the late eighteenth century, however, the People had found in the press their censor of the Government. The pressure of interest in Reform was such that the Lords allotted a separate row for reporters in its strangers' gallery in 1831 and, when the new Houses were erected in 1835, reporters got their own permanent galleries and no longer had to jostle with the casual public for seats.[13]

The *Morning Chronicle* had long been famous for the quality of its parliamentary reporting, and John Black (1783–1855), its editor for the years 1817–43, was universally respected. Understandably, Dickens's ambition at this time was to become a full-time reporter on the *Morning Chronicle*. Coincidentally, though, he was to attain this just when the writing career he had improvised for himself in the recesses between parliamentary sittings began to take on its own momentum. For, despite all the political excitement of the early 1830s, Dickens was generally left without work in the ebb-time when Parliament was not sitting. As he says in a letter of 6 June [1833] to the private secretary to Lord Stanley, who had praised Dickens's accuracy, "I am always entirely unemployed during the recess" (*Letters* I, 30). His request to Earle on this occasion for a recommendation to other shorthand work was unsuccessful, as were efforts at this time to be taken on at the *Morning Chronicle*. During the recess and election of 1832, he found work as a poll clerk. During the parliamentary recess of 1833, he seems to have produced his first sketch, "A Dinner at Poplar Walk," which appeared in December 1833. He finally became a reporter for the *Morning Chronicle* in August 1834, when the paper had been sold to John Easthope and two others.

During his tenure on this paper, in addition to his parliamentary reporting, Dickens covered a banquet given in Edinburgh for Earl Grey (September 1834), Lord Russell's campaign for a seat at South Devon (May 1835), a "Liberal" members' dinner at Bristol

(November 1835), and a Northamptonshire by-election (December 1835) – all "express" features requiring the alacrity for which Dickens was specially known among newspaper men. As Dickens himself described his life then,

Returning home from exciting political meetings in the country to the waiting press in London, I do verily believe I have been upset in almost every description of vehicle known in this country. I have been, in my time, belated on miry by-roads, towards the small hours, forty or fifty miles from London, in a wheelless carriage, with exhausted horses and drunken post-boys, and have got back in time for publication, to be received with never-forgotten compliments by the late Mr. Black ...[14]

The editor of the *Morning Chronicle*, whose leading articles were highly rated for intellectual ableness, was not the only one to compliment the young Dickens. Another newspaper man, James Grant (1802–79), singled out Dickens in a section on parliamentary reporting in *The Great Metropolis* (1836), saying that he "is one of the most promising literary young men of the present day."[15] Grant reiterated his opinion thirty-five years later in *The Newspaper Press* (1871–72): "a more talented reporter never occupied a seat in the gallery of either House of Parliament."[16]

Other sources for what we know about reporting during the 1830s include Charles Mackay's *Forty Years' Recollections* (1877), and S.C. Hall's *Retrospect of a Long Life* (1833). From these we learn, with hindsight, the excellence of Dickens as a reporter. But for a less selective and celebratory view of the reporter's life during this time, we may wish to turn to accounts in contemporary periodicals. "Place-men, Parliament-men, Penny-a-liners, and Parliamentary Reporters" (by William Maginn, perhaps with J.A. Heraud), in *Fraser's Magazine* of October 1830, is mostly a sketch of the Parliament of 1830 in the aftermath of Catholic emancipation, rendered in *Fraser's* typically querulous manner: "A more petty-larceny looking set of rogues never yet projected a small robbery, or debated on the division of sixpenny spoil" (2 no.9 Oct. 1830: 282). From the individual sketches drawn here of James Graham, Henry Goulburn, J.C. Herries, William Huskisson, Michael Sadler, James Mackintosh, Joseph Hume, and Daniel O'Connell, one derives some notion of the Parliamentary boredom and nonsense, making it clear that Dickens's own satires of the House cannot be accused of exaggeration.

Fraser's noted that the press was under attack from the House at this time. In response to one member's complaints about the press's misrepresentation of his speeches, the article goes on to describe how the reporters produced their copy:

There are only three papers in London that profess to give a fair and full account of the debates. – The *Morning Chronicle*, the *Times*, and the *Morning Herald*. There are from ten to twelve reporters engaged by each of these papers, at a salary of between three and four hundred pounds a year. They take notes in the gallery for three quarters of an hour, and returning to the office they spend four or five hours in writing those at large.

(*Fraser's Magazine* 2 no. 9 Oct. 1830: 292)

The article implies that this work is a sort of metaphorical alchemy, where the reputation for exact reporting is not easily maintained, and the reporter has as well to possess an "extreme facility of composition, to enable him on the moment to fill up the *lacunae* which must necessarily exist in the most perfect note-book" (293).

In a more sociological description of the types of men who became reporters, the article adds that reporting "is for the most part adopted merely as a temporary assistance by men engaged in some other pursuit. The reporters of the *Times* and *Chronicle* are, with scarcely an exception, law-students" (293).[17] This knowledge is helpful in allowing us to understand the context in which Dickens took up short-hand while employed as a law clerk during the years 1827–28, as well as the process by which he was to abandon the law. In 1828, when Dickens's uncle began the *Mirror of Parliament*, a rival to *Hansard*, John Dickens learned shorthand and began a journalistic career of sorts. In the wake of his father's new occupation, Dickens also learned shorthand, quit the law, and set up as a freelance shorthand reporter in Doctors' Commons till he could get a regular job as a newspaper reporter. Meanwhile, Thomas Mitton, his friend of these clerkship years, stayed on at Molloy's, one of two solicitors for whom Dickens had briefly worked, and became qualified as a lawyer in 1833.

Perhaps it was Mitton's example that kept up Dickens's attachment to the law, for, despite our retrospective insight that he was meant to be a writer, it was far from obvious to Dickens himself during these years. Even in 1834, a few months after he had obtained the long-coveted post on the *Morning Chronicle*, Dickens could write, "I intend entering at the bar, as soon as circumstances will enable me to do so" (*Letters* I, 43; 13 Nov. [1834]); and a few years later, when *Nicholas Nickleby* had just come to a triumphant close, he paid the fees and put himself on the books as a student at Middle Temple in December 1839. Much later, in the 1840s, in that dangerous fretful time between *Martin Chuzzlewit* and *Dombey and Son*, Dickens would half-heartedly consider resuming his legal training and reversing that transition made fifteen years earlier from law to journalism: "I am (nominally, God knows) a Law Student, and have a certain number of 'terms to keep' [*sic*] before I can be called to the Bar; and it would be well for me to be called, as there are many little pickings to be got – pretty easily within my reach – which *can* only be bestowed on Barristers" (*Letters* IV, 534; 17 Apr. 1846). The theatre was always a similar kind of vocational dalliance, from the time of Doctors' Commons when he arranged for an audition at Covent Garden. Its fascination later found its way into amateur theatricals at the same time when Dickens's work for the philanthropic Miss Coutts was itself becoming a kind of informal magistracy. As Dickens said jokingly to John Forster when confiding some of these ventures of early life: "See how near I may have been to another sort of life" (*Life* I, iv, 50).

Thus in the days of clerkhood, when his main vocation as a writer had not yet become clear to Dickens, he was one among any number of young men who looked about for extra money and went to the theatre every night. The shorthand training and the British Museum reader's ticket would not be uncommon features of the law student's life. Later, such experience, added to parliamentary reporting, was to serve the same function in supporting the pursuit of a writing life. The important thing to realize about Dickens's choice of profession at this time is that he was above all ambitious, regardless of what form that ambition took. Describing to Forster his decision to concentrate on reporting rather than go for another acting audition at that time, he said: "I made a great splash in the gallery soon afterwards; the *Chronicle* opened to me; I had a distinction in the little world of the newspaper, which made one like it; began to write; didn't want money, had never thought of the stage but as a means of getting it" (*Life* I, iv, 50). The emphasis here is on the determination to succeed, in whatever way possible.

Whether or not authorship could be considered a profession generally included the question as to whether or not a reporter could be considered a gentleman. Hence the *Fraser's* writer, citing all the prominent men who had once been reporters, felt it necessary to defend the parliamentary press, "As a body I know no charge which can be made against them, save that they are so poor as to be compelled to enter an intellectual tread-mill for a consideration of three hundred pounds a year" (294). Throughout his professional life as an author, Dickens was much concerned with the question of the literary man's status, and the editors of the fifth volume of the Pilgrim

Letters remark that Dickens and Forster did not distinguish the profession of authorship from journalism (V, ix). Despite, however, the great increase in professional literary men's societies during Dickens's lifetime, the consensus would seem to be that journalism was not a respectable way to make a living. Because of the party-mongering that went on among all the newspapers, slander was considered to be part of the stock-in-trade.[18]

A typical example of the process by which rumour and inference became news is described by *Fraser's* in an article called "Influence of the Newspapers" (Sept. and Oct. 1831). According to *Fraser's*, what appeared in the papers was no more than what was asked for by their readers, who generally did not come from the class that governed: "the lower classes are the most voracious readers of newspapers" (Sept. 1831: 136). Real understanding of events was to be sought in the pages of the quarterlies; only John Black, the editor of the *Morning Chronicle*, is exempted from this general charge that newspaper editors were but fawning and muddled commentators on public affairs. However, Black himself was to prove no exception to *Fraser's* rule that, "There is scarcely an instance of any individual, known as the editor of a newspaper, and known to the world for his talents as a public writer, who has ever acquired wealth by such a connexion" (Oct. 1831: 318). Indeed, Black's premature and forced retirement in 1843 was financed by the sale of his own extensive library.

If editors were not respectable, reporters were virtually invisible:

a class of hand-to-mouth gentlemen – geniuses of the first water, upon five guineas a-week – politicians of rare talents, living in second-floor lodgings – men who can catch your thoughts with a pen gliber [*sic*] than your tongue, but who vegetate in unknown places, maintaining their quality on a pittance which we are ashamed to name, and waging a perpetual war with tailors and a legion of duns.   (*Fraser's Magazine* 4 no. 21 Oct. 1831: 319)

This refers to reporters at large; parliamentary reporters were held to be a class slightly apart. For one thing, *Fraser's* considers that the integrity and accuracy of their work had a powerful effect in raising the reputation of a paper. For another, they had affinities equally with their political colleagues as with their journalistic ones. Much as they were complained about, even given the fact that they were crowded into the public gallery, "it is nevertheless true, that several of the most popular debaters in that house more frequently address their arguments to the gentlemen in the gallery – to their patrons of the fourth estate – to the hirelings of the newspapers – than to the speaker's chair" (Oct. 1831: 320). The reason would seem to lie in the aspirations of the reporters themselves, who used parliamentary reporting as a way of supporting their legal studies.

Therefore, however much Dickens may have hated the dullness of the lawyer's life from the stool of a clerk's hours, the initial decision to take up parliamentary reporting was still no break with that life. Similarly, Thackeray, in *The Adventures of Philip*, has Philip during one of his improvident stages resolve to learn shorthand in order to supplement his non-existent income as a barrister with reportorial work:

> Why should not Mr. Philip Firmin, barrister-at-law, bethink him that he belonged to a profession which has helped very many men to competence, and not a few to wealth and honours? ... We all knew instances of men who, having commenced their careers as writers for the press, had carried on the legal profession simultaneously, and attained the greatest honours of the bar and the bench.[19]

John Manning has pointed out that for Dickens the experience of five years' parliamentary reporting was something of a university education in itself.[20] This is perceptive, but it ignores the fact that Dickens's lack of a degree would have set him apart from his colleagues and from the status of gentleman. In fact, as Arthur Aspinall, in his article on the social status of journalists at this time, remarks, "Of the twenty-three persons who in 1810 were employed in reporting parliamentary debates for the newspapers, no less than eighteen were men with a University education."[21] His evidence is taken from a parliamentary debate of 1810 and illustrates the way in which these journalists were regarded. On 23 March 1810, there was a debate to withdraw an apparently hastily adopted by-law, which said that "no man who had ever written in a newspaper for hire, should be allowed to perform his preparatory exercises, in order to [obtain] his admission to the bar."[22] In the argument to have this by-law repealed, the names of Addison, Steele, and Johnson were invoked, and other instances were cited of prominent men who had temporarily supported themselves at their legal studies by taking up reporting. One debater, who had himself done so, remarked that "If the act of writing for the newspapers was immoral or dishonourable, he did not see how the doing it gratuitously could redeem the act from reproach."[23] There was no one who opposed the motion, and, in fact, it seems clear that the Lincoln's Inn benchers of their own accord were about to withdraw the regulation; it is of interest, none the less, to note the hierarchy suggested, from daily newspaper writing up to quarterly reviews – it was the notion of being a gentleman that was the standard invoked against writing for money.

Even twenty years later, in another debate, on 29 July 1833, a member replying to complaints about certain parliamentary reporters felt it necessary to say: "he had good reason to believe that they were gentlemen of education and integrity." In a similar vein, Peel himself said, "that there were forty or fifty reporters, some of them holding commissions in the Army and Navy, several at the Bar, most of them having received an academical education, and occupying, therefore, the situation of gentlemen."[24]

We have no record of the twenty-one-year-old Dickens's reactions as he sat in the gallery listening to these exchanges, about whether or not reporters could be considered gentlemen; one can only contrive to imagine what he thought about a debate that must have brought to the fore all the anomalies of his own position. The fact is that *pace* Manning, Dickens did not have a university education. He had managed to obtain his place among these men only because his great-aunt's lodger had enough pull to get him into the lowest realms of the law, and then again because one of his uncles had enough resources to set up the *Mirror of Parliament*, which eventually expired in any case a few years later. Like the other young Englishmen (not the ubiquitous Irish) in the gallery, he was on his way up, but, unlike them, he could always be reminded of where he came from, by the fact that his father, John Dickens – a middle-aged man whose salary barely paid to keep him out of the clutches of the parish and certainly not to finance any legal studies – also worked in the gallery at the same job. As the term was being used in these debates going on before him, therefore, Dickens was no gentleman.

Professionally, the move in 1833 to sketch-writing and away from law may be seen in retrospect to have been the right choice. Dickens's humiliating courtship of Maria Beadnell ended at the same time. Over the next year he cast about: the submission of a sketch to the *Monthly Magazine* and the acting audition were merely two throws of the dice. Ironically, by the time he finally did get taken on at the *Morning Chronicle*, it was only after the writing of sketches had become part of his reputation. In an article "Dickens the Beginner," F. J. Harvey Darton suggests that "right up to the end of 1835, Dickens was a Fleet Street man, first, last, and most of the rest of the time."[25] The change of proprietorship of the *Morning Chronicle* in the summer of 1834, from William Clement (also owner of the *Observer* and *Bell's Life in London*, two papers later to feature Dickens's sketches) to John Easthope, meant that a reputable career in journalism opened up to the young Dickens at last:

The development of the "Morning Chronicle" was a much more important thing to Charles Dickens, journalist, than it seems now to us in the evolution of Boz, man of letters. To a Fleet Street young man of twenty-one it was the kind of chance which comes seldom — the re-establishment of a substantial journal, with a determined policy, and plenty of money behind it.[26]

Undoubtedly, the decision to move into the realms of professional authorship had a great deal to do with meeting George Hogarth, the music and drama critic on the *Morning Chronicle*, and falling in love with his daughter Catherine. Just as meeting Maria Beadnell, a banker's daughter, had fired up the childhood hunger to be a gentleman, so the praise of Hogarth, who had been a friend of Sir Walter Scott, must have shown Dickens the possibilities of being a fiction-writer and man of letters. Dickens met Catherine in late 1834 or early 1835. At the same time, Hogarth, in setting up the *Evening Chronicle*, asked Dickens for a series of sketches for the new paper and eventually for the *Morning Chronicle*. Before going on to consider the reporter's transformation into "Boz" the sketch-writer, we might look at this literary scene onto which he self-consciously made his début in 1833.

2

Literature in 1833

I

The debate about whether or not Grub Street is a suitable place for the pursuits of gentlemen dominates the definition of literature in the nineteenth century. There seems to have been a consensus that anyone who frequented newspaper offices and taverns would never acquire wealth or respectability. The reporters who sat in the parliamentary gallery were admitted as an exception because of their legal studies. Yet, by the age of twenty-one, Dickens had decided to give up any pretence to studying law, and had instead begun to pursue full-time reporting. It was remarkable that in a few short years this irregular life of the Grub Street hack should bring him the acquaintance of some of the most respectable men of letters in the London literary world.

One symbol of this extraordinary rise is a copy of *Oliver Twist* extant from 1838, which is inscribed in friendship from the twenty-five-year-old Dickens to John Gibson Lockhart, the son-in-law of Sir Walter Scott. Scott is always to be found at the centre of any understanding of early nineteenth-century literary life: to understand Dickens's ambitions in his early manhood is to come round inevitably to Scott. Where Dickens dreamt for years of making the step up to full-time reporting, the son-in-law of Scott could afford to worry that the very editorship of a newspaper might be detrimental to a promising professional career. Coincidentally, the person who offered Lockhart this temptation was the equally ambitious Benjamin Disraeli; he was also intent on establishing the proper connections between the literary and political worlds so integral to the literary life of this time. In 1825 the bookseller John Murray sent Disraeli to Edinburgh to persuade Lockhart to become editor of *The Representative*, a new daily newspaper projected by Murray. Lockhart, though taken aback by Disraeli's jejune flourishes, invited him to stay and introduced him to Scott, while considering the matter. In the end Lockhart declined, for reasons that may be reflected in a letter Scott wrote to Murray afterwards. There, the general prejudice against newspaper work is

18

unmistakable: "It is very true ... that this department of literature may & ought to be renderd [*sic*] more respectable than it is at present but I think this a reformation more to be wishd [*sic*] than hoped for."[1] Murray then offered Lockhart the editorship of the *Quarterly Review*. This time it was Lockhart who travelled to London to negotiate the offer that would transplant him permanently to England, and it turned out to be a providential choice. The *Representative* failed after six months, Murray lost £26,000 and Disraeli was consigned to general opprobrium. His revenge took the form of his first novel, *Vivian Grey*, a fashionable *roman à clef* satirizing Murray and Lockhart. Lockhart, however, had secure connections in the Tory establishment world of which Murray, Scott and the *Quarterly Review* were a part, and he was able to ignore Disraeli for a number of years to come. Disraeli, for all his entrepreneurial visions, had meanwhile succeeded only in making himself notorious for blackguardism and ignorance. He dropped out of sight for the next few years before beginning again the hopeful assault on society, as a Radical politician (finally to be elected on his fourth attempt, as a Tory) and as a silver-fork novelist *à la* Bulwer (switching eventually to novels about the new industrial poor).

The brief intersection of the paths of the *Quarterly Review* editor and the fashionable novelist, both of whom were eventually to become kingpins in the Victorian political world, has its own fascination. Their choices of literary roles – Lockhart as quarterly editor and writer of realist novels, and Disraeli as newspaper entrepreneur and writer of fashionable novels – reflect contemporary opinion about the status of men of letters. The consequences of those choices show the gradations of the caste system, which ranked poetry, drama, and "serious" literature above the novel, and, in criticism, the quarterly editor above the daily newspaper controversialist.

Scott's own policy of refusing to treat literature as a profession was not unusual;[2] his consultations with English and Scottish legal colleagues about the possibility of Lockhart's combining the practices of law and literature show that this was still looked on unfavourably for anyone intending a serious career in law.[3] Lockhart made sure that he was called to the English bar when he moved to London, but it turned out that the *Quarterly Review* was to be his permanent livelihood, and he edited it from 1826 to 1853.

Meanwhile Disraeli followed the example of Edward Lytton Bulwer (1803–73), who during the late 1820s had also written a notorious specimen of silver-fork fiction, *Pelham* (1828). Robert Blake, in his biography of Disraeli, comments that Disraeli was "well aware that literature was not the passport to the highest social success, and he treated his fellow authors, apart from Bulwer, with indifference."[4] Disraeli's leading idea was ever that of success. Although his father and friends had always been Tories, Disraeli was a Radical during the early 1830s, when it was fashionable to be so,[5] and then gradually moved rightward again as the Whig Reform Parliament discredited itself and the Tories came back into office in 1841. Disraeli's career as a novelist shows the same sensitivity to public opinion: from London fashionable life in the 1820s to provincial industrialism in the 1840s, he is a sociologist's barometer. It is of interest to note that he was black-balled in a bid to join the Athenaeum Club (founded by Isaac D'Israeli, among others) in the early 1830s. Bulwer had predicted the outcome to Disraeli beforehand:

I think there is some chance of your not coming in because you have written books people have talked about. Had you compiled some obscure quarto which nobody had read you would be sure of success. But *il faut souffrir pour être célèbre*. These quiet fellows too have a great horror of us Novel writers. They fancy – the Ninnies – we shall clap them in a book. "Suspicion is the badge of all our tribe." For my part if I had not got into all my Clubs (at least the respectable ones) before I had taken to Authoring I should certainly be out of them all at this time.[6]

Here Bulwer is essentially talking about himself as a novelist of contemporary London manners in the world of the 1820s, where politics and literature seemed to bear about the same relation to one another as Byron to his half-sister.

At the same time one might look at Lockhart's remarks, on the contemporary novel and its relationship to politics, in one of the first reviews he wrote for the *Quarterly Review* after becoming editor. In 1825, Scott's prefatorial *Lives of the Novelists*, which had been appearing between 1821 and 1824 in ten volumes of the incomplete *Ballantyne's Novelist's Library*, were extracted and published in a single volume by Galignani, the Parisian publisher. Lockhart reviewed this one-volume edition in September 1826. (This was just after the publication of *Vivian Grey*, and Disraeli was being exposed as an *arriviste* author who, with the help of the notoriously fraudulent publisher Henry Colburn, had advertised himself as a blue blood – Christopher North, an ally of Lockhart, was having gleeful fun with this humiliating turn of events, in the pages of *Blackwood's*.)

Lockhart's review of Scott's *Lives* is far removed from the rarefied world of literary in-fighting and chooses instead to remind us of another kind of social history. Not unnaturally for someone writing in the aftermath of the French Revolution and popular domestic agitation, Lockhart discusses the genre of the novel in the context of the rise of the masses as a political force. Behind much of his argument is a consciousness of the growth of popular education and of forces such as the Society for the Diffusion of Useful Knowledge (formed 1825). Attempting to explain the decline of the drama since Shakespeare, for example, he attributes it to the growth of reading as a popular activity and puts forward the theory that anyone who regularly amuses himself with reading could not sit through the length of a public performance: "the drama is a form of composition originally intended and adapted for a state of society in which *reading* is not a general accomplishment of the *people*" (34 no. 68 Sept. 1826: 355). Obviously, Lockhart was no lover of the drama, but even he shares the apologetic opinion of his times, that the prevalence of novelists and romancers over dramatists meant a qualitative cultural decline in English literature. Still, he is less pessimistic than Scott about the supposed accompanying decline of morality on the popular level.

Lockhart is closer to what came to be the Victorian position than Scott, both in the worry that Fielding and Smollett might have a corrupting influence on the young reader and in complacency about the progress of an enlightened readership. Scott, in his *Life* of Fielding, had expressed no fears for the moral constitution of someone exposed to Tom Jones's debaucheries and remarked instead, Lockhart says, that " 'the worst evil to be apprehended from the perusal of novels is, that the habit is apt to generate an indisposition to useful literature and real history' " (371). Lockhart, on the other hand, draws out examples to show that the habit of reading, once established by whatever means, will soon stimulate in turn a taste for more substance and less sugar-coating. Scott himself is cited as the great instance of this. The popularity of his historical romances had encouraged the republication of his more obscure sources and created an entirely unexpected market for scholars and hacks of all disciplines. Lockhart is in fact surprisingly complimentary to the general reader and the expanding readership of democracy. The very attention he gives in this article to the novel as a tradition and an art form constitutes a judgement about its worth that is by no means to be expected from a quarterly reviewer. He even remarks that the level of romance writing itself has risen qualitatively in the last fifteen years, again because of Scott: "the example of one great author [Scott] has spread among our writers the feeling and perception of many principles of composition ... One genius, in a word, has made many clever artists" (378).

The judgement that the level of narrative writing has in fact risen is echoed elsewhere. One critic writing on the decline of the drama remarks,

The high rank which narrative fiction has of late years assumed in literature, – originally, perhaps, the merit and success of the Waverly [*sic*] Novels, – has undoubtedly induced an extremely large proportion of the literary talent of the country to devote itself to that style of composition.

(*Athenaeum* 1 no. 1 2 Jan. 1828: 13)

That there has been a decline in poetry after Byron is a cliché of contemporary criticism. In the same year, 1828, the *Athenaeum*, for instance, noted that Colburn the publisher had produced seventy-four volumes of novels and four volumes of poetry. It is Scott's example that has produced this: "From the moment that these novels began to operate strongly on the public mind, we think we can trace a decline of the interest which was taken in poetry."[7] This critic equates a declining interest in poetry with a general decline in intellectual vigour: when intellect is at its keenest, poetry is the natural expression of that, whereas tired intellects "court imbecility and inanition in the pages of a novel" (1 no. 47 17 Sept. 1828: 735–36).

Some reviewers, however, thought that the novel could provide instead something altogether more substantial and lasting than mere emotion: knowledge. Here again Scott had shown the way. He had raised the novel from inanition by his preference for truth to "Nature" over sensationalism. Thus, the *Edinburgh Review* wrote a few months before his death,

In consequence of this newly-enlarged view of the principles on which fiction should be written, we have, since the appearance of Waverley, seen the fruits of varied learning and experience displayed in that agreeable form; and we have even received from works of fiction what it would once have been thought preposterous to expect – information ... We have learnt, too, how greatly the sphere of the Novel may be extended, and how capable it is of becoming the vehicle almost of every species of popular knowledge.

(*Edinburgh Review* 55 no. 109 Apr. 1832: 77)

Such praise for Scott's learning and the way in which he used the more universalized concerns of history in stiffening the fabric of fiction is found throughout the criticism of the time.

One cannot help noticing in all such praise for Scott the emphasis on knowledge: the *Edinburgh Review*'s "information" and "popular knowledge," Lockhart's assertion in the *Quarterly Review* that the Waverley novels had led to an appetite for serious history and science, and the exception made by the *Athenaeum* for historical romance because of its ability to instruct. Concomitant with the decline of Byron and poetry had been the rise of James Mill and practical knowledge. However, this very predominance of practicality over imagination was also common cause for lament. The·late 1820s and early 1830s do not hold a high place in English literary history, and the critics of the time felt conscious of a general mediocrity. In a definitive series of articles on contemporary periodical writing, the Rev. Henry Stebbing in the *Athenaeum* issue of April 1828 was typical in introducing his subject by bemoaning the state of literature and the lack of any truly imaginative poet. Instead, it was the pulse of scientific research that was everywhere felt to be quickening. The publishing crisis of 1825–26 is not mentioned by Stebbing as a possible explanation for decline, but part of this taste for the useful lies in the fact that both publishers and readers were playing it safe. The appetite for materialism and for useful knowledge, Stebbing argues, made light fiction and popular science the most attractive commodities, and moral philosophy the least. Fiction is "the staple of English literature at present. Novels and romances are the bookseller's most valuable copy-right, and the author's surest stepping-stone to fortune and reputation" (1 no. 20 Apr. 1828: 305).

II

Even this, however, was a sanguine estimate of the literary market. The appetite for scientific knowledge and historical romance only modified the nature of the publisher's list; within the next couple of years politics and the Reform Bill were nearly to extinguish it. Agitation for the Bill began in 1830. By 1831 the *Athenaeum*'s "Weekly Gossip" of literary news was lamenting: "It must be owned that for these six months art and literature have suffered a sad eclipse" (4 no. 207 15 Oct. 1831: 667). Only cheap books were selling at all, for it was agreed that no man could "expect to read a large work leisurely through, when the very ground under his feet seems to have a touch of the earthquake ... in truth, till the great question of reform is settled, we need look for no commanding works in either literature or art" (4 no. 212 19 Nov. 1831: 755). Scott's works continued to sell since reprints were among the safer ventures for a publisher. Throughout 1832, the *Athenaeum*'s "Weekly Gossip" continued to publish bulletins about the sad state of Literature, which ricocheted between flimsy tales of fashionable scandal and those of democracy's low-life: "in poetry, there is nothing from any popular name, and, saving a few novels, prose is almost confined to pamphlets on Cholera and Reform'' (5 no. 223 4 Feb. 1832: 82).

The *Athenaeum* noted in January 1832 that its own feeling about the situation (see 5 no. 221 21 Jan. 1832: 50) was corroborated by the *Quarterly Review*, which that same month published an article reflecting on the agitation of the times and the general fear of civil warfare. There was a palpable threat of anarchy in the streets when the House of Lords refused to pass the Reform Bill.[8] Internal disruption, a cholera epidemic, and Continental trading uncertainties had brought on commercial stagnation just when it had seemed that the country was recovering from the economic crises of 1825. Publishing as a trade dealing in articles of luxury had declined to a degree that the *Quarterly* reviewer found unprecedented in his own lifetime. Anxiety about the apocalyptic rumblings of democracy meant that newspapers were nearly the only reading. This echoes the *Athenaeum*'s lament: ''No one talks of Literature in these stormy and changeful times ... Literature will gradually sink into pamphlets and papers; for such is the agitated state of the public mind, that no attention is paid to anything but speculations on reform and change of rulers'' (5 no. 237 12 May 1832: 307); and later: ''Literature, notwithstanding all our hopes, seems about to resolve itself into daily, weekly, monthly, and quarterly periodicals'' (5 no. 249 4 Aug. 1832: 507).

Thus, the study of literature as reflected in contemporary periodicals has its own ironies, when one considers that the periodical form of publication itself was revising the terms on which literature was produced. The intense political interest of the time meant that *news* in its regular bits and pieces was the most compelling reading and, consequently, that reading became a fragmentary experience, for the leisure associated with the quarterlies seemed to have receded into the past.

This was, above all, an economic phenomenon. The democratization of politics was not only reported but reflected in the press. In a series of articles on the newspapers in 1829, the *Westminster Review* analysed the developments taking place in readership. The *Westminster Review*, itself a liberal journal, assigns a large place to the weekly press in the growth of liberal sentiments in rural areas. Even though the Tory agitation against Catholic emancipation, for example, appeared vociferous and prominent, the circulation figures of the London Sunday papers in the provinces suggested otherwise. The circulation of the Sunday papers (which were *de facto* liberal at this time) is used as evidence of the existence of widespread democratic feeling. However, the *Westminster Review*'s intention to proselytize becomes evident, when we find it using the same argument in reverse, such that the papers are seen not only as passive reflections but also as agents of this new-born democracy:

How much are the present ministry, and the friends of Catholic Emancipation, indebted to the London and Provincial Press, for the success which has crowned their labours! But for the newspapers they might have laboured in vain for ever. (*Westminster Review* 10 no. 20 Apr. 1829: 471)

More interesting is the attempt to decide if in fact there had been a real increase in newspaper reading, based on the fluctuations between sales of daily papers and those of weeklies. If one assumes that newspapers are read most in periods of excitement, then the end of the Napoleonic wars is taken to be the best node of comparison:

At the close of the late war, the public, who appeared to have been satiated with news, and to imagine that a time of peace could never furnish sufficient incident to keep up the interest of a daily paper, evinced a pretty general indifference to news; and many persons with whom the purchase of a daily paper proceeded from mere excitement, discontinued their subscriptions, and contented themselves with reading the news once a week instead of once in every twenty-four hours, but this was only for a time; within the last four or five years there has been a good demand for daily papers, without any material decrease in the sale of Sunday papers; and we are able to assert that the number of readers has very considerably increased within the last six years. (*Westminster Review* 10 no. 20 Apr. 1829: 474–75)[9]

The *Westminster Review*'s conclusion is typically optimistic: "at no time during the peace, and in the absence of peculiarly exciting causes, has the sale of newspapers been so great as within the last two or three years," and it proudly notes, "Men read newspapers then for accounts of battles and sieges – they read them now for improvement" (475). The increase in readership is asserted to have been made up in the working classes, particularly in metropolitan areas. Even more specifically, this is tied to an increase in coffee-shops, where papers were made available. The presence of coffee-houses was particularly a feature of cities, unlike country towns, which could offer only public houses. Whatever a twentieth-century historian may make of the *Westminster Review*'s statistics, its own commentator confidently associates an increase in newspaper reading with progressive change, and specifically with such change among the lower metropolitan classes: "What does all this prove but that whatever may be the means of purchase, there is a great increase of readers – that the schoolmaster is indeed abroad, and that man is become more of a

reasoning animal?'' (476). The *Westminster Review* is here quoting
from Henry Brougham, who had said in a speech to the Commons
on 29 January 1828, that he had more faith in the ability of intellectual
than military force to rule mankind; his optimistic phrase "the
schoolmaster is abroad" quickly became one of the most quoted
phrases of Radical idealism.

The *Westminster Review* was not alone in its self-congratulation.
Brougham himself, as the self-styled "friend of human improvement," reflects happily in an article called "Progress of the People"
in the *Edinburgh Review* of April 1833, on the success of the penny
weeklies such as the *Penny Magazine, Saturday Magazine,* and
Chambers's Edinburgh Journal, all begun in the revolutionary year
of 1832. Like the *Westminster Review* commentator, Brougham sees
the existence and unprecedented circulation of these weeklies as
evidence that the People have learned to think for themselves, without
relying on the slanderous inbred accounts of the London papers. Like
the *Westminster Review,* too, he judges that there has been an increase
in newspaper reading over the last few years. Specifically, he says this
is because "The old Parliament had lost the confidence of the country;
and the sense of the people having no legitimate organ, the
Newspapers, especially those of the metropolis, had usurped that
office" (57 no. 115 Apr. 1833: 247). However, since the reforming
of Parliament, Brougham sees that the Government has regained the
confidence of the People, and the newspapers accordingly have
subsided in influence while flailing about ever more furiously in
scurrility and fulmination against the Government, as they perceive
that the People are now learning to keep their own counsel. Part of
Brougham's self-congratulation, no doubt as a founder of the Society
for the Diffusion of Useful Knowledge (1825), is that he sees the
People's thirst for knowledge and self-improvement being fed by the
cheap weeklies, which can only further gain at the London papers'
expense if the stamp-tax is repealed. It is not the masses, he says, but
the upper classes who have the London papers' appetite for "ribaldry
and libel" (241). Being on the spot, the fashionable classes see
everything Parliamentary as a matter of personalities. The only fear
of cheap publications Brougham admits is not that they will drive
out "higher" works, but that they will plagiarize them in the absence
of a stiff law of copyright.

It is useful to have Brougham's gloss on this subject but the
optimistic rhetoric of Reform in this article is slightly distasteful. Some
commentators, concerned less about popular education than about
literature as a tradition, found reason to bemoan these same trends

brought by an increasing readership. Cultivators of reading on useful matters are not always the cultivators of literature. The *Athenaeum* notes that the book trade was declining – its decline lamented by the very periodicals whose own circulation was increasing:

Some of our monthly periodicals lament the utter ruin which they imagine is coming upon literature: not one book in ten pays its expenses in these degenerate times: novels are a drug in the market: the day of romance is gone by, poetry has lifted its wings and departed for some more favoured land, and nothing will go down with the public but matters of utility. In truth, the British world, that used to bolt two guineas-worth at once, can only be induced now to swallow a penny-worth. (*Athenaeum* 6 no. 275 2 Feb. 1833: 74)

Perhaps, as suggested by the *Quarterly Review*, in times of great political excitement – and particularly excitement of a democratic nature – the upper classes were less inclined to spend lavishly on luxuries, while at the same time the lower classes were optimistically increasing their expenditure on the periodicals and educative reading that were seen as allied to the effort to raise themselves. In 1812, Francis Jeffrey had argued in the *Edinburgh Review*: "In this country, there probably are not less than two hundred thousand persons who read for amusement or instruction among the middling classes of society. In the higher classes, there are not as many as twenty thousand" ("Crabbe's Tales" 20 no. 40 Nov. 1812: 280). When Archibald Constable, publisher of some of the early nineteenth century's most successful literary properties, the *Edinburgh Review* and Walter Scott, began revolving the scheme for what was to become *Constable's Miscellany*, Scott remarked that he doubted if his rich Abbotsford neighbours spent £10 on contemporary literature in a year. Constable agreed:

"there is no market among them that's worth one's thinking about. They are contented with a review or a magazine, or at best with a paltry subscription to some circulating library forty miles off ... Twelve volumes in the year, a halfpenny of profit upon every copy of which will make me richer than the possession of all the copyrights of all the quartos that ever were, or will be, hot-pressed!"[10]

The *Miscellany* projected by Constable was to consist of alternating sections of the Waverley novels and Scott's *Life of Napoleon*, each section making up either one-half a novel or one of four sections of the *Life*, in duodecimo volumes to be published monthly at three shillings or one half-crown. Constable's scheme coincided with Scott's own weariness with fiction and interest in trying his hand at history. He too thought that the market could bear a good deal more: "'I am of opinion that historical writing has no more been adapted to the demands of the increased circles among which literature does already find its way, than you [Constable] allege as to the shape and price of books in general.' "[11]

Scott, as usual, almost as much an entrepreneur as an author, was thus at the centre of another publishing innovation. This scheme was the first among a rash of cheap reprinting schemes during the late twenties and early thirties, and Lockhart called it "nothing less than a total revolution in the art and traffic of bookselling."[12] Constable's own pronouncement gives the typical flavour of book-selling at this time, when the Society for the Diffusion of Useful Knowledge was its most notorious example of success: "'Literary genius may, or may not, have done its best; but printing and book-selling, as instruments for enlightening and entertaining mankind, and, of course, for making money, are as yet in mere infancy.'"[13] The popularity of Scott's writing as a historical phenomenon in all of this cannot be separated out from the question of how best to capitalize on the popular thirst for knowledge. Interestingly, when Murray began a similar series, the *Family Library*, in 1829, the first number consisted of Scott's *Life of Napoleon* abridged by Lockhart and illustrated by George Cruikshank. Later, Longman's publication of *Lardner's Cabinet Cyclopaedia*, the longest running such series, began with Scott's *History of Scotland* at 6s a volume.

By contrast, the publication of original fiction was struggling. In a short note entitled "General Bankruptcy of Literature," *Tait's Edinburgh Magazine* for February 1833 wrote: "Very few books of fiction, now published, yield the return of their expenses; and 'Eugene Aram,' the most favourite novel of last season, has not yet reached a second edition!" (2 no. 11 Feb. 1833: 662). *Tait's* also remarked that no new annuals (the 1830s version of coffee-table books) had succeeded, that Murray was publishing only reprints, and that the new publisher Richard Bentley, who had split from Colburn in 1832, seemed merely to be spinning novels out of Colburn's leftover sheets.

Bentley had indeed recently (February 1831) begun a series of reprinted fiction called *Standard Novels*, with each volume containing one complete novel and selling for 6s. An earlier experiment with monthly volumes of useful literature (Colburn and Bentley's *National Library* series) had failed barely a year after it had begun (1830–31) and, in any case, the rage for "useful knowledge" series was a short-lived phenomenon. A strong preference for fiction reprints in fact dominated the market and as much as 85 percent of the circulating library trade.[14]

Again, the model came from Scott – specifically, Robert Cadell's reprinting of the Waverley novels in 1829 with engravings and selling at 5s per monthly volume, with sales as high as 35,000 per month.[15] As Royal Gettmann remarks, "In short, Sir Walter Scott, whose influence is everywhere in the history of nineteenth-century fiction, was responsible not only for the three-volume novel priced at 31s 6d but for the inexpensive one-volume reprint as well,"[16] and he points out that Bentley's first advertisements called the *Standard Novels* series "A Companion to the Waverley Novels." Bentley had originally hoped to make the series primarily a reprinting of eighteenth-century classics, using Scott's prefaces from *Ballantyne's Novelist's Library*. Unable to obtain these, Bentley made the series a reprinting of contemporary novels and romances, beginning with James Fenimore Cooper.[17] Unlike Cadell's reprinting of Scott, which offered every novel in two volumes at 5s per volume, Bentley offered every novel in one volume at 6s. The formula of correlating price to volume was obviously crucial, and so was the fixing upon monthly intervals. The *Standard Novels* series lasted in this form until 1855, although the attempt by Bentley to imitate his own model, with a *Standard Library* series of non-fiction in 1839, survived less than a year.

What recurs in all these schemes is the notion of cheapness allied to regular, generally monthly, publication. *Tait's*, which had commercial reasons to interest itself in this phenomenon, helps to clarify some of the issues. In January 1834, it published an article called "Johnstone's Edinburgh Magazine: The Cheap and Dear Periodicals," which discussed the change in readership with some complexity. Of particular interest here is attention given in this article to cheap monthly publications. (The phenomenon of cheap weeklies at a penny each is a sociological issue in itself. Three of the most successful new weekly magazines, all of them heavily illustrated, *Chambers's Edinburgh Journal*, *Saturday Magazine*, and *Penny Magazine*, began in 1832 and had circulations of thousands. Simply to list all the cartoon-strip parodies of Dickens's shilling numbers that were to appear in such weeklies a few years later would have been a task beyond Dickens himself, had he overcome his own antipathy sufficiently to bother. Instead, it is a notable index to his ambitions that he chose to begin as a writer for a traditional monthly costing 3s 6d a month.)

It is mostly with the monthlies' readership that *Tait's* is here concerned. Interestingly, *Tait's* includes reprints such as Bentley's *Standard Novels* series among the monthly literature that was garnering a new readership: "The expensive quartos and octavos, which used to issue in such swarms from Albemarle Street, and The Row, and from the Edinburgh press in *Constable's* days, have given place to the *Waverley Novels, Lardner's Cyclopaedia, The Edinburgh Cabinet Library*, and some scores more of similar works, published in monthly parts, at cheap prices'' (4 no.22 Jan. 1834: 492). What is immediately noticeable is that there are no original works among these names: they are all compilations or reprints of standard favourites – a sign that the booksellers are playing safe. As the *Literary Gazette* remarks at this time,

We know not at the present moment the publisher who would undertake the risk of bringing out an extensive original work upon any important subject matter whatever. It must either be trimmed down to a six or three-shilling volume, to suit what is called the taste of the times, or it must remain in manuscript.   (*Literary Gazette* 17 no.866 24 Aug. 1833: 539)

In fact, the monthly market was going in two different directions at once. There were magazines that had as much repute and political bias as the quarterlies; these included *Blackwood's*, the *New Monthly*, *Fraser's*, the *Metropolitan*, and *Tait's* itself. All these sold for either 3s 6d (the more fashionable ones) or 2s 6d, and were generally, like the quarterlies (which sold for 6s per issue), taken in by the circulating libraries. Their circulation and rate of private subscription were not large, despite their prominence. They were neither as likely to have private subscribers as the quarterlies, though equally as prominent politically, nor to be as popular as the less prominent but cheaper monthlies and weeklies.

For example, *Fraser's*, as *Tait's* writer points out, received far more notice and employed more talented writers than a publication such as *Johnstone's Magazine* – and yet had a circulation a fraction of the latter's. This seems hardly surprising or unfair. After all, *Johnstone's, Chambers's Historical Newspaper, British Cyclopaedia*, and the other cheap monthlies all sold for 8d, 6d, or even less. What is interesting to a modern observer is that *Tait's* should single out as a phenomenon in itself the fact that circulation was dependent not on talent, controversiality or political backing – but on cost to the reader. A magazine such as *Fraser's* had the advantage of talent and prominence simply by being published in London; like most of the other magazines of its class, its reputation pre-dated those of the cheap monthlies, and it had political friends. None of this mattered. It was clearly more profitable to be the publisher of a *Johnstone's*.

It is notable that *Johnstone's* began publication originally under the title of *The Schoolmaster and Edinburgh Weekly Magazine*, in the watershed year of 1832. The writer of the *Tait's* article describes it as "having no politics" and "being addressed to every class" (496). This is disingenuous. *Tait's* had the same publisher as *Johnstone's*, and, in fact, the whole *Tait's* article is obviously an analysis of, not to say an advertisement for, the success of the experiment in cheap monthly publication conducted by William Tait. *Johnstone's* had no politics only to the extent that it was not based in London and published no articles on party politics, but its very effort to be instructive and its motto, "The Schoolmaster is Abroad," proclaim it as Radical and democratic. The quality of "being addressed to every class" – at the price of 8d – meant merely that its readers were middle class, not classless, and that the fashionable world was certainly not being solicited.

The whole argument is given another turn when one discovers that in fact *Tait's* and *Johnstone's* were to merge in June 1834, when their respective prices of 2s 6d and 8d became 1s. The notice that broadcasts this change in *Tait's* for January 1834 refers the reader specifically to the article "The Cheap and Dear Periodicals" and states:

we have noted the universal decline in circulation of the expensive periodicals, for several years; and have watched the astonishing progress of cheap literature, with attentive eyes. A powerful current has set in against the dear periodicals, and in favour of the cheap.

(*Tait's Magazine* 4 no. 22 Jan. 1834: ii)

The writer suggests that, because of the invention of the steam printing press, cheap publishing is for the first time more profitable than the traditional system of keeping to a small circulation and charging a high price.

In any case, the proprietors of this much praised new monthly had evidently decided that the healthiness of a monthly's sales lay with the cheap price and not with traditional prestige. For even the great increase in library reading-rooms had not forestalled the decline in readership of the expensive periodicals that the onset of high prices and establishment of the library system had encouraged. The higher priced monthlies suffered a decline in purchasers along with the quarterlies, but also increasingly, at the other end, competition from cheap penny magazines. The monthlies, like the libraries which took them in, were suffering from the fact that their former readers were now buying cheap periodicals "instead of *borrowing* a volume or two, on a leisure evening" (492). Thus, *Blackwood's*, the *New Monthly*, *Fraser's*, the *Metropolitan*, the *Monthly*, and *Tait's*, the six most prominent monthlies, all circulated at around a few thousand, with

Blackwood's claiming a high of nine thousand and the *Monthly* probably less than one thousand. The quarterlies, selling from three thousand (*Westminster Review*) to nine thousand (*Quarterly Review*) also knew a decline from earlier days – while *Johnstone's* and *Chambers's* claimed more than ten times the quarterlies' sales. This would not necessarily have made them the more profitable – until the new printing technology and the new call for educational knowledge. A cheap price would have been no advantage until large printings also meant a saving in expenses.

The monthlies at this time faced a dilemma. Having been prodded earlier in the century by the example of the quarterlies to flesh out mere lists of new books into article-length criticism, they had then learned to become organs of amusement to library readers who had not the same leisure as wealthy subscribers had for re-reading. Short fiction had therefore become their special province: "brevity" and "amusement" were the great bywords for a successful monthly. By 1832, however, it seemed that profitability was to be found, not in the wealth of country readers or circulating libraries, but in the odd sixpences of readers who had taste, not for party loyalty or metropolitan frivolities, but for instruction and sentiment.

The only point of debate, as we have seen from considering all the "Family Libraries" and "Cyclopaedias," concerned the form in which these new readers preferred to receive their instruction. The appetite for scientific treatises is astonishing to a twentieth-century reader, and it would have taken great prescience to see that *narrative*, preferably with illustrations, would be the format most likely to appeal. For, generally speaking, fiction and romance, as associated with the working classes, were seen as narcotics.[18] Only biography and history were thought to be respectable types of narrative. Given this, one appreciates anew the respectability that Scott brought to romantic narratives, and also the wisdom of Constable's proposed alternation of historical and romantic narratives.

Commentators repeatedly attest that since 1813 Scott had raised the status of the novel and at the same time encouraged the demand for historical studies. It is clear that Scott is at the conjunction of these two appetites for instruction and amusement. The acknowledgement of his genius is the more pronounced, inasmuch as the run of his imitators is usually condemned. Scott, after years of private researches and by the force of his memory, could call on amazing resources with which to contrive his historical romances. His very love for historical detail infused the minds of his readers with his

own curiosity. As the *Edinburgh Review* wrote on the Cadell edition
of the Waverley novels a few months before Scott's death,

History has been, in consequence of his works, much read by those who would
otherwise have neglected it. Still more, perhaps, has enquiry been directed
towards its adjuncts and subsidiaries — towards biographical and antiquarian
researches. Never has the press been more fertile than during the last ten years
in this species of agreeable lore — in memoirs, diaries, and letters; which
convey much amusing information, and some that may with truth be called
valuable.   (*Edinburgh Review* 55 no. 109 Apr. 1832: 78)

This readership was to be even further extended, as we have seen, with
the Cadell monthly issue of Scott's works. The gulf between this
popular history and what the *Edinburgh Review* carefully calls
researches "that may with truth be called valuable" could only
become larger.

   Where the *Edinburgh Review* on the eve of Scott's death breathed
sad thanks to the author of this cultural phenomenon, the *Literary
Gazette* a year later points out more irritably the less desirable
consequences of this cheap issue of such an author. By his own
preservation of anonymity Scott himself showed where *he* placed his
work on the scale of respectability. Whatever the scholarly faults of
his romances, he could always plead amateur status. What he could
not have foreseen were the effects produced by the conjunction of
his private popularity and Constable-like visions of cheap publishing
in an age of aggressive democracy. That is to say, he could not have
foreseen the symbiotic growth of professional authorship and mass-
market printing. The *Literary Gazette* complains that this new appetite
for cheap knowledge was not without malignant side effects:

the publishing trade is almost entirely confined to hasty compilations hurried
through the press ... One worthless volume after another issues from the press,
every page of which bears the stamp of incompetency, or of dishonesty, either
in carelessness or appropriation. Such, with few, a very few exceptions, is
the present depressed and deplorable state of the literature of England.
                    (*Literary Gazette* 17 no. 866 24 Aug. 1833: 539)

III

Scott cannot be held entirely responsible for the state of affairs
complained about. It would be more accurate to blame the grip of
a depressed economy and cautious booksellers in the midst of an
uncertain political situation. If anyone, Lord Brougham is as much to
blame. Greville writes in his *Memoirs*: "after the Duke of Wellington

and Peel carrying the Catholic question, Canning's friends advocating Radical Reform, and Eldon living to see Brougham on the Woolsack, what may one not expect?"[19] This was in 1831, when Greville felt the anticipation of anarchy enough to write daily in his journal and to note: "Nothing talked of, thought of, dreamt of, but Reform. Every creature one meets asks, What is said now? How will it go? What is the last news? What do *you* think? and so it is from morning till night, in the streets, in the clubs, and in private houses."[20]

The tension did not soon let up, however, and the Reform Bill did not pass until a year later, in the session of 1832. Subsequently, much of the 1833 Reformed Parliament's business seemed to consist in undermining the position of the Established Church (the Bishops had ostracized themselves by blocking passage of the Reform Bill). Concurrently there was an outbreak of cholera; this and the seeming attack on religion gave the early thirties an apocalyptic flavour: "The times were very evil and very exciting."[21]

The connections between the literary and the public states of affairs may be seen in the letters of Thomas Carlyle at this time. The unfortunate Carlyle chose the month of August 1831 to venture down from rural Scotland to London, where he intended to arrange for the publication of *Sartor Resartus*. By December 1831, he was writing to his family in Scotland that "There is still not the faintest outlook for *Teufelsdreck*, more especially till the Reform Bill get out of the way."[22] In January 1832 the refrain continued, "there *is* nothing in London at present but stagnation and apprehension, and Radical Reform ... British Literature is a mud-ocean" (VI, 87; 10 Jan. 1832). Carlyle was forced to conclude that the publishing of books had been "crippled" by the anxiety about Reform (VI, 97; 22 Jan. 1832), and by May 1833 resolved finally upon publishing his book in "hydra-hea[ded]" fashion — that is to say, in magazines (VI, 241; 16 Oct. 1832). He mourned to John Stuart Mill,

I had hoped that by and by I might get out of Periodicals altogether, and write Books: but the light I got in London last winter showed me that *this* was as good as over. My Editors of Periodicals are my Booksellers ...

(VI, 241)

The strangeness and awkwardness of the times are also registered by Mary Shelley's writing to John Murray, to ask if her father might be allowed to write a volume for Murray's *Family Library* series, the closest William Godwin could come to adapting himself to the times. Mrs. Shelley writes,

You are but too well aware of the evil days on which literature is fallen – and how difficult it is for a man however gifted, whose existence depends on his pen, to make one engagement succeed another with sufficient speed to answer the calls of his situation – Nearly all our literati have found but one resource in this – which is in the ample scope afforded by periodicals – a kind of literary pride has prevented my father from mingling in these – [23]

The Radical press, of course, took the diffusion of life and literature through periodicals as a matter for congratulation. The change in printing technology may have coincided with a dearth of "great works," but "for their absence, we have much amends made to us by the never-failing floods of our periodical literature" (*Bell's New Weekly Messenger* [*Reviewer*] 1 no. 1 Jan. 1832: 1). From this is projected a cultural Armageddon, in which democracy shall triumph. Periodicals were apparently to become the *sansculottes* of literary life.

Notwithstanding this intoxicating prophecy, the frenzy and the cholera finally did pass, and by September 1833 Greville could write with some relief, "the world seems in a state of repose."[24] The aftermath of the passing of the Reform Bill and the death of Scott, both in 1832, showed that an era had ended. To most commentators it was the end of much national anxiety but also of much romantic excitement – the French Revolution, Napoleon, the fear of invasion, Byron and the democratic experiments in Greece – it had been a surprisingly military age, considering the gentleness of those literary figures we remember from it. Wordsworth had French soldier friends during his time in France, and Jane Austen had two brothers who fought in the naval wars against Napoleon. These two most domestically English of our writers are only among the more famous examples of a generation that was forced to stay at home because of the uproar on the Continent. Indeed, as Marilyn Butler has shown, the reaction against things French and republican partially took shape in a cultivation of the homely spirit of *Gemütlichkeit*.[25] The celebration of German provincial life was England's propaganda against the gathering of French power unto worldly Paris.

This era came to an unlooked-for end, with the hero of Waterloo routed by the machine of Democracy, and the House of Lords forced to accede to the Reform Bill. When the Napoleonic wars ended, the masses recruited by them had come home again to protectionist taxes that kept the price of corn artificially high. The atmosphere of consensus and national thankfulness was broken by class warfare. Wordsworth, who could fight for the rights of the French working class in the 1790s, thought the Reform Bill and the weakening of feudal ties between classes a disastrous prospect. But Reform had come to seem inevitable even to William IV, who co-operated with the Whigs in ensuring that the Lords passed the Bill. When the Tories left office, they had not the support of a single daily paper; the shifting of *The Times*, which was notorious for veering with public opinion, was by then simply part of a new ethos, where the growth of middle-class commercial advertising meant that the papers no longer regarded themselves as conduits for Ministerial information.[26] Independence from everything except public opinion was beginning to pay, and in 1832 that meant that the Lords could no longer forestall Reform. What did this mean for the prospects of serious literature in 1832?

There were at least two major efforts within the next year to consider such a question. The *Athenaeum* published a "Biographical and Critical History of the Last Fifty Years" by Allan Cunningham (1784–1842), friend of Scott and Carlyle, and a journalistic factotum who wrote criticism, ballads, and biography for many London publications. Cunningham included very full lists under each genre of outstanding authors in each field. Such lists, showing the preference for certain authors over others, are interesting to the historian of taste. For one thing, authorship must have been defined quite differently from the way it is today. Cunningham's list in 1833 makes this explicit: the categories treated under the rubric of "Literature" are poetry, fiction, and drama – and include history, biography, and criticism. This is a more remarkable fact than the choice of authors named.[27] In his characterization of the times, Cunningham's themes are entirely conventional: the decline of poetry and drama, the encroachment of the novel (and its own fragmentation into specialized forms of poetic and historical), and the predominance of criticism ("This is the century of criticism: the age of brass has succeeded that of gold" [*Athenaeum* 6 no. 322 28 Dec. 1833: 891]).

The other survey of 1833 remarked by contemporaries was *England and the English*, by Edward Lytton Bulwer, who had recently been editor of the *New Monthly Magazine* (1831–32) and was still an M.P. (1831–41). *England and the English* is Bulwer's anatomy of the English character and institutions as they appeared just after the Reform Bill. It is of much interest, though it often reads as little more than a series of not particularly profound editorials full of optimistic proselytizing; Bulwer was a fashionable Radical, which meant that his clothes were Brummellish and his politics Benthamite.

In a chapter with the running head "Poverty of our Present Literature," Bulwer sets out to describe the contemporary state of English literature. Asked to name the great writers of the past twenty years, he cites Byron, Wordsworth, Scott, Thomas Moore (author of the popular metrical romance *Lalla Rookh* [1817]), Shelley, and Thomas Campbell (author of patriotic songs during the Napoleonic wars and editor of the *New Monthly Magazine* 1820–30). These are the representatives of what he calls "imaginative" literature, that is to say, poets and writers of fiction. He remarks, "In imaginative literature, then, we are peculiarly rich, in the graver letters we are as singularly barren."[28] For it becomes apparent again that "Literature" in 1833 comprehends serious works of prose quite as much as those of poetry and fiction. Criticism, *belles lettres* or "miscellaneous literature," history, moral philosophy: these are the categories under which Bulwer searches for literary talent. As examples of such writers in the early nineteenth century, Bulwer puts forward the names of Isaac D'Israeli, Hazlitt, Leigh Hunt, Lamb, and Southey.

His dilemma is, that "we cannot but feel impressed, while adducing some names in the non-inventive classes of literature, with the paucity of those who remain. It is a great literary age − we have great literary men − but where are their works?"[29] And the reply echoes Cunningham's judgement that it is an age of criticism: "we must seek them not in detached and avowed and standard publications, but in periodical miscellanies."[30] Here follow the names of Sydney Smith, John Wilson ("Christopher North"), Jeffrey, and Macaulay. Thus the salient fact of Bulwer's literary age is its ephemerality: its case to posterity will have to be made by compilation and republication.

The other feature, for Bulwer, of periodical literature, going back to Addison, Steele, and Defoe, is the close intercourse it keeps up between literature and politics; this is naturally of interest to someone who was both an M.P. and a novelist. The question why periodical literature should foster a "natural sympathy"[31] between literature and politics is not addressed to Bulwer − only assumed. One also notices that in speaking of literature Bulwer uses the term *intellect* frequently and commonly talks of literature as the "Intellectual Spirit of the Time."[32] Both *literature* and *intellect* are used by Bulwer in a wider sense than they would be now. *Literature* had for him a critical capacity as well as an imaginative one and did not exclude discussion of political matters.

If the periodical medium encouraged this intercourse, it also, in Bulwer's opinion, encouraged its devaluation. Articles written for a deadline could not be but hasty and superficial reflections on a problem, whereas "imaginative" writing could afford to be more truly analytical or "intellectual." It is to Scott's writing, for example, "that the wise historian will look not only for an epoch in poetical literature, but the reflection of the moral sentiment of an age."[33] Part of the "moral sentiment" of an era will include its politics. The writings of both Scott and Byron, whom Bulwer goes on to analyse, were widely perceived to have definite political consequences and moralities. Such was part-and-parcel of their notoriety. And when it comes to talking about Wordsworth, Bulwer uses the term *"toryism"* to describe Wordsworth's characteristic "disdain for the pettier cries which float over that vast abyss which we call the public, and of a firm desire for Peace as the best nurse to high and undiurnal thoughts."[34] The term *toryism*, with its political overtones, is here commandeered in a metaphorical sense to describe Wordsworth's well-known conservatism — just at this time when *Tory* as a political tag was giving way to *Conservative*. It is notable that Bulwer's vocabulary in his analysis of the poets is heavily political and never deviates from addressing the question of how these writers reflect their eras. Bulwer of course was himself living in a period of high political interest, and the stance of poets such as Wordsworth, Shelley, and Byron was far from being apolitical. Different as Wordsworth was from Byron, or Shelley from Scott, "each appertains emphatically to a time of visible and violent transition."[35] Bulwer's era of political action was a time when commentators were looking about anxiously for signs of what was preparing to come, and the passing of Byron was a signpost to this era's prospects:

When Byron passed away, the feeling he had represented craved utterance no more. With a sigh we turned to the actual and practical career of life: we awoke from the morbid, the passionate, the dreaming, "the moonlight and the dimness of the mind," and by a natural reaction addressed ourselves to the active and daily objects which lay before us ... Hence that strong attachment to the Practical, which became so visible a little time after the death of Byron, and which continues (unabated, or rather increased,) to characterize the temper of the time.[36]

Bulwer is not quite so naive as to ascribe the whole of the Utilitarian movement to the death of Byron; it cannot have escaped his notice that there was also a financial crisis in 1825–26 as well as increased leisure for domestic affairs after long anxiety about France, both of which might have encouraged Reformism:

the long Peace, and the pressure of financial difficulties, naturally inclined us to look narrowly at our real state; to examine the laws we had only boasted of, and dissect the constitution we had hitherto deemed it only our duty to admire.[37]

Scott had taken to writing prose, and the wayward Brougham stood for the typical great man of the age.

Perhaps, as Bulwer suggests, the reading public had already tired of the sickly imitations of Byron and was looking around to be amused more usefully. It was not the epic novel of Cervantes or Fielding that Scott produced or made popular — it was the novel at large: "It was not, however, as in former times, the great novel alone, that was read among the more refined circles, but novels of all sorts."[38] This confounding of categories was for Bulwer an expression of the age, and the novel was its most characteristic vehicle. In the post-war period of domestic self-examination, the novel had a secure place. Yet, as Alison Adburgham points out in her study of the silver-fork novel, "When the Napoleonic Wars ended, there were in London no novelists of any note."[39] The literary life was scattered across the provinces: Scott in Scotland, Maria Edgeworth and others in Ireland, Jane Austen in rural England. The success of Scott, and later John Galt, made scenes and characters of Scottish life all the rage.

What London produced during this interregnum was periodical literature and a less distinguished sub-genre of fiction called the "fashionable" novel. These gossiping forms were the particular contribution of the London metropolis to literary life in the 1820s — not surprisingly, for both are concerned with the description of manners and politics. The *romans-à-clef* simply provided fictional names where the newspapers used asterisks; both satisfied the London appetite for scandal and innuendo. This was also connected to the growth of publishers' advertising, or, to use a less polite term, "puffing." When Henry Colburn, whose name was synonymous with this term, hinted that the young author of *Vivian Grey* was a blue blood, he was only following his own well-established practice of enticing readers by playing on their curiosity about the inner circles of London high life. Part of this practice was, not only to place "excerpts" from favourable "reviews" in the papers, but also to discover which prominent families had ordered these novels from the circulating libraries. As *Fraser's*, in an article on "Fashionable Novels," noted, the "obsequious" librarian then "tells less considerable swallowers of the Colburnian jejune, unkneaded trash, that such and such first-rate fashionables have sought the perusal of such and such volumes." In this way, "the manipulated dainties of Henry Colburn and Richard Bentley obtain readers, and meet with an extensive circulation" (1 no. 3 Apr. 1830: 319).

These "manipulated dainties" combined the sensations of romance with close description of fashionable manners and current events.

Adburgham observes, "The world of politics was indistinguishable from the world of fashion. As both Bulwer and Disraeli knew full well, the entrance to Parliament lay through the drawing-rooms."[40] The periodicals and the silver-fork novels (a genre dominated by women authors) were the record of this. Drama had languished, and, as many commentators repeated, "At present the English, instead of finding politics on the stage, find their stage in politics."[41] Fastidious scholarship and Horace's rule of keeping a work nine years were wanted by neither contemporary publishers nor public, although lamentations for these losses are ubiquitous in the criticism of the time. *Fraser's* was not offering a compliment when it noted that, "*Reality* became the order of the day" (1 no. 3 Apr. 1830: 325).

Of course, the combination of Reform and steam printing made the contemporary scene itself compelling reading. The *Edinburgh Review*, reviewing a fashionable novel called *Recollections of a Chaperon*, states unequivocally:

It is no longer necessary to defend the novel against those sweeping denunci-ations by which it was once assailed ... Fictitious narrative can often better illustrate those general truths which experience teaches, than the bare relation of partial facts; and many a novel, devoid of every other merit, may not be without its value as a faithful portrait of the manners of the day.

(*Edinburgh Review* 57 no. 116 July 1833: 404)

The *Edinburgh Review* emphasizes that the value of novels as a record is not historical: "On the contrary, they are, perhaps, beyond all works, save the periodical essay, or the party pamphlet, written peculiarly for the present day" (405).

It is clear, then, that as publishing events novels were not con-sidered part of traditional literature, of poetry, drama, and arcane researches. They are above all political entities, in their subject matter, in their audience, and in their publishing ephemerality. The *Edinburgh Review*'s comparison with periodicals and pamphlets is a revealing and appropriate one to make. In fact, the constant lament of contemporary reviewers – that the public craved only "light" reading, or alternatively, only "useful" reading – may be seen as different sides of the same coin: that the public of the 1820s and 1830s wanted to read only about themselves. There was no time for research during the upheavals of the early thirties; what was wanted was news. In particular, parliamentary news.

As the era of the Napoleonic wars receded, and in Bulwer's phrase, Britain began to look round itself, this looking-round meant a gradual intensification of the focus on government and London. Provincial agitation only placed increased pressure on Parliament. Scott, Edgeworth, and Austen yielded to silver-fork scandal. At the same time, the new technology meant also that the London newspapers could more easily dominate the reading matter in the provinces.[42] Thus, the period between 1814 and the early 1830s was one which increased the focus on London life and came to a climax with the Reform Bill. The collapse of the Edinburgh publishing scene in 1826, coincidentally just when fashionable noveldom was approaching its zenith, is perhaps symptomatic of the yielding of the provinces to the metropolis. In March 1830, *Fraser's Magazine* complained that "Our publishers of the proud northern metropolis seem to have lost all pluck since the lamented death of their great father, Mr. Constable ... the vaunted Modern Athens is fast dwindling away into a mere spelling-book and primer manufactory" (1 no. 2 Mar. 1830: 236).

As *Fraser's* noted, the activities of John Wilson and Susan Ferrier had faded from prominence, Scott had taken to writing history, John Galt was busier as an entrepreneur than as a novelist, and Lockhart had moved to London. *Fraser's*, as might be expected, was scornful of the novels of fashionable London life. They were reflective of real life, to be sure, but only of "an elaborate raree-show of ostrich feathers and silk stockings, cashmere shawls and moustaches ... négligées and fiddle-de-dee's, ottomans, Turkey carpets, and silver forks" (1 no. 2 Mar. 1830: 236). The reader, claimed *Fraser's*, hesitated to "buy a book bearing the title of a novel, lest he should be sickened by a repetition of the elaborate nothings which have become ipecacuanha even to the very watering-place libraries" (236).

It is noteworthy that *Fraser's* remarks are uttered in a review welcoming Galt's *Lawrie Todd*. But, as sharp as *Fraser's* criticism usually was, it here appears sentimental in its tastes. Here in the 1830s, in the midst of all the agitation of Reform and the vortex of London scandal-mongering, *Fraser's* welcomes a picaresque tale of a Scotsman abroad, as a return to the times of Fielding and Smollett, when writers did not scorn "to draw much, as was done of old, from the wide and deep wells of nature and of truth" (242).

Fraser's nostalgic celebration of realism and morality was both out of date and about twenty years premature. Before the British reading public could relish *Vanity Fair*'s moralistic second look at the post-war era, things got worse. Galt faded, Scott died, and the obsession with London and political news intensified. Thackeray's career as a writer is perhaps the typical one of the times. During the 1830s he indulged in Pierce Eganish low-life adventures and consorted with the debauched William Maginn. In fact, he lingered a good fifteen years longer at this improvident apprenticeship in journalism before *Vanity Fair*, his satire of the Regency world, made him a Victorian literary lion in 1848. Perhaps it was not until then — eleven years after Victoria came to the throne, and the *annus mirabilis* also of *Dombey and Son* — that the British reading public was ready for the return to Truth that *Fraser's* pined for in 1830. In the meantime, there was Dickens.

3

1833 – 1836 The sketch writer

I

Dickens's first published sketch, "A Dinner at Poplar Walk," appeared in the *Monthly Magazine* in the last month of 1833. The transformation of Dickens from parliamentary reporter to author coincides with the gradual re-emergence of interest in things literary. The first Reformed session, said to have conducted the largest amount of parliamentary business ever known, was finally prorogued during the summer months. In practical terms, it was not until the Parliament elected in the hectic atmosphere of Reform had shown it too could be undemocratic that political excitement died down.[1] During the recess, Dickens found himself without employment despite strong applications to Lord Stanley and the *Morning Chronicle*. Nor had his suit of Maria Beadnell come to anything after four years. Thus, in the aftermath of love and politics, idle for the first time in years, Dickens sat down to the writing of sketches.

Dickens's sketches may be divided into two critical categories: those for which he got paid, and those for which he did not. Those he wrote as an "idler" appeared in the *Monthly Magazine* between December 1833 and February 1835; those he wrote as a professional literary man appeared in newspapers between June 1834 and October 1836. The collected *Sketches by Boz* blurs the difference by mixing them together, but discussion of their chronological appearance will make clear how Dickens's originality in choice and treatment of his subject matter is grounded in his financial circumstances and contemporary politics. Dickens was part of the general Radicalism in which both Whigs and Tories participated at this time. This appetite for reform moved out of the parliamentary arena after 1833 and into humanitarian agencies during the 1840s: the pull into sympathy for the unfortunate is the force that animates Dickens's pull into narrative. In his story-telling he may have begun with Gothic effects left over from the eighteenth century, but by

43

the 1830s Gothicism is distinctly Tory; Dickens's most sublime effects were to be achieved in realizing his own Radicalism.

The editor who first published Dickens's work was a Captain J. B. Holland, who had bought the "old" *Monthly* earlier in 1833.[2] Our fullest contemporary source for information about this magazine and other periodicals during the 1830s is James Grant's *The Great Metropolis* (1836). This book is a feast for the historian, although one should be cautioned that contemporary reviewers professed to find it full of errors. Like Dickens, Grant was a parliamentary reporter on the *Morning Chronicle* during the early 1830s; he later became editor of the *Monthly* for a brief period in 1836. The *Monthly* paid Dickens nothing for his contribution, as was the practice with amateurs. Coincidentally, the *Monthly* was transferred to James Grant's editorship just about the time that Dickens requested payment for his tales; Grant later claimed there was an exchange of correspondence between them, in which Dickens, citing his new duties on Chapman and Hall's serial, set his terms for any proposed series in the *Monthly* at no less than 8 guineas a sheet (*Letters* I, 131; [16 or 17 Feb. 1836]).

In considering how the *Monthly* might have appeared to a young author choosing a vehicle for his first submission, we should note that there is some reason for believing Dickens in fact intended to send his first story to the *Metropolitan Magazine* (*Letters* I, 34). At the very time when Dickens would have been thinking out plans for his writing, the *Metropolitan* ran an article satirizing the various types of unsolicited contributions typically received by a literary monthly. The "editor" in this dramatic dialogue bemoans the pedant producers of endless tracts on the *Faerie Queene*, the rural homilists, the authors of Gothic tales and "light" papers, the political purveyors of privileged gossip — each certain that his paper, being both gratis and original, will be received by the editor with breathless thanks. The article is a succinct analysis of the literary clichés of the period, with its rhymed swoonings of "poor curates — apprentices in love — blue virgins past thirty — bookworms — disappointed swains — and idle persons of all sorts" (8 no. 30 Oct. 1833: 125).

It is unlikely that the twenty-one-year-old Dickens could have offended on the score of pedantry, but he was certainly capable of doing so under the other categories of Gothic and domestic tales, trite verse, and polemical essays — by 1836 he had published all of these. Fortunately, he also had his sense of humour, and it is with "light" monthly tales that his publishing career began. We do not know if any of these were ever seen or refused by the *Metropolitan* itself – certainly these tales fall in the category of those kinds of "light papers" which in their straining after humour are described by the *Metropolitan* as being "the *heaviest* of the whole set" (125).

In fact, it becomes apparent when looking over the *Metropolitan*'s list and considering the *haut-monde* tone of the "editor's" conversation, that the magazine is a good notch of "fashionability" above Dickens. Only in the theatrical gossip do we find one part of its world with which he could confidently have been conversant. The "editor" is correct in seeing that a monthly magazine's pool of contributors was traditionally filled by "idle persons of all sorts" (125). Robert Mayo's study of magazine literature from 1785 to 1815 finds that most writers for miscellanies were "graduate amateurs," kept in a state of "egregious unprofessionalism" by editors who preferred not to pay money to these reader-correspondents:

At least half of the so-called "original" material printed in the miscellanies from about 1770 to 1815 was produced by industrious amateurs whose names were unknown, often, even to the editors ... All that was needed to become an editor, apparently, was an understanding with the printer, a desk, a pair of scissors, and a mailbox to receive the favors of the writing public.[3]

Mayo contends that Samuel Johnson's pride in his professionalism as an author derives from impatience not only with the old style of patronage but also with the late eighteenth-century flood of scribbling amateurs, who might have led anyone to observe that "no man but a blockhead ever wrote, except for money."

II

Dickens's own status as an amateur and an idler was merely a function of his youth and unemployment. Close as he might have come to being an occupant of the Inns of Court with an income supplemented by parliamentary reporting – a common enough description, as we have seen, of the lives of the young men in the gallery – he simply could not afford to remain an amateur contributor. He never was a *flâneur* in any aspect of life, not even in his voracious theatre-going. He fretted at his unpaid status with the *Monthly*, which lasted only until the advent of the *Morning Chronicle* series began to pay him a regular as well as a supplemental income.

It is notable, then, that Dickens's early *Monthly* tales project a more elevated social scene than any he was actually familiar with on a daily basis. The bachelor hero of "A Dinner at Poplar Walk" (December 1833) is a clerk at Somerset House, with £10,000 invested and a first floor in Tavistock Street, Covent Garden.[4] The other guests at the dinner party in Stamford Hill assume that this civil servant must possess inside knowledge of the Cabinet machinations (16 Dec. 1833: 621). The class of persons at this party approximates that found in the humorous tales of Theodore Hook − who had been educated at Harrow and Oxford and was an intimate of the Prince of Wales's circle.

In Dickens's second tale, "Mrs. Joseph Porter, 'over the way,'" Mr. Gattleton lives in a suburban villa at Clapham Rise and is "a stock-broker in especially comfortable circumstances" (17 Jan. 1834: 11). One of the guests in the family's private theatricals is said to work at the post-office in a civil-servant position. At this point one wonders if Dickens's characters simply consist of lower-class persons arbitrarily assigned a higher status. With "Horatio Sparkins" (February 1834), the Beadnell-like pretensions become farcical. There is satire on connections with the City, the West End (Mr. Frederick Malderton has "an intimate friend who once knew a gentleman who formerly lived in the Albany"), a Lord and an M.P. ("I couldn't stop to talk to him as long as I could wish though, because I was on my way to a banker's, a very rich man, and a member of Parliament, with whom I am also rather, indeed I may say very, intimate") (153; 158). The young ladies call Sparkins "a second Pelham" (160) and try to guess whether he is a clergyman, a barrister, a travelling foreigner, "a surgeon, a contributor to the magazines, a writer of fashionable novels, or an artist" (153). That "the metaphysical Sparkins" turns out to be a shop assistant has often been taken as Dickens's hit at the mutual humbugging of the Beadnells and himself.

By April 1834 and "The Bloomsbury Christening," we are back to a middle-aged bachelor hero, but this time one who has only a salary of £500 and a "'first floor furnished' at Pentonville" (17 Apr. 1834: 375). The main event of the story concerns a christening among his relations, who live − depending upon the maliciousness of the speaker − off Russell Square or Tottenham Court Road. However, the real action is set further out, among the clerks who commute to the City from Islington.

In the progress of publication during the course of 1834, the heroes of these tales gradually assume a status closer to Dickens's own. With this change and Mrs. Tibbs's "Boarding-House" (May and August 1834) in Great Coram Street, Dickens finally stakes out his peculiar caste and territory. The world of his early tales is still very much that of the Regency, Byron, and Waterloo, but such fashionableness as there is becomes blatantly hand-me-down. One of the boarders is a dandy, and the other a quoter of *Don Juan*. Mr. Tibbs is mysteriously said to be "engaged in the City," but the lack of a suburban villa and the necessity of boarders openly precludes any illusions. If anything, his wife's industry and his own helpless servility irresistibly suggest what we know about Dickens's own parents, down to Mr. Tibbs's inability to finish his one tale that begins "'I recollect when I was in the volunteer corps, in eighteen hundred and six'" (481). When Mr. and Mrs. Tibbs come to their irreconcilable differences in No. II (August 1834), Mr. Tibbs retires to Walworth and a small tavern, where his volunteer story is reported to attain its conclusion. The setting of "The Boarding-House," which is the first tale Dickens seems inclined to extend, is a good distance from the comfortable situation of a bachelor civil servant and his £10,000 (Mrs. Tibbs establishes her boarding-house on a legacy of £700). It is also notable that we are shown the weekday domesticities of the Tibbs household, not just its special occasions. Dickens is both more detailed in his depictions of Tibbsdom than of Clapham Rise or Tavistock Street, and also much kinder in his judgements of Great Coram Street's foibles.

III

Not surprisingly, the newspaper reviews of these pieces were light critical work. *Bell's New Weekly Messenger* called his first sketch, "A Dinner at Poplar Walk," "a choice bit of humour, somewhat exaggerated" (2 8 Dec. 1833: 98). The *Sun* called the second sketch, "Mrs. Joseph Porter, 'over the way,'" "a capital quiz" (1 Jan. 1834), and "Horatio Sparkins" was said to be "clever" (1 Feb. 1834). In these descriptions, questions of literary merit seem hardly to matter alongside the entertainment value of the piece. It was enough that the reader laughed with recognition at Dickens's invocation of suburban entertainments. But, as early as April 1834, this brand of wit had palled somewhat on the reviewers. In continuing to call Dickens's work "clever" (1 Apr. 1834), the *Sun* expresses our reservations about these tales generally: "the author is too ambitious of saying smart things – is too much on the strain."

Undoubtedly the effort to play up to the pretensions of Bloomsbury and the need for lightness does bring out a sense of strain in Dickens's writing. He continued to offer up tales to the *Monthly*, but with August 1834 and the advent of the "Street Sketches" in the *Morning Chronicle*, not quite a year after Dickens had begun to produce his *Monthly* tales, the shift in literary and social caste is confirmed. The tales had shown the Stamford Hill and Somerset House world of which Dickens could only have had glimpses, perhaps in his weekend moments at the Beadnells. The *Morning Chronicle* "Street Sketches" (published September to December 1834) are thankfully less facetious, and for the first time reveal Dickens's originality. Freed from the need to construct elaborate plots or plausible characters, he gave himself up to the recording simply of his great knowledge of London. Later, when all the sketches and tales were reviewed in their collected form, it was this acuteness of observation that reviewers praised far more highly than the early cleverness.

Still, in the fourteen months' intermittent sketch-writing that led to *Sketches by Boz*, it was the earliest pieces, the *Monthly* tales, which drew the most attention from Dickens's colleagues on the London newspapers. From December 1833, with the publication of "A Dinner at Poplar Walk," to February 1835, when a second episode in the adventures of Watkins Tottle appeared as Dickens's last contribution to the *Monthly*, his nine sketches there received about forty notices. By contrast, his five *Morning Chronicle* "Street Sketches" (September to December 1834), his twenty *Evening Chronicle* "Sketches of London" (January to August 1835), and his twelve *Bell's Life in London* "Scenes and Characters" (September 1835 to January 1836) received no public notices at all from the reviewers. In fact, there is a gap of approximately a year after February 1835 until Dickens begins regularly to be reviewed again. The reviews resumed with *Sketches by Boz* and *Pickwick*. This has nothing to do with judgements of comparative merit. There was no convention of reviewing the amusements of a "daily contemporary." At best an author could only receive the dubious compliment of having his work pirated by another paper, something which Dickens's work suffered from the start and ever afterwards.

The simplest distinction to be made between these newspaper sketches and what Dickens wrote for the *Monthly Magazine* is that the newspaper narratives were sold as essays rather than tales. From August 1834, Dickens's work was thoroughly that of the newspaper man with a reporting job and a by-line. It is important not to ignore the stability and professional progress that Dickens achieved in these months as a reporter on a prominent daily paper. His job at the *Morning Chronicle* was the first one since Doctors' Commons that did not leave him high and dry with the closing of the parliamentary session. John Black, its editor, and George Hogarth, its music critic, were perhaps the first professional men of letters to praise his work.

By contrast, Dickens's unpaid submissions to the old *Monthly*, written in his periods of unemployment during the parliamentary recesses, would have seemed the doubtful pastime of a highly uncertain time in Dickens's life. Along with the friendship of George Hogarth came the courtship of Catherine Hogarth, a far less vulnerable affair than the one with Maria Beadnell. The extra income from *Pickwick* enabled Dickens to marry Catherine, but it was only the guaranteed salary of the projected *Bentley's Miscellany* that permitted Dickens to give up the security of reporting in late 1836. The emphasis on detailed realism in his writing of 1834 – 35 went along with an emphasis on financial realities.

It was the training that Dickens received as a reporter and a sketch-writer during these months that changed his work from the kind spoken of as "amusing" or "clever" to that praised for its "acuteness." These differences were noticeable when the newspaper sketches received their first comments, with the collected publication of the *Sketches* in volume form. Dickens's powers of observation were preferred to his facetious humour − and it is doubtful if he would ever have been encouraged to republish his sketches had they all continued in the vein of the *Monthly* tales.

The streets, more than any suburban drawing-room, were the indigenous setting of the domestic scenes he knew best. He could not summon up any pathos about a bachelor with £10,000. His first "Street Sketch," on "Omnibuses" (26 Sept. 1834), is also flippant in tone (the humour is at the expense of an "old swell" run about by two omnibus cads, who regularly tyrannize all their passengers between Oxford Street and the City), but in the second, "Shops and their Tenants" (10 Oct. 1834), Dickens moves unhesitatingly into pathos. Whereas he would never have solicited sympathy for Mrs. Joseph Porter, he manages to find a great deal for the tenants of small shops. Much of the sketch chronicles the slide of lower-class proprietors into poverty, especially as the sketch becomes caught up with the plight of a fancy stationer and his daughter:

We often thought, as her pale face looked more sad and pensive in the dim candle-light, that if those thoughtless females who interfere with the miserable market of poor creatures such as these, knew but one half of the misery they suffer, and the bitter privations they endure, in their honourable attempts to earn a scanty subsistence, they would, perhaps, resign even opportunities for the gratification of vanity and an unmodest love of self-display, rather than drive them to a last dreadful resource, which it would shock the delicate feelings of these *charitable* ladies to hear named.

("Shops and their Tenants" *Morning Chronicle* 10 Oct. 1834)

In this single sentence, Dickens sets at odds the Malderton-type "heroines" of his *Monthly* tales and the "fallen" women who form a recurring subject in his street sketches.

We see his progression from caricature to succinct thumbnail narratives in this dichotomy. This sketch begins with the keenest expression of Dickens's own fitness for his avocation – "What inexhaustible food for speculation do the streets of London afford!" – and the condemnation of those people who might walk the streets of London and notice nothing. His scorn is not entirely light-hearted; it is the condemnation of a class. This class is described by Dickens very specifically as consisting of "Large black stocks and light waistcoats – jet canes and discontented countenances" – he is describing young swells, in other words – and their only source of animation can be found in a "west-end cigar-shop in the evening":

There they are, lounging about on round tubs, and pipe-boxes, in all the dignity of whiskers, and gilt watch-guards; whispering soft nothings to the young lady in amber, with the large ear-rings, who, as she sits behind the counter in a blaze of adoration and gas-light, is the admiration of all the female servants in the neighbourhood, and the envy of every milliner's apprentice within two miles round.

("Shops and their Tenants" *Morning Chronicle* 10 Oct. 1834)

As any reader of the enormously interesting *Town* (1842) knows, cigar-shops were euphemistically named places.[5] Dickens describes the kind of haunt in which Sir Mulberry Hawke might have placed Kate Nickleby, had he had his wicked way; it is perhaps the kind of translation which is yet to come for the stationer's daughter. Dickens's narrator sees her now in the candlelight of her humble parlour; he may presently see her in the brilliant gaslight of the West End. In either setting, such a woman becomes the occasion for Dickens's sympathetic polemic.

The "Street Sketches," unlike the smart "Tales," consistently offer up such tableaux to Dickens's curiosity and indignation. "The Old Bailey" (No. III; *Morning Chronicle* 23 Oct. 1834) centres around such glimpses as the ordinary man may get of "fallen" life and its mingled pity and terror. In this case, the "fallen" characters are young boys, one to be seen as he is released to his suffering mother:

The woman put her hand upon his shoulder in an agony of entreaty; the boy sullenly raised his head as if in refusal; it was a brilliant morning, and every object looked fresh and happy in the broad, gay sun-light ... he burst into tears; and covering his face with one hand, and hurriedly placing the other in his mother's they walked away together.

("The Old Bailey" *Morning Chronicle* 23 Oct. 1834)

Nothing observed in Dickens in the *sanctus sanctorum* of a Russell Square mansion equals this scene for intimacy.

The inevitable outcome of this thumbnail sketch, and that of the prisoner pronounced guilty in the "Old Bailey," is in a sense followed out in "The Black Veil," a tale written specifically for the first volume of the *Sketches by Boz* two years later. In the third and final part of "The Old Bailey," a "Dodger" aged thirteen protests his innocence:

"S'elp me God, gen'lm'n, I never vos in trouble afore – indeed, my Lord, I never vos. Its all a howen to my having a twin brother, vich has wrongfully taken to prigging, and vich is so exactly like me, that no vun ever knows the difference atween us."

("The Old Bailey" *Morning Chronicle* 23 Oct. 1834)

The young vandal's pleading proving ineffectual, he shows his feelings for the society that has sentenced him to transportation with a final flourish not unlike the careless arrogance of the omnibus cad – "'Flare up, old big vig!'" In lieu of any firmer victory, St. Giles will always be able to embarrass St. James.

Dickens's sympathy is, in fact, reserved for neither of these characters, but for those in between – the "Shabby-Genteel People" of the fourth *Morning Chronicle* "Street Sketch" (5 Nov. 1834): "A glance at that depressed face, and timorous air of conscious poverty, will make your heart ache – always supposing that you are neither a philosopher, nor a political economist." He advises readers not to be taken in by "swells" of any class, who are pleased with their own confidence-tricks on society, whereas those who genuinely suffer from their own sense of misplaced caste (like Dickens himself) catch his eye and his pen. The defining characteristic of a shabby-genteel man is that he is a "miserably poor man (no matter whether he owes his distresses to his own conduct, or that of others) who feels his poverty, and vainly strives to conceal it."

Thus Dickens is sympathetic towards the pretensions of the poor in a way he can never be towards those of the upper middle class who might also happen to resent their deprivations. Dickens exempts shabby – as opposed to suburban – gentility from moral culpability for this decline. He spins romantic stories instead of satiric caricatures. The hidden sufferings, not the pretensions, seem to come to the fore in these sketches. This sense of the decline in station and self-esteem among the resentfully poor, and the milestones of their downward path, are the theme of the last *Morning Chronicle* "Street Sketch," "Brokers' and Marine Store Shops" (15 Dec. 1834). The sketch progresses downwards from rather grand Long Acre Mews furniture shops to poorer, second-hand Drury Lane shops of apprentices' theatrical costumes, to Ratcliff Highway dealers in sailors' gear, and finally to a King's Bench Prison pawn shop, where the clothes speak only of "the misery and destitution of those whom they once adorned." Again, pretension becomes less reprehensible when it is the cast-off theatrical costume of a stage-struck pot-boy in Covent Garden, than when it consists of a smart bachelor's sofa bedstead in Bloomsbury. Dickens will later write with sympathy, in one of the *Evening Chronicle* sketches that succeeded the *Morning Chronicle* ones, of those poorer people who "really believe that the privilege of wearing velvet and feathers for an hour or two at night, is sufficient compensation for a life of wretchedness and misery" ("Astley's," "Sketches of London" No. XI, 9 May 1835).

IV

The sensitivity to pathos — which emerges as Dickens writes more about the lower classes of London and less about the middle classes of its suburbs — leads into satire and polemic. The tears shed over poverty and the fall into it shade into anger. Where the misfortunes of his suburban heroes or heroines are caricatured as the fumblings of morally culpable individuals, the misfortunes of poorer people are treated apologetically as a class problem. The lower classes are used enough to having their shortcomings treated as vices, by suburban people who confidently excuse their own sins as venial. Dickens never applauds vice, but he is readier, in the case of his street-life characters, to give an explanatory narrative of external causes.

Like the *Morning Chronicle* series, the *Evening Chronicle* "Sketches of London" commence with a sketch (31 Jan. 1835) on one of the metropolis's most obvious features, its hackney coaches (in the *Morning Chronicle* series, it had been omnibuses). But the second sketch, on "Gin Shops" (7 Feb. 1835), like the second *Morning Chronicle* sketch, "Shops and their Tenants," begins with an essay on the exteriors of shops, and builds its interest on the shock of contrast between the splendour of gin-shops and the squalor of the neighbourhoods in which they are found. The sketch ends with a lecture pointed at those members of the middle class who cannot bear such topics: the behaviour of the gin-drinking classes is not so invidious as the self-righteousness of Temperance

Societies who have yet to find "an antidote against hunger and distress."

This is perhaps the most polemical line Dickens had yet taken with his readers. At the same time, one notes on the page of the *Morning Chronicle* where this appears a review of the most recent *Monthly Magazine* issue (Feb. 1835). The review is presumably by George Hogarth, and the greatest space is given to a long extract from "Watkins Tottle" – a "low" passage almost unique in Dickens's *Monthly* tales, because it shows the interior of a sponging house. Indeed, within the tale itself, which begins as nothing more than the usual matrimonial mix-ups of a bachelor among City men and the clergy, the confrontation with real poverty comes as a mild surprise. One notes that the descent into this sheriff's underworld, recounted as Gabriel Parsons arrives to rescue Tottle, is coincident with the story's first real touch of romance. Tottle's own story may be a tale of match-making but the only glimpse of passion occurs in the Cockney factotum's inset tale of a young girl who meets her brother's friend from college, marries against her father's wishes, and sinks into poverty.

The third sketch, "Early Coaches" (19 Feb. 1835), resorts again to comic coaches, but with the fourth, "The Parish" (28 Feb. 1835), Dickens settles into his most comfortable mingling of comedy and pathos. The beadle's pomposity provides the satire, and the schoolmaster's decline into shabby gentility, the sadness. As usual, Dickens ends with an apology for length in these sketches, but now he also suggests that he might create further tales out of the same materials. He makes a tentative approach to continuity in the next sketch, on "The House" (7 Mar. 1835). It is noticeable that he assures his readers of no intention to be "political." A reviewer's complaint on the same page where this sketch appears, that monthly magazines are no place for political disquisitions, reminds us of a standing complaint of the 1830s. Remarkably, Dickens does manage to avoid politics as he describes the country's centre of political debate. His description makes its purlieus sound little different from lower-class London streets, and his scepticism of the whole business is suggested by the fact that his most persistent analogy is to Babel. The posturing of men before other men is what comes before the mind's eye; if such Pickwickian business has anything to do with the lives of their constituents, it is only tangentially so.

Dickens, in fact, raises more politically sensitive topics when he comes in his next sketch to talk about "London Recreations" (17 Mar. 1835). This turns out to be a lecture on class divisions. The opening thesis, that "The wish of persons in the humbler classes of life to ape the manners and customs of those whom fortune has placed above them, is often the subject of remark, and not unfrequently of complaint," becomes very quickly a defence of the lower classes by means of a satire on the middle ones. It is not the lowest of classes who have aspirations above themselves, but the middle ones,

Tradesmen and clerks, with *Court Journal*-reading families, and circulating-library-subscribing daughters, get up tavern assemblies in humble imitation of Almack's, and promenade the dingy "large room" of some second rate hotel with as much complacency as the enviable few who are privileged to exhibit their magnificence in that exclusive haunt of fashion and foolery.

("London Recreations" *Evening Chronicle* 17 Mar. 1835)

Dickens denies that any degenerate fashion for aping prevails, except among these people "and a few other weak and insignificant persons." The end of the article contains a hit at the hypocrisy of the middle classes who invoke propriety to deprecate the pleasures of the working classes.

The sketch on "Greenwich Fair" a few numbers later (16 Apr. 1835) contains no apologies for its very full catalogue of lower-class enjoyments. Dickens admits, in his sketch "Thoughts about People" (23 Apr. 1835), to interesting himself particularly in the pleasures of London apprentices. He describes their fancy-dress recreations, promises sketches of them (readers of *Barnaby Rudge* may take note), and once again takes a hit at the Sabbath Bill. Thus, the innocuous topic of recreation contains more gunpowder in Dickens's politics than the very House of Commons where the Sabbath Bill was being debated. We know that, indeed, he felt strongly enough about it to publish the pamphlet *Sunday under Three Heads* a year later.

The sketches of "Our Parish" that multiply in these last numbers of the *Evening Chronicle*, curiously enough, show less of the working classes' distress than the other sketches. They also show less sense of developing narrative. The sketches of the Misses Willis (18 June 1835), the election for beadle (14 July 1835), and the ladies societies (20 Aug. 1835) are unified only by their title, "The Parish," and the tone of gossipy cheerfulness. There is a truer pull into narrative in a sketch that has nothing to do with the "Our Parish" series, "The Pawnbroker's Shop" (30 June 1835), where we are shown the descent into vice that in a female history often accompanies the descent into poverty. Here, he juxtaposes in two booths a young girl learning to part with her personal belongings, and a prostitute – and the moral drawn from this juxtaposition is that poverty means the end of a woman's self-possession. This could stand for an extension of the earlier scene in "Shops and their Tenants." By comparison with these sketches, the "Our Parish" sketches are simply a series of Pickwickian adventures strung together.

The twentieth and last sketch of the *Evening Chronicle* series, called simply "Our Parish" (20 Aug. 1835), concludes, "To be continued," and, in fact, Dickens had announced in the ninth sketch ("Greenwich Fair," 16 Apr. 1835) that he planned to write *two hundred* sketches altogether. In the fourteenth sketch ("Our Parish," 18 June 1835), he announced not only a promise of future happenings in the parish but also a hope "that an attempted delineation of character now and then will vary the numerous scenes" of London. With that, he launches into the four Misses Willis – who collectively turn out to have less development of character in two columns than the nameless young girl in a single paragraph of the "Pawnbroker's Shop." What sorts of characters Dickens is drawn to project narratives from, and why, is a separate question (though we may glimpse Oliver Twist and young David Copperfield in the boys who inhabit "The Streets – Morning" *Evening Chronicle* 21 July 1835): what is to be remarked here is that, after a number of "scenes," he feels drawn back to "character." The most obvious reason is that even London runs out of "scenes," and that the formal justification of each subject at beginning and end becomes onerous; he says, in announcing the plan to repeat sketches of "Our Parish," "that from this time forward we shall make no further apology for an abrupt conclusion to an article under the title of 'Our Parish,' than is contained in the words 'To be continued'" (No. XIV, 18 June 1835). These words would also, of course, excuse any seemingly abrupt shifts in a single character: there would always be more to be discovered in an accumulation of sketches.

Whatever Dickens's formal notion of character at this time, after the announcement in No. XIV, the characters described in the *Bell's Life in London* series of "Scenes and Characters" are disappointing. We are essentially back to the sense of "character" found in the *Monthly* tales. The first, "Seven Dials" (27 Sept. 1835), seems simply a pleasing continuation of the *Evening Chronicle* "Sketches of London." One wonders if Dickens has found another "Parish," from which he will draw his characters.

However, the second, "Miss Evans and 'the Eagle'" (*Bell's Life in London* 4 Oct. 1835), although set in north London, has characters far closer in their pretensions to those of the *Monthly* tales. And indeed the next five sketches all read very much like the *Monthly* tales of 1834, but with a lowering of class and a better handling of detail – the flirtatious straw-bonnet maker in Camden Town (No. II, 4 Oct. 1835), the middle-aged bachelor of Fetter Lane who thinks he will go into society (No. III, 11 Oct. 1835), the two City clerks who make a night of it (No. IV, 18 Oct. 1835), the retired "old boy" of Cursitor Street, Chancery Lane, who fancies himself as a lover (No. V, 25 Oct. 1835), and the dressmaker in Euston Square who sets up as a vocalist in society (No. VII, 22 Nov. 1835). "Some Account of an Omnibus Cad" (No. VI, 1 Nov. 1835) is more a sketch of manners than a tale – Dickens has already told us he is genuinely fascinated by these cads, and this results in a less condescending piece than the others. In considering the pretensions of both Dickens and his characters in this series, it might be recalled that the venue of publication, *Bell's Life in London* (full title: *"and Sporting Chronicle"*), was a paper established in 1822 to take advantage of the fad for Egan's *Life in London*; there was still an air of 1820s swelldom about it. Dickens was, of course, more kindly disposed towards the lower classes' aping of aristocratic manners than towards the snobs themselves.

Beginning with "The Prisoners' Van" (No. VIII, 29 Nov. 1835), we are back to "amateur vagrancy" and real sympathy with the characters. In fact, with this sketch we are back to another glimpse of the fallen woman. Dickens's account of the omnibus cad's crimes and sentence for transportation is mostly facetious, but his rhetoric becomes serious at the tableau of a woman on the way to ruin. The paragraphs describing the two young sisters flaunting their way into the van form only part of the whole column, which is one of the most humorous of the series, but it alters our whole feeling about the sketch and gives it its title. Poverty is seen by Dickens with a genial eye up to the point where his amusement turns into anger.

The remaining four sketches in the series are not tales. "Christmas Festivities" (No. X, 27 Dec. 1835) and "The New Year" (No. XI, 3 Jan. 1836) catalogue the pleasures of the season and throw a glow of acceptance around our condition. "The Parlour" (No. IX, 13 Dec. 1835) begins with a celebration of hearthside snugness in the cold season, but ends rather unexpectedly with an expression of disgust at men who retail in clichéd terms the issues of the day: "'dastardly Whigs,' 'sanguinary Tories,'" and "depreciation of the currency." From this, we would conclude that in Dickens's view the manners of political times and debate have nothing to do with the moral conditions of daily life. Alongside this picture of politics in a snug parlour, we must juxtapose the real suffering of "The Streets at Night" (No. XII, 17 Jan. 1836). There, we are shown a woman with a baby attempting to win a few coins by singing ballads to passers-by. This is the last of the individual sketches to appear before Macrone's volumes collected them, and Dickens winds up "The Streets at Night" with a discreet puff:

Scenes like these are continued until three or four o'clock in the morning; and even when they close, fresh ones open to the inquisitive novice. But as a description of all of them, however slight, would require a volume, we make our bow and drop the curtain.

("The Streets at Night" *Bell's Life in London* 17 Jan. 1836)

V

Dickens was obviously attracted by the idea of a series and a steady place for his work. Looking back at those first hesitant efforts for the *Monthly*, the desire to introduce continuity is apparent. "The Boarding House" appeared as a story on its own in May 1834. After a gap of two months ("Sentiment" appeared in *Bell's Weekly Magazine* in the interim), another sketch entitled "The Boarding House" appeared in August and was labelled "No. II." (When reprinted, the first sketch was relabelled "Chapter the First.") Only two more sketches appeared in the *Monthly* until January and February of 1835, when "Passage in the Life of Mr. Watkins Tottle" appeared with the labels "Chapter the First" and "Chapter the Second," and a promise of further adventures. The intervening sketches, which appeared in the *Morning Chronicle*, began with "Omnibuses," which was labelled "Street Sketches – No. I." Thus the idea of a series by title and number was this time present from the start. A signature, "Boz," had appeared for the first time with "The Boarding-House " in August 1834. With the *Morning Chronicle* series, "Boz" appeared consistently. This distinguished his sketches from his work as a reporter in two ways. It kept the sketch-writer's fancy separate from the reporter's reputation for accuracy, and removed the sketch-writer from the ranks of anonymity, for it meant that his way of writing acquired a trademark.

The tendency to seriality was also part of this movement towards a writing identity. It is not surprising that the system of continuous numbering and the advent of the pseudonym should have coincided. Before he ever took on *Pickwick* or began his own magazines, Dickens had grasped that principle so dear to a publisher's heart: the establishment of a market by repetition to satisfy an appetite created by that repetition. Given a reasonably proficient writer, this need not have led necessarily to a Dickensian success or notoriety, but it will none the less often make a comfortable profit for both publisher and writer, as twentieth-century formula fiction continues to demonstrate.

Hence, when the *Morning Chronicle* owners began the necessary work to establish their new evening paper, the thought that it might feature a series of Boz's sketches would not have been an uncommercial one, however green the writer. To judge by the apparent lack of fuss, Dickens's offer of a series cannot have been too startling or unwelcome (*Letters* I, 55; 20 Jan. [1835]). Indeed, it would have been up to him to offer his employers anything extra beyond his regular week's work and time as a reporter. In return, his salary rose from 5 to 7 guineas a week. So by February 1835, the time of his last unpaid appearance in the *Monthly*, Dickens had acquired an identity as a writer worth approximately a third of his weekly income.[6]

In August 1835, the twentieth and last sketch had appeared in the *Evening Chronicle*. Between September 1835 and January 1836, Dickens was occupied with a further twelve sketches, which appeared in *Bell's Life in London*, and with plans for a collection of the sketches, to be published by Macrone, whom he had met in the autumn of 1835. The first letter we have projecting the collected *Sketches* is dated [?27 Oct. 1835] (*Letters* I, 81–84).

Meantime, though Dickens's augmented salary continued and he apparently submitted a new series of sketches to the *Chronicle* proprietors, none of his creative work appeared in either the *Morning Chronicle* or the *Evening Chronicle* during this time. He continued his reporting work for the paper, wrote two sketches for the *Library of Fiction* (31 Mar. and 31 May 1836), prepared the collected *Sketches* for publication, and took on *Pickwick* (adding £14 a month to his income). His engagement to Catherine Hogarth in May 1835 had made Dickens anxious for extra income, and the final setting of the date of marriage, after some postponement, for April 1836, indicates that only such a level of income and commitments was felt to be at all secure.

The magazine articles were not, like those demanded by the quarterlies, learned and leisurely considerations of a political or critical subject. Research was not commonly a feature, and therefore there was nothing comparable to compel the pause of reflection. Consciously or not, Dickens demonstrated his qualifications for this kind of writing and his talent for the kind of serial-fiction career begun by *Pickwick* merely by his ability to work to a deadline. Before *Pickwick*, the profitability of novel-writing had nothing to do with being written "on time."

A vivid description of the typical magazine-writer's mind is to be found in *Tait's Edinburgh Magazine* for May 1833. Here was warning of the weariness that was to overcome Dickens in a few short Pickwickian years: "The brain of an article-monger is on the everlasting rack of thought" (3 no. 14 May 1833: 257). A "crack Magaziner" is apparently supposed to be "a droll of the first water": he is, in fact, a man unhappily always on the look-out for verbal conceits, and "for one good thought he turns up, he will launch fifty of the vilest, vapidest, preliminary stupidities it ever fell to the lot of mortal to listen to" (257). Variety, the genius of miscellany writing, was no more than a taskmaster; and it cannot be denied that its exigencies are frequently felt in *Sketches by Boz* and *Pickwick*. In another *Tait's* article, a few months later, the difficulties of magazine writing are blamed on a general deterioration of the old monthlies because of competition from a new class of periodicals – the cheap ones. It was the monthlies, rather than the quarterlies, which suffered:

On the Quarterly Reviews, no great change has been produced. They are conducted in the same manner as when a larger proportion of their sales were to private subscribers ... Rarely is a *flash* article, under pretence of being a review, admitted into the pages of the great Reviews. With the London monthly magazines, to speak generally, the case is reversed. Flash articles are the rule ... (*Tait's Magazine* 4 no. 22 Jan. 1834: 499)

Such, then, was the market that Dickens chose to write for in his spare time, and for a long while without pay. He was not so quixotic as to strive for the unattainable; magazine writing was something he did without a long apprenticeship. In the letter outlining the first collected edition of *Sketches by Boz*, Dickens does not hesitate to promise Macrone extra sketches at short notice should there not be enough to make up two volumes – "a day's time is a handsome allowance for me – much less [*sic* (more)] than I frequently had when I was writing for The Chronicle" (*Letters* I, 83 [?27 Oct. 1835]).

Two letters to Catherine Hogarth at this time echo this boast and also remind us of *Tait's* description of the miseries of a "crack Magaziner" – the miseries that were to be a daily part of Dickens's writing life from then on. In a short note penned at night, Dickens frets, "It is nearly eight, and I have not yet even begun the Sketch; neither have I thought of a subject" (*Letters* I, 85 [?29 Oct. 1835]). The next day he laments the onset of a cold and the fact that a friend had dropped in that evening, staying until midnight. A week later, he is off with another journalist to file an express report for the *Morning Chronicle* on Lord John Russell's speech in Bristol. Dickens never appears more thoroughly the newspaper man than in his directions here for the extra saddle-horses, night coaches, and porter laid on to make that "scoop" (*Letters* I, 90–93). Back in town, by 19 November, he was again writing to Catherine Hogarth of work on another sketch that was due three days later. As he says in another note of this time, excitement – the daily fare of a reporter's life – was also a necessary condition of his creative work: "I never can write with effect – especially in the serious way – until I have got my steam up, or in other words until I have become so excited with my subject that I cannot leave off" (*Letters* I, 97 [25 Nov. 1835]). The young Dickens seems positively to have thriven on "express" writing: the habits of a shorthand reporter were to become those of the crack magaziner and the editor of *Pickwick Papers*.

4

1836 – 1837 The qualifications of a novelist: *Pickwick Papers* and *Oliver Twist*

I

Where we might be used to thinking of Dickens as the first writer to bring the humour of the working classes of London into literature, his early reviews show that such a subject was already well worked before 1836 and *Pickwick Papers*. When the collected *Sketches* were published, the critics were not slow to accuse Boz of excessive caricaturing. The *Atlas* damned his writing as "clever of its kind" but none the less "sheer vulgarity" (11 no. 510 21 Feb. 1836: 123). The *Examiner* wrote of the collected *Sketches*: "The fault of the book is the caricature of Cockneyism, of which there is too much. This broad, common-place sort of thing is unworthy of the author, whose best powers are exercised obviously with great facility on the less hacknied subjects" (no. 1456 28 Feb. 1836: 132). Whatever these "best powers" might be, there are no hints in these reviews that Boz had any talents to cultivate as a novelist. These reviewers did not anticipate the innovations Dickens was to bring to the novel through his portrayal of working-class pathos. He had entered the literary stakes as a humorist, and his humour put him in his literary place – the genre of "entertainment."

However, the care taken over "A Visit to Newgate," a sketch written especially for the collection, and George Hogarth's comments on it in the *Morning Chronicle* (11 Feb. 1836), ought to have told them otherwise about Dickens's ambitions. Hogarth had observed in his review that it was "the most remarkable paper in the book," and apparently Dickens was of the same opinion when he wrote the advertising copy for the *Sketches*: the one sketch singled out by name was "a very powerful article, entitled 'A Visit to Newgate'" (*Letters* I, 123n; [2 Feb. 1836]). Dickens had already given special instructions to Macrone regarding review copies for the *Chronicle*, and he enclosed a personal note to go with the copy to the *Sun*.[1] The *Letters* show that he forwarded to Macrone a copy of "Hogarth's beautiful notice" and looked out for other notices in both the morning and evening papers (I, 129; [11 Feb. 1836]). The highlighting of Dickens's pathetic powers in Hogarth's review is thus to some extent a reflection of Dickens's own hopes for his work. He was equally eager to solicit opinion on another elaborately macabre sketch of the Newgate variety, "The Black Veil" (*Letters* I, 115–16; [7 Jan. 1836]), and began a new series in the *Morning Chronicle* two months later with a sketch of similar morbidity ("Our Next Door Neighbours" 18 Mar. 1836).

The commencement of this "New Series" in the *Chronicle* proved abortive, and there were no more sketches written for it. This may have been due to the press of business in the House (March saw controversy over the Irish Municipal Bill) or, more likely, in the affairs of Dickens himself. In February 1836 *Pickwick* burst upon Dickens. Where a series for the *Morning Chronicle* might have meant the production of two sketches of approximately 2,000 words each twice a month, the first instalment of *Pickwick* ran to about 13,000 words, or three times the amount of two newspaper sketches. Notwithstanding this, at the same time, he wrote a long sketch, "The Tuggs's at Ramsgate," for the first issue of the new *Library of Fiction*, and another for the June 1836 issue.

Still, perhaps because Dickens had not yet made the qualitative leap to sustained narrative, the first instalment of *Pickwick* consists, in effect, of two individual sketches: the parliamentary satire of the Pickwickians and the stage-farce jaunt to Rochester. After the death of Robert Seymour, the length required of Dickens expanded from twenty-four to thirty-two pages (12,000 to 16,000 words); he was faced with writing the equivalent of virtually seven to eight sketches per month. It was an impressive leap for a young author to make.

The content of the early *Papers* is acknowledged to be unsatisfactory. The three chapters in each part are virtually discrete sketches. In Part II there is a Gothic tale of a dying pantomime actor, slapstick comedy in a field-day bivouac, and a comic episode with a shying horse; in Part III, a poem ("The Ivy Green"), and another tale ("The Convict's Return"), a cricket match, and a *Monthly Magazine* style tale of a comic courtship. The next three parts contain a stage-farce elopement, satire on antiquarian discoveries, and a Gothic tale, satire on political elections, another comic tale of a bagman's romance, satire on literary lionism, midnight slapstick in a girls' boarding school, and a tale of a parish clerk's romance.

Thus, the advent of *Pickwick* in April 1836 did not change the view of Dickens as a humorist. A number of papers excerpted the scene at Golden Cross in Part I, which ends in the Cockney cabman's description of his forty-two-year-old horse:

"He always falls down, when he's took out o' the cab ... but when he's in it, we bears him up werry tight, and takes him in werry short, so as he can't werry well fall down, and we've got a pair o' precious large wheels on; so ven he *does* move, they run after him, and he must go on – he can't help it."

(*Pickwick Papers* Part I; ch. 2)

Such an excerpt, widely circulated under the title "A Cabman's Description of his Horse," sustained Dickens's reputation as a sketcher of cockneys. Indeed, the *Atlas* complained, "the wit of the writer has no wider range than through that melancholy region of exhausted comicality, which HOOD, and POOLE, and SMITH, and CRUIKSHANK, have reaped, until they have left not a single laugh behind" (11 no. 516 3 Apr. 1836: 220).

Some reviewers claimed, particularly after the introduction of Sam Weller, that these sketches would be no novelty to anyone who had read John Wight's *Mornings at Bow Street*, the police street reports printed in the *Morning Herald* in the early twenties and illustrated by George Cruikshank upon their publication in collected form in 1824 and 1827. Certainly, *Pickwick*'s passing stories are closer in humour and spirit to these collections of cockney anecdotes than to Pierce Egan's *Life in London* (1821), a more commonly cited precedent. Egan's lavishly printed *Life*, with its coloured plates, follows the slangy adventures of two swells cavorting in the gambling and pugilistic haunts of Regency London; it is a book such as Thackeray's *Vanity Fair*, not *Pickwick Papers*, which is more properly to be regarded as the bowdlerized sequel to this upper-class comic-book. Anyone who was to treat the swells in *Nicholas Nickleby*, Lord Frederick Verisopht and Sir Mulberry Hawk, with so much vehement indignation as Dickens does could not have taken Egan's *Life* as a model. Nor is there any resemblance between Egan's upper-class louts and Seymour's cockney sportsmen, which are, after all, the earliest form of the *Pickwick* characters. *Mornings at Bow Street* contains swells, but its heroes, like those of the Boz *Sketches* and *Pickwick*, are hackney coachmen.

Pickwick's success was not immediate, and there is no great quantity of notices until September 1836. In June, *John Bull* predicted it would hold a "high place in the ranks of comic literature" (16 no. 809 13 June 1836: 190), and in August, *Bell's Life in London* compared it to William Hogarth, but nowhere was *Pickwick* hailed as one of the future classics of the literary canon (7 Aug. 1836).

In general, reviewers seemed to be satisfied to see *Pickwick* as simply more of the humorous sketches for which Boz had already been distinguished. It is of interest to notice that *Pickwick* is generally described in these reviews as a "periodical."

The introduction of Sam Weller coincided with *Pickwick*'s leap into popularity but did nothing to change the perception of it as a humorous sketchbook. The August number (Part V) was excerpted under the heading "A Contested Election," and, perhaps because it featured an anecdote of election bribery, appeared in no fewer than seven London papers between 10 and 21 August. Most of them reprinted the single-line summary which constituted *The Times*'s notice and identified *Pickwick* merely as "a publication distinguished by much humour rich and genuine, though somewhat coarse and uncultivated" (10 Aug. 1836). The *Sun* reviews over the next few months continued to speak of *Pickwick* as "tales and sketches of characters" (4 July 1836), "amusing periodical sketches" (2 Sept. 1836), and "sketches of low life" (1 Oct. 1836). Along with this was always some remark about the humour. The "Boots" of the July number was noticed immediately, and his appearance as Sam Weller in the September issue received emphatic praise. Lengthy excerpting was a much more frequent practice in reviews than it is now, and Sam's comic soliloquies proved highly extractable. Thus, though it might be a long time before *Pickwick* would be given the space of a review in a paper like *The Times*, it was easy enough to give one of Sam's stories its own heading and place it in the middle of a column headed "Varieties" or "Miscellaneous." The remarkable thing about *Pickwick* was that in this homely way it received more numerous and more regular notices than if it had been published as a "novel" between two covers.

If *Pickwick* was not a book destined to receive considered critical attention in a column under the rubric of "Literature," neither was it a magazine with a changing stable of writers, which could be commended in a brief remark or two every month. Still, Dickens's newspaper sketches and *Pickwick* extracts, despite their comparatively low pretensions, received more sustained attention than his *Monthly* tales. This is because, although the sketches for the *Morning Chronicle*, the *Evening Chronicle*, and *Bell's Life in London* may have been discrete commodities in themselves, their linking together in a numbered series gave them a sort of byline. And the excerpts from *Pickwick*, especially of Sam's sayings and doings, gave Dickens a continuing exposure that a three-volume novelist might have envied. By October, it is worth remarking, the *Sun* called Sam "as well sustained a character as is to be met with in any of the novels of the present day'' (1 Oct. 1836). This also marks the first time that *Pickwick* was seen as comparable to a genre other than that of magazine ephemera.

By the November number, the *Sun* declared Sam Weller its favourite of all the Boz characters (1 Nov. 1836). But more interesting than the by now commonplace praise of Boz's "comic genius," was the excerpt chosen to accompany the review. It was not of the usual anecdote length – in this respect Sam Weller was eminently quotable and therefore reviewable – but instead filled a whole newspaper column. The attention given to *Pickwick* here was thus longer than that given to any other publication in this set of reviews, including *Blackwood's, Fraser's*, or any of the works reviewed under "Literature." What is more notable, *Pickwick* is here the only "periodical" made up of "contributions" written entirely by one author.[2]

The actual status of *Pickwick* was perhaps most accurately expressed by the *Morning Chronicle* in October 1836. Like many of the newspapers, the *Morning Chronicle* had favourably reviewed the collected *Sketches* and had excerpted *Pickwick* from time to time. Its formal review of *Pickwick* occurred, though, in the "Magazines" column, along with other notices of magazines such as the *New Monthly Magazine, Monthly Representative, Scottish Monthly Magazine*, the *Monthly, Alexander's East India Magazine, Fraser's*, and *Tait's*. Yet "The Pickwick Club," as it was labelled, was nothing like any of these, and the reviewer remarks, with some self-consciousness, of having to justify his inclusion of *Pickwick* in this column, that it was "entitled in every way to be placed among the periodicals; it is, in fact, a magazine consisting of only one article" (5 Oct. 1836).

Pickwick was an anomalous entry as a magazine: it had no political affiliation or editorials, no useful information or scholarly notes, no critical notices or literary gossip – its only qualification as a periodical among the others mentioned above was that it was published at the same monthly interval and numbered. However, it was not to be continued indefinitely as these other magazines were, although the initial contract was uncertain about the exact length of its run; nor were its numbers collected in yearly or half-yearly numbered volumes with an index. It was advertised as being "edited" by Boz, but he was editor of no one else's contributions except his own.

The reviews of the time classified *Pickwick* as a "magazine." We have come to know it as a "novel." Under either classification in a contemporary newspaper it was an oddity. It was a periodical with only one article. It had started out as a series of sporting engravings with some text, but it was not even clearly that, for the amount of text had made the engravings secondary. Nor was the length that of a typical novel, for the quantity of text was dependent more on the length of time that *Pickwick* kept its audience than on any similarity to the three-volume Scott product or even to the Minerva Press volumes. This uncertainty about the length of its run was something Chapman and Hall had written into the original contract.

The very binding of *Pickwick* expresses its anomalousness. The 1830s, as it happens, was a decade of key developments in binding technology, and *Pickwick* was one of these. It is a matter of common knowledge that the publishing history of the *Waverley* novels marks the settling down of the multi-volumed eighteenth-century novel into the nineteenth-century three-decker, the levelling-off of a rise in the price of novels to 31s 6d, and the shift from 12mo to 8vo. None of this explains or applies to *Pickwick*'s format.

Once *Pickwick*'s periodical run was finished, it was bound together in a single volume selling at one guinea. The binding together of these twenty parts was done in cloth. This would not have been possible before the technical innovations of 1830–32. Until the end of the eighteenth century, all books were issued in sheets; both Michael Sadleir and John Carter emphasize that the term "publisher's binding" is a dubious one to use in the descriptive bibliography of any book issued before the 1850s. The 1830s were a transitional period, when books were issued in a mixture of sheets, paper boards, and cloth. The first major innovation had occurred at the end of the eighteenth century, when the issuing of works in boards as well as sheets occurred; Sadleir marks 1802 as the year when boarding started to become as popular as the conventional issuing in wrappers. Even then, labels were not always provided or were supplied separately, suggesting what was taken for granted: that the form in which a publisher issued a work was not permanent and remained to be determined by the buyer. Carter thus makes a distinction between publishing, which was highly international, and binding, which was entirely local or personal.

Sadleir describes the years 1815–40 as "the vital period in the evolution of binding from ephemerality to permanence."[3] Cloth binding appeared in isolated instances during the 1820s, but even then the smooth cloths and the glue used were not presentable enough to encourage acceptance. Sadleir cites the first thirty to forty volumes of Bentley's *Standard Novels* series as a rare example of smooth cloth binding. Experimentation with the creation of grained cloths that would not show the glue can be seen in the ribbon-embossed style derived from dressmaking and used on both Lockhart's *Life of Scott* (1837–38) and Dickens's edition for Bentley of the *Memoirs of Grimaldi* (1838).

The *Standard Novels* series suggests another factor discouraging the issuing of fiction in any sort of binding that implies permanence. There was a *Library of Romance* series begun on 1 January 1833 by Leitch Ritchie (published by Smith & Elder) which issued each octavo volume of "original" romance in cloth at six shillings. Ritchie's advertisements mentioned Bentley's *Standard Novels* series but made the point that these were no more than reissues of old works, whereas Ritchie was proposing to provide *new* fiction at the same cheap price. Moreover, in doing so, he was also attacking Colburn's practice of ensuring that each new novel reached the often inflated length of three volumes, for the *Library of Romance* novels were to be completed in no more than two volumes each. Indeed, for the first few months, Ritchie put out a complete novel every month. But by April 1833, he was forced into multiple volumes and then irregular issue, a long silence during 1834, and then the end of the series in August 1835. Its unsold sheets were distributed a few years later. In an age when "cheap knowledge" was on everyone's lips, Smith & Elder had tried to sell "more cheap books to wean novel readers from borrowing more expensive ones. They imagined that the public would as readily buy new novels for 6s as they bought Bentley's Standard Novel reprints."[4] But, Sadleir explains,

the novel reading public liked to sample fiction from a library before they bought it and ... there was no similarity, save one of price, between the appeal of Bentley's editions of tried favourites and Smith, Elder's neat little volumes of unknown romance.[5]

The next attempt to issue original fiction in this way was undertaken by Chapman and Hall in 1845 (see advertisements in the *Athenaeum*, November 1844): the reviewers applauded, the series failed. (Sadleir claims never actually to have come across any of these Chapman and Hall volumes.)

Pickwick was thus no attempt to introduce cheap volumes of fiction. The paper wrappers in which it was issued did not make any appeal to the "library" notion of permanence, and the cover illustrations by Seymour were designed to appeal to the poor man's gallery, the crowd of gawkers always surrounding the London booksellers' windows where artists' prints were displayed.[6] The issuing of *Pickwick*'s parts in paper allowed leather binding at the end; the issuing of the whole in cloth was in effect a reprint of familiar fiction by the time December 1838 rolled around. In fact, Sadleir goes so far as to link the general change to cloth binding directly to the success of *Pickwick* – and so does Carter.

There is no record of why Chapman and Hall chose to issue *Pickwick* in a single volume cloth-bound. Nothing in the early advertisements suggests that they would. *Sketches by Boz* had been issued so, and Carter takes this as one more sign of Macrone's innovativeness, in the decade during which the technical possibilities of cloth binding and embossed gilt lettering of titles on cloth covers were struggling for commercial recognition. Sadleir remarks that Colburn and Bentley, the two biggest publishers of fiction, were much slower to abandon boards for their new fiction. Macrone, and Chapman and Hall were young publishers who had established their businesses only in the early 1830s; they were not part of the older book-trade (which had got into publishing only through the cautious expansion of the antiquarian book-trade during the Napoleonic years). There was no tradition before the 1830s of a publisher routinely concerning himself with binding; and indeed both Carter and Sadleir are rather severe on the pitfalls of assuming that the binding of any book published before the 1850s dates from the same time as the issue of its sheets. The lack of this tradition is, Carter explains, why cloth binding, even when technically perfected, did not immediately catch on. The trade price of a novel in the early nineteenth century was the same whether bound in paper or cloth, since it was always assumed the buyer would replace the outer envelope. Indeed, a contemporary guide to publishing says of cloth binding only that "until a Book is Bound in Leather, it certainly forms a very agreeable substitute."[7] Leather was more fashionable than either boards or cloth (a result, perhaps, of the antiquarian movement of the 1810s and 1820s) and, if boarding was to be included, it cost the publisher more, until at least the mid-thirties, for no foreseeable gain.

The final step which seems to have made cloth a selling point over cardboard was the possibility of embossing gilt lettering onto the cloth. Paper labels were associated with the ephemeral stage leading to leather; gilt labels could allow cloth to compete directly with leather in the appeal of permanence. The development of rapid, that is to say, mechanical, gold lettering onto cloth took place in 1832. The changeover is usually dated by Murray's issue of Byron's collected works (1833): the first two volumes had paper labels, while the rest used embossed gold lettering. But its real popularity is associated with the publisher's exploitation of the appetite for illustration. The most spectacular examples of this are to be seen in the elaborate naval motifs embossed in 1837 into the covers of Marryat's *Peter Simple* and *Jacob Faithful* (both novels which had been issued partially in serial form in the *Metropolitan Magazine* a few years earlier). *Oliver Twist* in 1838 and *Jack Sheppard* in 1839 are also remarkable for the fact that the publisher's name (Bentley) is printed in gilt on the spine, another sign that the concept of publisher's binding was taking hold. By 1841, the trend towards cloth was established, but it should be noted that this was far more the case for non-fiction than for fiction.

In retrospect, the use of cloth can be linked to *Pickwick* in two ways: the appetite for its illustrated parts is the same one exploited by mechanically printed gilt; and its twenty parts could never have been bound into a permanent board form without the use of something stronger than cardboard. Sadleir remarks that copies of the Dickens novels in this original cloth binding are difficult to obtain; most are in poor condition or have been rebound, because the volumes are really "too heavy for their cases."[8] Sadleir and Carter also point out that innovations in cloth binding of fiction reflect the part-issue market (associated with the selling of reprints), not the traditional three-volume form of the novel: "The three-decker [before 1860] is anything but representative of the general tendencies of publishers' cloth."[9] And, in fact, the *Author's Printing and Publishing Assistant*, a handbook for authors put out in 1839, advises that cloth binding "general as its use has become, has not, however, been adopted for Novels, which are still usually published in Boards."[10]

Therefore, when Chapman and Hall for whatever reasons decided to re-issue *Pickwick* in volume form, they may have been responding to its immense popularity and attempting to gratify those who had missed the early issues; as it stood, there was no pressure on them by the publishing conventions of the day to provide anything more than wrappers or cardboard. Had they chosen the latter, they would have needed to go for a number of small volumes. The surprising thing remains that they did not.

Bentley's publication of *Oliver Twist* was more traditional in every way. Marryat had already published a couple of novels serially in the *Metropolitan Magazine* before *Bentley's Miscellany* came on the scene, and the more permanent form of *Oliver's* publication took the shape of three volumes – cheapness being given a nod by its price of 25s. It was also sold in sheets. Such a mixture of formats was conventional. If Chapman and Hall had meant to hit the traditional circulating-library fiction market, the obvious choice was to go for three volumes. Thus, even in its binding, *Pickwick* belies its classification as a novel as the 1830s publishing world understood it. Leitch Ritchie's failure to sell original fiction in something resembling traditional volume form was too recent to be ignored, and 1837 was a year of depression in the publishing industry. When Chapman and Hall ultimately tried a similar experiment in 1845, they sold volumes, not wrapped parts. Both *Pickwick*'s part-issue and its final volume format suggest that other genres were in the minds of both publisher and author. In *Pickwick*'s first preface, Dickens later said he had been thinking of old novels hawked in parts by the pedlars of his childhood, but these had been reprints, not original publications.

On the difficult question of structure in Pickwickian narrative, Chesterton has astutely observed that all the reader really wants of Dickens in any case are "flowing lengths,"[11] and this is strikingly borne out by the first reviewers of *Pickwick*. There was no eagerness among them to see how the story would "turn out," for Pickwick was a "club," not a story. The categories or images used to describe *Pickwick* in its first long review by a magazine, the *New Monthly Magazine* for September 1836, are typically contradictory and confirm the confusing intersection of genres suggested by its binding. *Pickwick* is announced as a periodical, "edited" (but clearly, written) by Boz, whose "spirit" resembles those of two novelists – "our Fieldings and Smolletts" (102) – from the past but in the present can be likened only to that of the humorist Theodore Hook. And in the next paragraph it is described as a book – but one modelled on an eighteenth-century periodical:

The hint of this book (for such it is, though published in monthly numbers) seems to have been taken and improved upon from the whimsical descriptions of various clubs, consisting of humourists of different kinds, given in the "Spectator." (*New Monthly Magazine* 48 Sept. 1836:103)

This took no great perception, for indeed the advertisements projected *Pickwick* as no more than a series of discrete adventures and transactions.

At the same time as the *New Monthly Magazine* article was struggling to classify *Pickwick*'s achievement, in August 1836, Dickens received another sign of the reputation this anonymous publication had gained him. Just as Sam Weller was appearing on the scene (Part V), Richard Bentley paid a call to sign Dickens up as a Bentley author. Despite *Pickwick*'s success, Chapman and Hall at this point seem not to have had the perception that Bentley did, of Dickens's potential. They were probably waiting to see if *Pickwick* would "go" after the disasters of the first few months and may rightly have been dubious about committing themselves to another periodical, let alone anything else. From the *Letters*, it appears that they roused themselves only after the call by Bentley (I, 169; [?24 Aug. 1836]). But Bentley, encouraged by his chief clerk, Edward Samuel Morgan, had already signed up Dickens for two novels.

Morgan, admitting that it was he who had drawn his employer's attention to Dickens, was none the less aghast:

... I felt it was somewhat rash on Mr. B's part to agree to give so high a price for works of fiction, as yet unnamed, to a writer then almost unknown, & who had certainly not yet written a novel – for the "Pickwick" papers, could not be then considered in that light.[12]

A naive point, but a pertinent one: Dickens had *not* yet undertaken anything like a novel. His letter to Bentley the next day, while obviously written in bargaining terms, also expresses some of the difference between the matter-of-fact commitment to the supplying of *Pickwick*'s requisite letterpress and the more solemn effort he saw as appropriate to writing a novel. There he speaks of "the anxiety I should feel to make it a work on which I might build my fame" (*Letters* I, 165 [17 Aug. 1836]). There had been no mention of this kind of fame when *Pickwick* was taken on.

It would be of interest to know if the suggestion that Dickens appear in Bentley's list as a novelist came from the publisher or the author. In the contract for the novel, the title is "not yet determined," while the amount of letterpress very definitely is. The contract also specified that Dickens was to undertake no other literary work until it was completed (*Letters* I, 648–49; 22 Aug. 1836). The idea of asking Dickens to appear in his list as the editor of a periodical seems not to have occurred to Bentley until October, when Bentley himself had got comfortable with the notion of setting up his own magazine. Meanwhile he had made, in his own words, "a bold venture"[13] in asking the young supplier of copy for a sporting gallimaufry to move into three volumes. Morgan, it turns out, was perfectly right: Dickens never in fact produced the conventional three volumes of the Bentley contract. Instead, by continuing to write Pickwickian periodicals, he rewrote the form of the novel itself.

II

The agreement in August 1836 to produce two novels for Bentley did not prevent Dickens from writing to offer Chapman and Hall "future periodicals" and speaking heartily of them as "my periodical publishers." The success of *Pickwick* was encouraging to both author and publisher, but there are hints that relations were somewhat strained by Dickens's finding it difficult to be prompt with his instalments during the last quarter of 1836 (*Letters* I, 188–89; 1 Nov. 1836). Moreover, his first publisher, Macrone, was still expecting the second series of *Sketches by Boz* in December, and Bentley, his latest publisher, the promised novel within a year. These commitments, plus the business of rehearsals for *The Strange Gentleman*, which opened at the end of September, and *The Village Coquettes*, which opened in December 1836, were all defeating even Dickens's efficiency. None the less, by the appearance of the ninth number of *Pickwick* at the beginning of December, Dickens had also signed a contract to take on the editorship of *Bentley's Miscellany* (*Letters* I, 649–50; 4 Nov. 1836).

This marks the end of an era in Dickens's life, for it was the final sign that he was no longer intent upon a reporting career. It was the *Morning Chronicle* work and not *Pickwick* that was ultimately eliminated in order to give Dickens enough time to fulfil his obligations to the *Miscellany*. As Bentley's editor, Dickens could not be at the beck and call of newspaper reporting that might send him out of town at a moment's notice. The sketches in *Pickwick* were reviewed every month whereas the *Morning Chronicle* ones could never be, and Dickens perhaps had a feeling of being better appreciated by Chapman and Hall than by John Easthope. The letter to Chapman and Hall announcing this resolution is full of high spirits and warmth towards his publishers – its only spot of sullenness comes when Dickens reminds them that he has "many other occupations; and secondly that spirits are not to be forced up to Pickwick point, every day" (*Letters* I, 189). The continuation of *Pickwick* was possible only if the high jinks were not to be perpetual. This reminds us once again of the fact that *Pickwick* had originated essentially as a comic monthly and of how, by inserting serious tales, Dickens had taken it in a direction quite different from Seymour's rural sporting sketches.

Thus, October 1836 saw the rationalization of *Pickwick*'s plan. The mere fact that Chapman and Hall could ask for "another" periodical meant that the stopping point of *Pickwick* itself must now have come into sight. It was at this point that its final form would have become clear, and Dickens could have seen ahead to a monthly schedule alternating between the *Miscellany* and *Pickwick*, with work on the novel for Bentley filling up spare corners of his time.

The dates of these agreements, the friendly letter of 1 November to Chapman and Hall, and the formal contract of 4 November with Bentley, mean that Dickens was mulling over such plans through the writing of *Pickwick*'s eighth number during October. The effect of these resolutions is seen in the ninth number (December 1836) of *Pickwick*, in its greater attention to matters of plot. In the seventh number, the introduction of new adventures had still been casual: "'we may as well see Ipswich as any other place'" says Pickwick, for example, in chapter 20. Nearly a hundred pages and a matrimonial misadventure later, they expose Jingle as an impostor. At the end of this action, Dickens takes up the reins of the plot more firmly. In the ninth number, chapter 26 begins with the legal proceedings against Pickwick. Thus, the Bardell v. Pickwick action is given a stronger grip on the narrative. Up till this point, the exposure of Jingle had been the tenuous main thread – one rather inclined to give out – of the original narrative. In this particular episode, it ends in a mock trial of the Pickwickians by an Ipswich magistrate, in a spoof of legal-parliamentary mannerisms. The Bardell intrigue is also eventually ended in such a manner, with the pseudo-parliamentary linguistic formula that Dickens is prone to co-opt when invention dwindles.

The Club and its legalistic proceedings progressively fade from the scene, while the figures of Sam and Mr. Pickwick acquire interest against an increasingly chiaroscurist background. Instead of dis-jointed Pickwickian antics punctuated by staged macabre inter-polations, the character of Pickwick himself is gradually educated in the world's sorrow. When the narrative brings us round to Dingley Dell again in the Christmas chapter of Part X, the lighthearted pleasures of the season are almost overwhelmed by the recollection of time's vagaries. The "Man of Feeling" stance of the narrator here, which becomes more and more explicit in the narrative, is not an original Pickwickian feature. Pickwickianism, originally, consists of high spirits and pomposity. Mr. Pickwick's "scientific" interest in mankind, though benign, is far from being an intimate one. But for Dickens, it becomes apparent, an intimate knowledge of men means a knowledge of their sorrows and how men contend against them. Such is the moral of the story of Gabriel Grub. Grub, a predecessor of Scrooge, is made to see that his moroseness is selfish, when others who have greater reason to be so continue to practise contentedness. This is not cheerfulness in the Pickwickian sense. There are no men in boyish clubs in the vision given to Gabriel Grub. Men in clubs are forever boyish and can remain so because privileged, whereas what Grub sees is a vision of men in the working world.

The split between things Pickwickian and things Dickensian is also to be seen in Dickens's first contributions to *Bentley's Miscellany*: it is present in the contrast between the adventures of Mr. Tulrumble, a pompous small-town public official, written for the January 1837 issue and the adventures of Oliver Twist, a small parish pauper, written for the February issue. "The Public Life of Mr. Tulrumble, Mayor of Mudfog" is little different from the first chapter of *Pickwick* – a satire of public official bumblings and speechifying. "Oliver Twist" is introduced the next month as a kind of sequel, inasmuch as the first number is also a satire of Mudfog officialdom, substituting Mr. Bumble for Mr. Tulrumble. There is a difference, however, in that the second treatment of Mudfog has a rhetorical purposiveness. No longer are we in a vague literary land of gentle village life; we are in contemporary England, where the traditional unit of the parish has been bureaucratized into a new and disagreeable shape.

Oliver Twist might be seen as the earliest of Dickens's condition-of-England novels – with the qualification, however, that although it might depict Dickens's idea of England, it does not demonstrate his notion of the English novel. His contribution to the February 1837 issue of *Bentley's Miscellany* is an article, not the opening segment of a novel ("Oliver Twist," not *Oliver Twist*). And, although the story of Oliver Twist seems very far from the original *Wits' Miscellany* notion of merriment, Bentley obviously approved (see his puff in the *St. James's Chronicle*, 31 Jan. 1837). The New Poor Law, which isolated wives from husbands, parents from children, and then separately starved them was a law brought in by the Whig Reform Parliament. It was criticized by Radicals and Tories alike. Dickens was close to being a Radical, Bentley was certainly a Tory, and so "Oliver Twist" suited them both. *Sunday under Three Heads* (1836), Dickens's first venture into polemic, had been an anonymous pamphlet scarcely noticed; now six months later, his "Oliver Twist" polemic was receiving enthusiastic attention in a well-circulated monthly. The *Constitutional*, a Radical paper, praised Dickens as highly as the Tory *St. James's Chronicle*.

Not surprisingly, there are far more January notices of the new *Miscellany* than of *Pickwick*, which was into its tenth month. By this time, most review columns were carrying only excerpts of *Pickwick*. The *United Services Gazette* was one of the few papers which noticed both serials, praising *Bentley's Miscellany* as "one of the pleasantest of the London periodicals" and *Pickwick* as a "very droll miscellany" (no. 209 4 Feb. 1837: 3—4). Both notices appeared under the "Magazines" column.

The succeeding number (March 1837) of each periodical was favourably received. In both instalments the satirical element was prominent: there was more facetiousness over the New Poor Law in "Oliver Twist," and a parody of the Norton v. Melbourne case of 1836 in *Pickwick*. Most readers, however, preferred the comic passage between Sam Weller and his father on writing valentines in chapter 32, which certainly made a convenient extract. The only extracts taken from the trial of Pickwick consisted of Sam Weller's testimony. Even the Wellers could be objected to, however, in the Temperance Association scene, when Mrs. Weller's shepherd preacher was shown drunk. As with the workhouse satire in *Oliver Twist*, the objections to it were on the grounds of "coarseness" or "nastiness." *Bell's New Weekly Messenger* complained that such vulgarity would have "the effect of excluding the author's Mr. Pickwick and Mr. Weller from every decent room in the country" (6 no. 271 5 Mar. 1837: 154). The *Examiner*, too, another weekly that went out to provincial readers, complained about the meanness of Dickens's satire in *Oliver Twist* (no. 1519 12 Mar. 1837: 165—66). Thus, the pressures over "lowness" that Dickens was to complain about in the *Oliver Twist* preface of 1841 had begun as early as Oliver's second appearance in 1837.

The *Examiner* was consistently to complain of this fault in *Oliver Twist*, right up to and including its review of the story in book form. At the same time, the fact that *Oliver* was even noticed in the *Examiner*'s pages was extraordinary; unlike many papers, the *Examiner* did not have a consistent policy of regular excerpting. This attention paid to *Bentley's Miscellany*, and particularly to *Oliver*, directly reflects the interest of John Forster, who had been the paper's dramatic critic since 1833, and its literary editor since 1835. These early reviews, though written before Forster and Dickens had met, often temper their criticism by suggesting that Boz could do better. The attention paid to the trivial productions with which Dickens was associated during 1836 and the perpetual exception made for Dickens himself were flattering.

What makes this *Examiner* review of *Oliver Twist*'s second instalment (there appears to have been no review of its first) additionally interesting is that it was precisely about this time that Dickens and Forster became acquainted. We can guess that this occurred sometime early in March when Dickens sent Forster copies of *Sketches by Boz* as a token of the "desire to cultivate and avail himself of a friendship which has been so pleasantly thrown in his way" (*Letters* I, 243; [?23 Mar. 1837]). Both had worked for the *True Sun* in 1832 (though Dickens was there only from March to July) but apparently did not meet then. Dickens was a parliamentary reporter; Forster had been its dramatic critic. This perhaps warns against assuming introductions through any number of mutual acquaintances, however plausible. It is generally thought that Ainsworth, who had introduced Dickens to his first publisher, made the introductions between Dickens and Forster. Dickens was shortly to find Forster's friendship more useful than he could have imagined.

Notwithstanding Forster's fears in his *Examiner* reviews about the coarseness of Dickens's Poor Law satire, most reviewers seemed to respond favourably to the pathos emerging out of the satirical context. The April number includes a macabre tale about the death of a beloved wife, not unlike the interpolated tale of the pantomime actor in *Pickwick*'s second number. Dickens was evidently trying to impress his readers with his best Newgate powers. The *Carlton Chronicle* caught this intention and wrote about it in its review of the April number,

We come to "Boz;" but stop, reader! you are going to burst into a guffau! – Stop, we say, for your own credit's sake – you do not understand "Boz" ... The surface of the stream seems bright, and cheerfully bubbling as it rushes on – but in its windings you come ever and anon upon some place of depth, which is dark at top ... he possesses in his sketches the power Rembrandt had, of bringing out to stand forth visibly masses of dark by a few strokes of light.   (*Carlton Chronicle* no. 40 8 Apr. 1837: 635)

That month Macrone (with whom Dickens was no longer on speaking terms after having transferred the publishing rights for "Gabriel Vardon" to Bentley) had published a second edition of *Sketches by Boz, Second Series*. As a second appearance of the work, it was not widely reviewed. But one notice, in the *Weekly Dispatch*, used the appearance of the second edition as an opportunity to note the changing shape of Dickens's reputation: his early celebrity as an original humorist was being altered by the recognition that he could write pathos too (no. 1851 9 Apr. 1837: 178). The extract given, from "The Hospital Patient," is a gloomy one, and it is significant that the last word should be of Dickens's powers of pathos. The *Sunday Times*, too, praised Dickens's evocation of the "philosophical subtleties of human nature" (no. 757 23 Apr. 1837).

The culmination of this second period of Dickens's fame after he had become editor of Bentley's flash *Miscellany* can be seen in retrospect to occur with the Literary Fund dinner of early May 1837. At this dinner were a number of literary men who had become Dickens's friends within the past eighteen months: Ainsworth, "Father Prout," Macrone, Bentley, Samuel Lover, William Jerdan, and R. H. Horne. The toast from the Chair was to "the health of Mr. Dickens and the rising Authors of the Age." Dickens's reply was suitably modest for a man who would have been passed by on the street a year before by any one of those who were drinking his health now.

A short summary of Dickens's career to date is given by *Chambers's Edinburgh Journal* in the same month. This account is factual rather than critical, being intended primarily to bring country readers up to date on a London phenomenon, who "is unrivalled in the peculiar line he has selected, and, to the wonder of every body, has risen from comparative obscurity to a high point of fame in the short space of a single year" (6 no. 274 29 Apr. 1837: 109). His fame, according to this account, consists in being a humorist and an observer – a "contributor to the public amusement." There is no reference to novel-writing, and *Pickwick* is called "a series of monthly pamphlets." Such was *Chambers's* introduction of Dickens to readers outside London.

Pickwick, by now in its thirteenth number, was still commonly referred to as a "popular periodical, for so it may be called" (*Morning Advertiser* 1 May 1837). In fact, it is apparent that for all the comparisons made to eighteenth-century novelists, these allusions refer at least as much to their journalistic writings as to their novels. The *Sun*, reviewing *Oliver Twist*, wrote of "this clever series of articles," that "Boz has great and ready powers of invention, combined with a felicity of touch that not unfrequently reminds us of the 'Citizen of the World'" (1 May 1837). This review is reprinted in the *Morning Post* as one of Bentley's puffs and shows that Dickens's publisher at least thought the *Sun*'s description of the *Miscellany* for May a suitable one. Nor would the comparison to *Citizen of the World* have been unwelcome to Dickens. A few years later, when projecting *Master Humphrey's Clock*, he wrote to Forster that he wanted it to be "something between *Gulliver's Travels* and the *Citizen of the World*" (*Letters* I, 564; [14 July 1839]).

With Mary Hogarth's death in May, there occurs the well-known break in the serial appearances of both *Pickwick* and *Oliver*. In fact, May and June 1837 mark a significant juncture in Dickens's career.

More importantly, the events of these months brought him into closer friendship with John Forster, who stayed with Dickens and Catherine while they recuperated at Hampstead and who after this became much more closely involved in Dickens's business affairs. Coincidentally, there was suddenly an increase in such affairs. Dickens's relationship with Macrone had earlier broken down when Dickens transferred the property of his first novel to Bentley. Now Dickens heard that Macrone intended to reissue the *Sketches* in a monthly format identical with that of *Pickwick*. As the indignant Dickens saw it, Macrone was insensitive to the commercial greed such a transaction would impute to Dickens: "the fact of my name being before the town, attached to three publications at the same time, must prove seriously prejudicial to my reputation" (*Letters* I, 269–70; to Forster [?9 June 1837]). Dickens asked Forster to intervene and threatened to publish a disclaimer in all the papers where Macrone advertised the new work. We see from this episode, not only the great success of *Pickwick*, but also the fact that Dickens was associated in the public mind with a specific formula: he was not a novelist at this stage, but a monthly producer of public entertainments, the serial format of which was close to being overexploited.

At this time when Dickens began to see himself as the abused commodity of his publishers and was planning how to protect himself against Macrone, he cast an eye over his obligations to Bentley (*Letters* I, 271; to Forster [?14 June 1837]). When Macrone's plans came out, Bentley seemed inclined for a while to help Dickens out by bidding for the copyright of the *Sketches*, but in the end it was Chapman and Hall who bought them. Despite his high moral tone earlier, Dickens agreed to allow their reissue in monthly parts, with the explanation to Forster, that if the *Sketches* were going to appear in such a form it might as well be undertaken by Chapman and Hall, who unlike Macrone, would give Dickens part of the profit (*Letters* I, 273; to Forster [?17 June 1837]). And so it happened. *Sketches by Boz* was republished in twenty monthly parts from November 1837 to June 1839. The agreement with Macrone also specified that Chapman and Hall buy up his remaining stock of the *Sketches*, one hundred copies of the First Series in two volumes, and 750 copies of the Second Series in one volume.

In the end, Dickens, pressed by circumstances, was faced with his name appearing everywhere in green covers. At least the reprint series of the *Sketches*, which was started just in the interval between the end of *Pickwick* and the start of *Nicholas Nickleby*, used pink covers. Nevertheless, it caused Chapman and Hall unforeseen expense for an old property, which their author thought he had left behind him as an apprenticeship effort. It was *Pickwick* that had made Dickens a name to conjure with, not the *Sketches*, and it was in a sense to keep the trademark of *Pickwick* – monthly green covers – identified as their property, that Chapman and Hall bought up the *Sketches by Boz* copyright. Certainly, neither they nor Dickens had shown any previous inclination to obtain *Sketches by Boz* in the volume format. Assuming that Macrone gave every appearance of firmness, they must have feared the real dissipation of *Pickwick*'s cachet, were its distinctive green covers to appear under another publisher's name. Dickens's early determination to advertise against Macrone, and the allowing of Chapman and Hall to do the very same thing shows not only the inevitable enticement of profit but also the identification of a publisher with a recognizable property: that is to say, of Chapman and Hall with Dickens and *Pickwick*. As Dickens explained in his letter to Forster, Chapman and Hall with "all the *Pickwick* machinery in full operation" (I, 273), were likely to turn a better profit than Macrone on the same venture – or, as Sam Weller said, "Pickwick and principle."

Forster presumably agreed. At this point we begin to see the sudden full force of a lawyer's interest in Dickens's affairs. It is with the fifteenth number of *Pickwick*, the first number to appear after Mary Hogarth's death and the visit at Hampstead, that Forster began to read the proofs of Dickens's monthly work. It was also in July that Forster's "beautiful notice" of *Pickwick*'s fifteenth number appeared in the *Examiner* (see *Letters* I, 280; to Forster, 2 July 1837).

The fifteenth number of *Pickwick*, then, marks a critical leap forward in recognition of Dickens's narrative skills. The *Sun*, one of the closest critics of Dickens's writing, praised the particular polish of this number and invoked a comparison with Fielding. There were also exceptional words of praise for *Oliver Twist* and a comparison made to Scott (1 July 1837). As Dickens advanced into the tales of the Fleet prisoner and the orphan, and settled both narratives among specifically London scenes, his emotional effects became the more intense and sustained. At the same time that Chapman and Hall were intent on exploiting their Pickwickian property of monthly green covers, the writing itself was moving on into the fields of more coherent narrative.

This contradiction was well marked in the first review of Dickens's work to appear in a quarterly. In this way too, July 1837 signifies a substantial turning point in Dickens's reputation. That the bustling young John Forster should have taken up Dickens now was fortunate;

that a quarterly should have taken up a cockney sketch-writer without a serious book to his name was astonishing.

The *London and Westminster Review*, in reviewing Dickens in July 1837, shows some consciousness of this anomaly. The review, written by Charles Buller, Carlyle's young friend and pupil, begins with the observation that this was attention "more serious than is generally accorded to the anonymous writers of productions given to the world in so very fugitive a form" (194). As far as quarterlies were concerned, *Pickwick*'s method of production should have more than disqualified it from serious critical attention, whatever its ephemeral success. Carlyle commented on this fact, saying: "An intelligent kind of youth in Dumfries expressed his amazement that '*this* Review,' as he reverently named it, had taken notice of Pickwick at all" (IX, 256; 18 July 1837). Carlyle himself sent for a copy of *Pickwick* on the basis of what Buller said. After reading the instalments to date, he forswore any faith in Buller's reviewing – and continued to read *Pickwick* (IX, 268; 28 July 1837). Buller's review assumes most of its readers would have read *Pickwick*, even while recognizing that such an assumption was unusual. The announced purpose of his article was to attempt to understand "a popularity extraordinary on account of its sudden growth" and also in its ability to cut across classes (196). Dickens is here being considered more as a cultural phenomenon than as an individual artist. The fact that he had appeared before the public over the previous fifteen months, month in and month out, and latterly, in two monthly places at once, that he appeared in the daily and weekly papers at the same time in the form of long excerpts to be read by people who would not have picked up the *Pickwick* pamphlet itself: all this meant that Dickens attracted regular and widespread critical notice in a way that simply would not have happened had he appeared in three volumes during just one of those months. The *Sketches* had already made their own reputation serially before Macrone's publication of them in collected form caused them to be considered in the polite literary columns; ironically, their appearance in book form had brought such attention to a conclusion: "excellent as they are, they are rather too like one another; the same kind of objects are described in each, in much the same tone and same manner; and the effect of the entire volumes is, therefore, somewhat monotonous" (198). But *Pickwick* in its seriality went on stimulating the appetite for things Dickensian.

In analysing the Boz phenomenon, Buller starts by comparing Dickens's qualities as a comic writer and observer to those of Theodore Hook and Washington Irving. He goes on from these to consider Dickens's ability to delineate character and incident. It is interesting to note that the charges of caricaturing and inability to sustain a plot are to be found here as much as they are in the 1850s. What is more remarkable is that even so, and even at this early stage, the *London and Westminster Review* saw that Dickens might attain the qualifications of a major novelist. The question of what distinguishes a novel from a progress overshadowed the reception of *Pickwick* during 1837 and changed the course of Dickens's plans for all his future work.

III

The *London and Westminster Review* speaks of neither *Pickwick* nor *Oliver* as novels but simply as continuous narratives. And certainly their publication format was that of magazines, not novels. As late as 1 May 1837, the *Sun* reviewer, who is consistently noticeable for his close attention to Dickens's intentions, called *Oliver Twist* a "clever series of articles." However, during June and July, prodded by the state of his arrangements with Bentley, Dickens set out to change that.

The first agreement Dickens had ever made with Bentley (22 Aug. 1836) had been for two novels, each in three volumes of 320 pages and 25 lines per page, and for £500. No date of delivery is mentioned, although it specified that "no other literary production" was to be undertaken by Dickens until the novel was completed" (*Letters* I, 649).

The next two agreements with Bentley (4 Nov. 1836; 17 Mar. 1837) concerned the *Miscellany*. Dickens, in addition to his editorial duties, committed himself to providing "an original article of his own writing" (*Letters* I, 650) of sixteen pages every month, at 20 guineas a sheet, the copyright to become Bentley's. The last clause, in providing for the possibility that Bentley might abandon the *Miscellany* before a year was up, said that the monthly sheet of original work and the 20 guineas would continue with the under-standing that these monthly payments for "unpublished Numbers" would be set against the amount to be paid "for a literary work which the said Charles Dickens Esq engages to write for the said Richard Bentley, should such a contingency arise" (*Letters* I, 650). The wording of this does not suggest that such a literary work would be one of those already contracted for.

This clause was cancelled in the agreement of 17 March 1837. By this time it was apparent that the *Miscellany* would "go," and so many of the provisions for that uncertainty could be eliminated. The period guaranteed was changed from one year to five. It was agreed therefore that if the *Miscellany*'s publication lapsed before the end of this time, then Dickens was to receive twelve months' notice or £250, £125 of which was "to be reckoned as a set-off against a literary work" written by Dickens (*Letters* I, 651).

Such was the agreement in effect when Dickens in a letter of 14 July 1837 proposed two new arrangements. The first novel, "Gabriel Vardon," was now named *Barnaby Rudge*, and the payment was raised to £600; Dickens was to finish it by 1 March 1838. The second novel was now *Oliver Twist*, for which £700 was requested, except for what "may have been paid to me for the appearance of different portions of it, in the Miscellany up to the time of my furnishing the whole MS" (*Letters* I, 284).

Should Bentley not concede these points about the novels, Dickens proposed to exert his own freedom over the regularity of the muse's visits to the *Miscellany*. Dickens wished to put into effect a clause which ordinarily would have applied if the *Miscellany* had failed; in so doing he set off a train of events that effectively brought an end to the *Miscellany* as a source of income for him. Bentley of course wished to stick with the old agreement, because it cost him less: "Moreover I [Bentley] objected to 'Oliver Twist' being considered as his 2nd. novel on the ground that portions of that work had appeared in the Miscellany and the Copyright had therefore become my property as far as was already published" (*Letters* I, 292–93n). Perhaps Bentley was also doubtful about trying to flog *Oliver* as a novel after its appearance in the *Miscellany*. It had after all started out merely as a topical article in fable form.

In the context of this private dispute, it is noteworthy that one reviewer at this time should complain of the system of "continuations" in magazines. The *Weekly Dispatch* wrote of *Bentley's Miscellany* for August: "It is true that he [Dickens] has contributed an able paper, in continuation of the adventures of 'Oliver Twist,' but these 'Continuations' in Magazines are annoying to the reader" (no. 1869 13 Aug. 1837: 394). It was presumably the same reviewer who had written the previous week complaining of the *New Monthly Magazine*:

There is a practice growing stronger every day with magazines, which must eventually destroy all such periodical publications. We allude to the abominable habit of writing at book-making by bits and driblets, in a magazine. An author, resting on the oars of his reputation, writes loose papers for a Magazine, intending afterwards to make a book of them.

(*Weekly Dispatch*, no. 1868 6 Aug. 1837: 382)

Captain Marryat in particular is singled out as being "with one exception" the author who has done the most of this. Marryat had begun the practice with the appearance in 1832–33 of his novel *Peter Simple* in the *Metropolitan Magazine*. He had judged it wise, however, not to allow the novel to finish in the magazine but rather to supply the conclusion in its three-volume form only and to bring in a new serial, *Jacob Faithful*. In an authorial note that appeared between the two serials in the *Metropolitan*'s September 1833 issue, Marryat took the opportunity to defend the practice of "continuations":

there is no system so likely to produce a good work as that of continuations in a Magazine, and then publishing the whole. A narrative may appear in three volumes, and if there is one good chapter out of three, the public are generous and are satisfied; but when every portion is severally presented to be analyzed and criticised for thirty days, the author dare not flag.
(*Metropolitan Magazine* 8 no. 29 Sept. 1833: 69–71)

Dickens meanwhile, whether or not any complaint about the continuation of his serials had reached him, was contemplating the suspension of *Oliver*'s continuation. If Bentley refused to accept *Oliver* as a novel, then neither should he have it as a feature of the *Miscellany*. It is likely that Dickens would have been encouraged by comments such as that of the *Observer*, also of 13 August, that "*Bentley's Miscellany* improves: the great attraction of this number is the continuation of the story of 'Oliver Twist,' by Boz."

With September, the split between these two points of view became even more pronounced. The *Weekly Dispatch* quite hammered away at the vicious practice it had seized upon. Whatever the praise due to *Oliver*, "we must protest against publishing a long story, bit by bit, in a Magazine, and then reprinting the whole in the shape of a novel" (no. 1872 3 Sept. 1837: 430). *Bell's New Weekly Messenger* did not like the inserted story of the "Bagman's Uncle" and warned, "There is much straining at something new, but the subject is already exhausted, and if 'Boz' be regardful of his reputation, he will speedily wind the story up" (7 no. 297 3 Sept. 1837: 67). And *Bell's Life in London* commented cynically on Chapman and Hall's announcement for *Nicholas Nickleby*: "Nothing like striking while 'the iron is hot:' but even iron may be worn out" (3 Sept. 1837).

For the first time, however, one becomes aware that the skirmish of critical opinions is being conducted on unequal ground. The most favourable reviews to appear in the month of September 1837 are pronouncedly biased. On 2 September 1837, the *Morning Chronicle* commented on the "disadvantageous advantage" in *Bentley's Miscellany* of having one contributor such as Boz who shows up all the rest. In the specific absence of anything by Dickens appearing in that month's *Miscellany*, Hogarth's partisanship could not have been more pointed. The *Sun*, too, singled out *Oliver*, which it said, "bids fair to become Boz's master-piece" (1 Sept. 1837). The most emphatic of all Dickens's defenders was Forster in the *Examiner* of 10 September 1837, which opened, "The story of *Oliver Twist*, so far as it has yet proceeded, is its author's masterpiece, and mean as the subject appears to be − the account of the Progress of a Parish Boy − promises to take its place among the higher prose fictions of the language" (581). Specifically, Forster praises *Oliver*'s realism and descries a resemblance to Fielding in the adherence to truth: "In his writings we find *reality*." Here Forster anticipates, or more properly speaking provides, the aesthetic defence that Dickens was to summon up throughout his early career: that of telling the truth. Even Forster was uneasy about the "lowness" of the parish boy's haunts and never stopped reminding his readers of the allowance being made, but in the end he found a justification for the depiction of vice by ascribing moral purposes to Dickens.

This review is a long and assured piece of writing, such as any writer would be glad to see. Although its heading suggests that the review is to be a treatment of the *Miscellany*, the magazine is only cursorily mentioned in the last paragraph and, if the point had not already been made, its "distinguishing feature and support" is said again to be *Oliver Twist* (582) although, strictly speaking, *Oliver* had not appeared that month. The timing of this review was acute: Dickens had broken off correspondence with Bentley and resigned as editor in mid-September. Ultimately, a new agreement was reached on 28 September 1837 (*Letters* I, 654). It treated of both *Bentley's Miscellany* and the novels. Besides a rise in salary and a share in profits of sales over 6,000 copies, Dickens was conceded *Oliver Twist*'s status as a novel. However, Bentley was given full copyright in both for three years; after which Dickens received half. Bentley was forbidden the possibility of publishing either novel as part of his *Standard Novels* series.

Considering the ultimate publishing history of both *Oliver Twist* and *Barnaby Rudge*, the fact that in this contract Bentley was to be allowed to publish them neither in numbers nor in parts is notable. *Barnaby Rudge* was from the first to be a novel in three volumes (due October 1838). Bentley agreed to pay £700 for it, but the price for *Oliver* remained at £500. Unlike *Barnaby Rudge*, its length was not stipulated; and it would appear from the seventh clause of the contract that this was not known in advance. For Dickens – or was it Bentley? – won the point that it was to be continued in the *Miscellany* until midsummer 1838. The phrasing of the clause specifies that it is, "Then to be collected and the remainder of the Copy to be furnished" by Dickens once he had received his price of £500. So the price of *Oliver* did not rise – but Dickens may privately have determined that Bentley would not receive any more than his *Miscellany*'s worth.

Bentley was to pay the £500 by 1 May 1838. In effect he would be paying for *Oliver* twice, excepting whatever Dickens wrote after midsummer 1838. Kathleen Tillotson conjectures that "It cannot have been intended that the serialization would be complete by midsummer, since further instalments even of the full 16 pages would not have brought it anywhere near three-volume length."[14] At approximately fourteen pages of *Miscellany* copy per month (Dickens did not start writing up to the maximum monthly quota until after June 1838), from February 1837 to July 1838 inclusive (with two months' instalments missed), the amount of copy completed might be projected at sixteen instalments totalling 224 pages (at approximately 500 words per page) – a total of 112,000 words. *Barnaby Rudge* had originally been specified at three volumes of 320 pages each and 25 lines per page. The number of words per line was not specified. A page of *Bentley's Miscellany* generally came to about 500 words, as did *Pickwick* (see the contract for *Pickwick*, *Letters* I, 648), but a novel might have fewer than 200 words per page. At 24,000 lines per volume, Dickens might have been expected to deliver 180,000 words, but in fact *Oliver* came nearer to 160,000 words.[15]

Thus, by July 1838, Dickens apparently had between 50,000 words or something more than a volume to complete. As it turned out, in fact, by midsummer 1838 he had eight instalments or one-third more to go. He wrote 114 more pages (500 words per page) or 57,000 words. The total came to about 338 *Bentley's Miscellany* pages or 159,000 words. When *Oliver* was divided into volumes, Volume Three began with the August 1838 number. The instalments after June 1838 are consistently the full sixteen pages, but this was due to Dickens's exasperation with Bentley's "meanness" (*Letters* I, 401; to Bentley [?31 May 1838]) in deducting payment for anything less than the full sheet of original work.

In any case, the contract for September 1837 shows that Dickens and Bentley agreed to midsummer 1838 (approximately sixteen instalments; eighteen, if June and October 1837 were included) as completing the time that *Oliver* ought to appear in *Bentley's*

Miscellany. Beyond that Dickens would simply provide the necessary additional text to make up a novel.

George Cruikshank was drawn into the dispute (on Bentley's side) before this contract was drawn up, and his advice to Bentley was to accept *Oliver* as a novel, on the grounds that "the public are heartily tired of 'Oliver Twist' long before he reached to three Volumes and I should say more likely to injure the Miscellany than otherwise – People like *Novelty*" (*Letters* I, 308n [16 Sept. 1837]). Cruikshank calculated that, if *Oliver* were carried on till midsummer 1838, that would come to £350 of the total bill for the novel. Bentley would then have to pay only £150 beyond what he had already paid for it in the *Miscellany*. This suggests that Dickens would have another third (five more instalments) to write.

Events went quite differently from the way this contract with Bentley specified. Although we tend to lump together all Dickens's novels as being written in parts, it is clear that Dickens had no desire to make *Oliver* another *Pickwick* – indeed, there would have been no obvious benefit in running it as a feature of *Bentley's Miscellany* for an overly long time such as twenty months. Cruikshank was wrong, though, about the public growing sick of *Oliver*. A tenuous association with Mudfog was kept up by the appearance of "The Mudfog Papers" and the "explanation that its length left no room for the serial" (*Bentley's Miscellany*, Oct. 1837). Meanwhile Hogarth in the *Morning Chronicle* observed,

we are bound to say that we grieve bitterly for the absence of "Oliver Twist," and we are confident that the majority of readers will think that nothing, however good may be the substitute, can compensate for the absence and continuation of that eventful history. This month Boz has given us, to be sure, a capital piece of satire and ridicule of the recent proceedings of the British Association at Liverpool. It is full of wit, drollery, and severity, but what of that? – it is not "Oliver Twist." What a pity that he could not afford us Oliver into the bargain. The Rowland for the Oliver is unexceptionable, and has made us laugh from the time we took it up till the time we laid it down, but *it is not Oliver*, and there is an end of the matter.

(*Morning Chronicle* 5 Oct. 1837)

Dickens won his point, and if Thomas Beard had proved a weak ally in Dickens's battle with Macrone, Forster did not fail him against Bentley. Forster was valiant in private and in print. When *Oliver* resumed in November 1837, the *Examiner* wrote of *Bentley's Miscellany*, "This is a very stupid magazine, but like a certain other stupid and unpleasant thing, it 'wears a precious jewel in its head' " (no. 1555 19 Nov. 1837: 740).

The October break in the narrative, like the one in May 1837, became important to the shape of the story. In taking up the connections between the Brownlow family and the original chapters describing Oliver's birth, Dickens was making the satirical "Progress" into something like a history. That he had to make a conscious effort to do this is shown by the fact that he was forced to ask Bentley's clerk for a copy of the February 1837 *Miscellany* to remind himself of the original details of Oliver's life (*Letters* I, 319; to E. S. Morgan [?13 Oct. 1837]). The September number had left Mr. Brownlow and Mr. Grimwig in suspense, as they waited for Oliver to come back from his first venture out since his convalescence at the Brownlows'. Dickens's last chapter before the break (ch. 15) commenced with an aggrieved digression on misplaced trust and pointed remarks about his "long-considered intentions and plans regarding this prose epic." He added the parenthesis: "for such I mean it to be." This preamble must have had its point solely for the villain Bentley; it does not appear in later editions.

What Dickens does seem to have thought about carefully is the character of Nancy. Tillotson, drawing attention to this in the introduction to the Clarendon edition, says "the novel had become more than a serial."[16] More precisely, the serial had become a novel. It was in the character of Nancy, not Oliver, that this development took hold; the coming of good out of evil marked the end of the parish satire. To Forster, Dickens wrote, "I hope to do great things with Nancy" (*Letters* I, 328; 3 Nov. [1837]). And in his review on 19 November, Forster obligingly singled out the portrayal of Nancy for both its "power" and its "discrimination." In another part of the review, Forster also commented on the improvement in the narrative in its "management of a sustained plot" (no. 1555 19 Nov. 1837: 740). Forster also expressed his opinion to Dickens personally, perhaps even before the review appeared, and Dickens's letter of 3 November is an expression of his pleasure at hearing this.

At the same time he was able to say, "I think I may defy Mr. Hayward and all his works" (*Letters* I, 328). Abraham Hayward (1801–84) had just published a critical consideration of Dickens's work in the *Quarterly Review* for October 1837. It is to this that Dickens refers. Of course, it had appeared anonymously, but Dickens had known about the writer and his intentions for a while. In a letter to Ainsworth, Dickens relates how he had "declined the honor of his [Hayward's] intimate acquaintance when he came to inform me about four months ago with a patronising air, that Lockhart had requested him to write it; and I think he has not quite forgotten or forgiven the circumstance" (*Letters* I, 325; 30 Oct. [1837]).

Thus, Dickens's reputation had advanced to the point where one of the two great quarterlies of the age felt it necessary as early as July 1837 to discuss his fiction-writing seriously – when the twenty-five-year-old Dickens had yet to produce a novel. Even *Pickwick*'s parts had not yet been collected. The only permanent volume by Dickens that had appeared so far was *Sketches by Boz*. None of Dickens's publishers was at all venerable (all had been established since 1831) or particularly respectable, nor were the types of publications in which he had appeared distinguished ones.

A partial explanation for the *Quarterly Review*'s interest is to be found in the first sentence of its review: "The popularity of this writer is one of the most remarkable literary phenomena of recent times" (59 no. 118 Oct. 1837: 484). The review concerned itself chiefly with *Pickwick*, which, it noted, had succeeded in getting itself talked about in spite of its anonymity, its vulgar subject, and lack of reference to political or fashionable topics and personages.

In what way *Pickwick* had succeeded was another matter – and here perhaps lay the part that rankled with Dickens. At a time when Forster in the *Examiner* was applauding his Fieldingesque feats of realism in *Oliver*, the *Quarterly Review* chose instead to revert to *Pickwick* and the *Sketches*, and to treating Dickens entirely as a humorist: "Of Fielding's intuitive perception of the springs of action, and skill in the construction of the prose epic – or Smollett's dash, vivacity, wild spirit of adventure and rich poetic imagination – he has none" (484). This was galling, when the names of Fielding and Smollett had been sounding in Dickens's ears for months, a fact which Hayward would have known by following the papers. Instead, Hayward reverts to comparisons of Dickens with humorist contemporaries such as Sydney Smith, Theodore Hook, and Washington Irving. The *Quarterly* was, strictly speaking, quite correct in its categorization and taste. Hook had already made the subject of Bloomsbury his own before Dickens appeared on the scene, while Marryat, Crofton Croker, and "Christopher North" had long ago beat him to the title of "originalist."

More interesting is the *Quarterly*'s difficulty in classifying *Pickwick*. The serial had started out as a rather eighteenth-century topical quiz on learned societies and then become a series of adventures which verge only now and then (in the Bardell v. Pickwick numbers) on becoming a narrative – "it can hardly be as a story that the book before us has attained its popularity" (494–95), says Hayward. Once again, the descriptive word chosen for *Pickwick* is "anomalous" (494). Whatever critics of subsequent decades, or

Dickens in his prefaces, might say about the monthly green covers that became his "first" novel, it is important to recognize that at this point *Pickwick* fell into no recognizable literary genre. The criticism of the day as represented by the *Quarterly Review*, an acknowledged arbiter of it, reflects this fact.

Having demonstrated, like the *London and Westminster Review* in July, that Dickens had no particular gift for sustained narrative or character description, the *Quarterly Review* concludes (with a great many Wellerisms) that Dickens has made available the literary possibilities of a new sort of language hitherto excluded by its lower-class origins. He had made the vulgar palatable. Only in his attention to things low does the *Quarterly Review* allow a resemblance to Fielding, who also "writhed" (507) under the reproach of lowness: "With such testimony in his favour, Mr. Dickens may well afford to disregard the imputation of vulgarity, invariably and indiscriminately levelled by the tawdry affecters of gentility against every man of genius who ventures to take human life, in all its gradations, for his subject-matter" (506). Warning Dickens not to allow too much of repugnance (such as the description of the Fleet, which the *Quarterly* calls exaggerated and out-of-date) in his scenes and characters, and also having cited sources for some of Dickens's imitative manners and stories, the *Quarterly Review* reiterates its opinion that Dickens's originality and popularity lie in the literary depiction of lower-class speech.

The review then goes on to add that "indications are not wanting that the particular vein of humour which has hitherto yielded so much attractive metal, is worked out" (514). One can imagine Dickens bridling at this charge of faddishness. The review states,

The essential question, therefore, seems to be, whether Mr. Dickens is endowed with the quality for which Lord Byron gave Sir Walter Scott credit, when he said, that the moment the public interest in Sir Walter's poetry began to flag, he turned about and flashed forth as a novelist, and were it possible for the public to become satiated with his novels, he would find or make for himself a third road to popularity – in other words, whether Mr. Dickens be a true man of genius ...   (*Quarterly Review* 59 no. 118 Oct. 1837: 514–15)

This rhetorical question rather coldly straddles the border between insult and compliment. The references to genius and to Sir Walter Scott are backhanded praise, when coupled with the underlying sneer at Dickens's insubstantiality. After this, one can hardly wonder at his determination to defy Hayward.

Coincidentally, the review concludes with a glance at *Oliver*, though, strictly speaking, it is not *Oliver* that is being reviewed. While lamenting "the decline visible in the later numbers of the Pickwick Papers" (518), Hayward sees *Oliver* as manifesting "a sustained power, a range of observation, and a continuity of interest in this series which we seek in vain in any other of his works" (518). Thus, this major article of early criticism ends with a mixture of encouragement and provocation. The reviewer warns Dickens against accepting too many engagements at once ("Mr. Dickens writes too often and too fast" [518]), something that Dickens himself was to complain about very soon. Indeed, it was to become a major worry as it became more and more apparent that his "first Novel" was receding further and further into non-existence. This – three volumes – was the shape of the promise Dickens held out to himself and others, of "a high and enduring reputation" (518). However, notwithstanding, it seemed likely in October 1837 that Hayward was foretelling a self-evident truth: "he has risen like a rocket, and he will come down like the stick" (518).

The *Quarterly Review* was itself regularly reviewed in the newspapers. The *Observer* of 24 October 1837 briefly remarked, "We do not think the reviewer has done justice to Mr. Dickens." The paper also carried an extract from the *London and Westminster Review*, "The Comic Writers – The Novelists," dwelling on the originality of Dickens. The *Sun*, too, thought the *Quarterly Review* could have been more eloquent (30 Oct. 1837). The *Sun* was itself particularly appreciative of *Oliver* and, unlike the *Quarterly Review*, saw every reason to think of Fielding:

From certain unequivocal indications in the "Oliver Twist" of this month, we find that Boz has been applying himself diligently to the perusal of Fielding's novels, which we are glad to see, for in the department of literature which he has chosen, he will find no one who will be of such benefit to him, by disciplining his fancy, and maturing his judgment, as the author of that prose epic "Tom Jones," ...   (*Sun* 1 Nov. 1837)

"Prose epic" seemed to be a phrase much on the lips of Dickens and his defenders this month.

In fact, as we have seen, *Oliver*'s form remained to be determined. This point is demonstrated by a review in the *Atlas*, which begins: "The romance, novel, history, or narrative, or whatever else it may be called, of 'Oliver Twist,' is assuredly an invention *per se*. It bears no sort of resemblance to any other fiction, looking like truth, with which we are acquainted" (12 no. 598 5 Nov. 1837: 713).

If November was important for marking the resumption of *Oliver*, it was also noteworthy for the winding-up of *Pickwick*. The reviewers generally praised Dickens and his work for its warmth of sentiment. *Bell's New Weekly Messenger* said that Dickens was "evidently a clever man, and perhaps capable of giving to our literature superior things" (7 no. 306   5 Nov. 1837: 138–39). What these "superior things" might be was left unspecified. The *Examiner*'s notice, however, was explicit in welcoming Dickens into the body of "established English novelists" (no. 1553   5 Nov. 1837: 708–09). And, in the preface to the first edition in volume form of *Pickwick*, Dickens, who there seems preoccupied with excusing the disconnected nature of the "papers," used not only the obvious explanation that the book was originally written "almost as the periodical occasion arose," but also, finally, the reflection that "the same objection has been made to the works of some of the greatest novelists in the English language."

This is a rather contradictory but revealing pairing of explanations. If later critics have tried to explain away many of *Pickwick*'s structural peculiarities according to the categories of traditional criticism of the novel, without considering the appropriateness of their models, it is at least partly because Dickens and his closest colleagues deliberately set the first example. *Pickwick* may not have been a novel in its original idea or composition, but by the end of its run nearly two years later, and after a visit by Mr. Bentley only a month before the preface was written, Dickens had decided that he was going to be known as a novelist.

5

1837–1838 The editor of *Bentley's Miscellany*

I

Neither Chapman and Hall nor Bentley asked for the innovations they found on their hands with *Pickwick* and *Oliver Twist*; nor do we have reason to believe that Dickens intended to produce other than what these publishers commissioned from him. In signing a contract with Bentley in August 1836, Dickens tied himself to a publisher reared in the prosperous antiquarian trade with a natural caution and a predilection for proven formulas. The palmy days were gone when Constable and Murray, the publishers of Scott and Byron, spread around thousands of pounds in speculative ventures. The crash of 1825–26 had been followed by Constable's death and Scott's decline; in the aftermath of the crash, Murray put out only biography and travel and went in for profit-sharing arrangements with his authors. In 1831, John Taylor, the publisher of Keats, was describing himself as "no publisher of poetry,"[1] and Blackwood wrote, "There never has been so slack a year in our trade ever since I have been in business."[2]

The only venturer to set up in the immediate aftermath of the financial crisis of 1825–26 was Thomas Tegg, who made his business by being a pirate publisher and a seller of remainders. Henry Colburn survived by publishing novels written by titled people and then puffing them in all the papers. It was against this background that Richard Bentley, the son of an antiquarian and younger brother of a printer, attempted to make his start in publishing during the late 1820s. Samuel Bentley, his brother, was already doing a great deal of printing business for Colburn, and in 1828 Colburn and Bentley negotiated a partnership. Their *National Library* series of non-fiction (1830–32), set up in imitation of Murray's grander *Family Library* (1829), shows the entrepreneurial poverty of Bentley and Colburn's partnership. Bentley had allied himself with a publisher notorious for the practice of puffing, which was perhaps necessary to the flogging of silver-fork fiction but anomalous when applied to the "March of Intellect."

Bentley was a man who practised publishing by following in the footsteps of others such as Murray and Constable, but whose natural competitors often turned out to be no more than men like the despised Tegg. His natural caution must have been confirmed by the losses of two short years with Colburn, and their partnership dissolved in 1832. Edward Samuel Morgan, Bentley's chief assistant for many years and the one who claims to have put forward both the original title and concept of the "Wits' Miscellany," says that Bentley was needled by Colburn's use of the *New Monthly Magazine* to advertise his publishing activities after their breakup and decided in 1836 to buy up the old *Monthly* to retaliate. Morgan advised him not to take up with an "old harridan" but to start his own new magazine. Morgan, by his own account, drew up the prospectus one weekend at the end of October 1836 for a magazine cheaper than the *New Monthly* (2s 6d a month instead of 3s 6d) and "to contain no notices of new publications nor any records of 'Bankrupts &c.' but to be devoted to humorous papers by popular writers." He also suggested the name of Boz, whose writing he had followed since the days of the *Morning Chronicle* sketches, and of Cruikshank. Bentley was apparently "overjoyed" with the scheme, if we are to believe an old man's proud "Retrospect."[3]

Bentley showed perhaps the only spark of innovation of his publishing career by signing up the young Dickens as the editor of a new miscellany he projected to get back at Colburn. In January 1836, Dickens was looking forward to the publication of two little volumes of sketches not particularly well advertised, and his literary acquaintance might be said to consist of three men. By January of 1837, only a year later, Dickens was editor of a successful miscellany and conferring with contributors such as Samuel Lover, William Jerdan, William Maginn, Father Prout, Charles Ollier, Theodore Hook and others. All of these literary men were well established long before Dickens had so much as settled on the pseudonym of Boz – none of them had ever solicited material from him while he was still the young writer of sketches.

Bentley was not a publisher of original ideas; to understand his *Miscellany*, we need to look at the formula behind it. What is immediately noticeable about the names of all these literary celebrities is their common association with the most successful monthly of the time: *Fraser's Magazine*. Bentley's choice of Maginn and Prout rather than Dickens to write the first words of the *Miscellany* encountered by new readers may seem odd to a twentieth-century reader, for whom Dickens is the real celebrity. But to someone contemplating the expense of one shilling for a new magazine in the 1830s, the advertised resemblance to *Fraser's* suggested by the names of Maginn and Prout would have been something more to conjure with than the mention of Boz. The fame of *Pickwick* as a periodical was still of less venerable vintage than that of *Fraser's*. *Pickwick* was a periodical with only one article; *Fraser's* was a coterie of all the brightest literary stars of "town and country," and it defined the quintessence of the new post-war monthly, which casually "mixed riotous fun with abuse as to have the effect of playful irresponsibility."[4]

II

Fraser's came into existence the year of George IV's death and is Regency through and through in its boisterous coarseness, whereas *Bentley's*, born six months before Victoria's accession, possesses the self-assurance of neither the Regency nor the Victorian period. Unlike the young Dickens, *Fraser's* editor Maginn was not sentimental about the eighteenth century: in introducing *Fraser's* to the public, Maginn explicitly avoids the fiction of both a *Spectator*-like Club and of "a very old gentleman as the eidolon of an editor," such as Dickens used in *Pickwick Papers* and *Master Humphrey's Clock*. The opening editorial of February 1830 makes a virtue of its offhandedness, and refusing to be caught in any tender gestures towards its readers, merely remarks, "it would be waste of time to say that we are to be a literary miscellany, embracing &c. &c. &c. &c." What *Fraser's* does not decline to name is its politics, confidently pronouncing that this was essential to the definition of any magazine. It indeed goes on to regret the conciliatory mentality among the political parties of its time: "The Whigs have been un-whigged; the Tories un-toried." Five-and-a-half pages out of the seven comprising this opening editorial are spent on describing the magazine's political policy. This spate of vehemence wound up, the editor goes on to the first article – which turns out to be a review of American poetry. And lest one should be tempted to expatiate on the deeper significance of this choice, the article is introduced by saying, "We have not the least notion what we are to begin with, and almost at random take the following. Positively we do not know what it is about." The magazine's second article, however, is on "the Philosophy of Catholicism."

Fraser's was nothing if not habitually disingenuous. For all this professed disdain of clubs, the portrait of its own "Fraserians" was perhaps the most famous of the "Gallery of Illustrious Literary

Characters'' series commissioned by William Maginn for *Fraser's* during the first half of the 1830s. Daniel Maclise (later a friend of Dickens) drew portraits of the most prominent men of the age, one sketch appearing in each issue from June 1830 to December 1836 (and for two months in 1838), and Maginn wrote the biographical sketches for all but a few. The group portrait of ''The Fraserians'' (January 1835) depicts the magazine's circle of twenty-five contributors as they are supposed to have appeared at their regular dinners. Maginn is its master of ceremonies, and Lockhart his side-kick. Ainsworth, Carlyle, Prout, and others recite verse, sing comic songs, exchange learned quotations, and generally malign the Whigs.

To a twentieth-century reader – who is probably most intrigued by the unexpected appearance of the young Thackeray among this group – the prominence of Maginn and the esteem in which he was held at this time is surprising. If any figure can be said to symbolize the bohemian spirit of journalism in the 1820s and 1830s, it is William Maginn: he was *the* example against which young writers such as Thackeray, Dickens, and Lockhart measured themselves. Thackeray was perhaps fascinated longest by this spectacle of self-destructive high spirits, and much of his writing seems but the attempt to record what went on at those Fraserian dinners of the 1830s. Dickens, separated more by ambition and class, reacted against such bohemianism, ultimately by becoming a self-sufficient Victorian magazine proprietor.

When Murray and Disraeli projected the *Representative* in 1825, it was Lockhart and Maginn whom they were especially eager to secure for the paper. Lockhart, as we know, declined the proposal but seems to have encouraged Maginn to accept the post of foreign correspondent in Paris, fearing only that the regularity of Maginn's contributions would not match that of his generous salary. And indeed, whatever else Maginn did while receiving his seven hundred pounds a year from Murray, he seems to have applied himself to the study of Hebrew in the Bibliothèque Nationale. Maginn was very much the literary adventurer and wrote indiscriminately for the highest to lowest publications, from the *Quarterly Review* to Radical rags. He was on informal terms with both Barnes of *The Times* and Westmacott of the infamous *Age*, and caroused with Carlyle as easily as with the thieving classes of Paris and London.

Poor Murray, who had already once had to take Maginn off a favourite project (the biography of Byron, a plum commission of the decade), recalled Maginn after seven months, offering him a supplemental editor's job in London at even more money. There, Maginn continued to write for *John Bull*, the *Quarterly Review*, the *Literary Gazette*, as well as for the *Foreign Review* and the *Foreign Quarterly*, and of course, *Fraser's*. He became the acknowledged centre of the most brilliant literary coterie of the day. He later produced the *Shakespeare Papers* for *Bentley's Miscellany* (May 1837–May 1838), a series of seven critical essays of impressive acuteness. But the steadiness of tone in these papers is perhaps their most remarkable aspect, for intemperance and improvidence were the only regular features of Maginn's life. The anarchical nature of his writing and opinions breached the political decorum of even the 1830s. The fierceness of his Tory Protestantism reads quaintly now, but his abuse of the party itself and of his country's government read dangerously then. He was thrown into the Fleet prison for debt in 1842, where he seems to have been as careless and jovial as John Dickens. His friends obtained his release, but he died four months later. Prime Minister Peel, who for years had been maligned in Maginn's columns, gave one hundred pounds of his own money to a subscription for Maginn just before his death and obtained a commission for his son. Lockhart, whose respect was not easily given, loved Maginn, and it fell to him to write the brief epitaph, "bright broken Maginn," and memoir by which the learned Doctor is usually recalled.

In view of the paradoxes of this man's career, therefore, we should perhaps not find it surprising that Bentley, who was himself long a butt of Maginn, should have been eager to have him write for the *Miscellany*. It was a reputation for Tory outrageousness that Bentley coveted for his new monthly when he co-opted Maginn. Their association, such as it was, dated back at least to 1830, when Bentley had asked Maginn's assistance with the *National Library* series. This had not stopped the latter from beginning a *Fraser's* article in the same year with an attack on Bentley. There, Maginn asserts that the literary world must pick itself up from its worship of poseurs, and specifically from "attending the morning levees of Mr. Richard Bentley, who (as he styles himself) is the first publisher in London, turning up his nose in utter contempt at 'such small gear' as the Murrays, the Longmans, the Hursts, and the Baldwins." He maliciously describes Bentley at these levees as being "unkempt, unshorn, and decently attired in his night-gown and slippers" (1 no. 3 Apr. 1830: 318–19).

The review is a hit at the silver-fork novels published by Colburn and Bentley. The firm's puffing was associated most closely with Colburn, although not stopped by Bentley, who had no pretensions to any literature other than the amusing and selling kind, as one can see from the original name of his magazine: the *Wits' Miscellany*.

The account of how Dickens tussled with and finally broke the circle of "Wits" is the account of how a new literary age emerged from the old one.

III

Gordon N. Ray, in relating the story of Thackeray's literary apprenticeship, remarks of this period:

The 1830s were a painful interregnum in the history of English literature. The success of Byron in poetry and Scott in fiction had created a new mass reading public. When these great men died, they left behind them no obvious successors. Yet the appetite for print that they had aroused offered commercial opportunities too tempting to be ignored, and enterprising publishers were quick to take advantage of them. Thus a generation of naive and half-educated readers came to be exploited by a generation of business men who were hardly better trained.[5]

Ray also notes that severity among contemporary critics was generally "motivated by political partisanship rather than by literary discrimination."[6] Hence the virulence of "puffing," or the recognition that the criticism found in contemporary journals was more a public ideological matter than an individual critical one – *vide* Maginn to the defence of Bentley.

Despite *Fraser's* attack on Bentley's levees in 1830, it is notable that when in that same year Colburn and Bentley began the non-fictional *National Library* series, *Fraser's* was the only prominent magazine to defend its first publication, Galt's *Life of Byron*. If a defence of Bentley sounds strange coming from *Fraser's*, it may sound less so when one recalls that the author of the *Life*, Galt, was himself a Fraserian. His portrait appears in the *Fraser's* December 1830 issue, and throughout these months *Fraser's* is filled with articles by Galt, including his own two-part defence of the *Byron*. In fact, defence of Galt's work on Byron seems unlikely to have been undertaken by anyone except by *Fraser's*. The *DNB* notes that Galt's *Byron* went through four editions, "though valueless." Moreover, in defence of Galt, *Fraser's* also took on the *Edinburgh Review*. This was a way of getting at the demon Whig, Lord Brougham, who had used the occasion of the *National Library*'s inception to vaunt the publications of his own Society for the Diffusion of Useful Knowledge. In its own article "The Edinburgh Review *versus* Galt's Life of Byron," published in November 1830, *Fraser's* called Brougham's article an advertisement for the Society. But in fact Brougham's criticisms of the *National Library* were not far off those that *Fraser's* itself had made.

None of these criticisms altered Bentley's notion of what a "National" Library ought to be. The fourteen volumes in all, published from 1830 to 1832, included "instruction" on chivalry, chemistry, Napoleon, and conversations with the ubiquitous Byron. As Maginn was to say in a review of another useful knowledge series, the preference for safe publishing formulas had brought the entry of the "slap-dash of periodicalism" into the writing of reference works: "We have reared among us a class of men who sit down to toss off history, biography, philosophy, in all their branches and subdivisions" (*Fraser's* 16 no. 95 Nov. 1837: 530). Such men, many of them prominent in literature, became hacks in the general fixation with cheap publishing and mass marketing: "Left to themselves, they would never have thought of such task-work; but their *names* were wanted, and their names accordingly they gave, and scarcely any thing else" (531). Fielding, as ever, represents the beacon of light; Scott, the darkness of the present age: "Fielding made no 'series,' but Scott, unfortunately, did; and, from the time that the Waverley novels assumed the character of a periodical, they rapidly deteriorated" (529).

Ray describes Thackeray as turning to Maginn because he spoke out against bookmaking and puffing, but even Maginn does not come out as irreproachably principled. Maginn, certainly, like the *Athenaeum*, named influence-peddling where he saw it but could also ignore it where personal loyalties ruled. For all that Maginn may have shown Thackeray how to steer an independent path among the powers that be, the espousal of political interests was a creed with him, as it never was with Thackeray. Thackeray himself recognized this. In 1839, he was to say about Carlyle's *Critical and Miscellaneous Essays*: "Criticism has been a party matter with us till now ... and literature a poor political lackey − please God we shall begin ere long to love art for art's sake."[7] And it was to Carlyle, not Maginn, that Thackeray looked for leadership in such a reformation.

Thackeray's great dislike of party and religious politicking was something he shared with Dickens; they were both of the generation that had known only the divisive era after the War. Against this, we must place Maginn's rabidly Orange Protestantism and his insistence on the importance of politics in defining periodical writing. Because, Maginn said, magazine writing is necessarily defined by its interest in "what *is* actually going on around us":

There may be periodical collections of nouvellettes, or essays, or criticisms, or drolleries, or verses, good or bad as the chance may be, but they do not fall under the definition of what is generally considered to be *the* magazine.   (*Fraser's* 16 no. 95 Nov. 1837: 528)

By this definition, of course, *Fraser's* is *the* magazine.

It is in this, the attitude to politics, that we find more than anywhere else the divergence between the old journalism and the new. Maginn and Bentley had been raised in the era of Napoleon, when the very rise of journalism and increase in reading were associated with eagerness for news of the French foe. With the Peace had returned many ambitious young men, and there arose a fad for naval reminiscences and the naval novel (still to be seen in early issues of *Bentley's Miscellany*, but dying out after 1840), as many stories censured during the War now found an audience. However, with the Peace also came renewed internal dissension − and this, represented most clearly by the agitation throughout the 1820s and 1830s for repeal of the Corn Law, is what Dickens and Thackeray grew up with. Reform, not Napoleon, was the warcry of their 1820s youth. The use of the term *Conservative*, rather than *Tory*, to describe the inclination of the *Miscellany*, is a word denoting conciliation in the 1830s. If the Duke of Wellington, the vanquisher of Napoleon, was the head of the old Tory party, so Peel, a consistent subject of Maginn's abuse, was to be the head of the new "Conservative" party and the man who ultimately gave in to Corn Law agitation and destroyed eighteenth-century Toryism.

Maginn had passingly remarked on Dickens's politics in a *Fraser's* article as early as August 1836. There he had remarked on "Boz the magnificent": "what a pity it is that he deludes himself into the absurd idea that he can be a Whig! − Mr. Pickwick was a Whig, and that was only right; but Boz is just as much a Whig as he is a giraffe" (14 no. 80 Aug. 1836: 242). The context of this remark is of interest to Dickens's politics. The article is a famous review by Maginn, "Mr. Grantley Berkeley and his Novel," of *Berkeley Castle*, a historical romance in three volumes. We may notice, the publisher was none other than the detested Bentley, in the very month that Bentley and Dickens were to sign their first contract.

Berkeley (1800−81), the sixth son of an earl and a godson of the Prince Regent, had recently resigned his commission in the Coldstream Guards and entered Parliament in 1832, becoming a Member for the next twenty years. He was also an active sportsman and a bully to the degree that even the names of his hunting dogs were notorious. Towards the end of his life he wrote *Anecdotes of the Upper Ten Thousand* (1867), and the seventy-year ambition of his life was to succeed to the earldom of Berkeley. Maginn draws attention to the bad taste of Berkeley in writing about his family seat when it was widely known that his mother was the daughter of a butcher and had been the earl's mistress long before she became his wife. Much of the review is open abuse of the pretensions of Berkeley to blueblood lineage.[8] In short, Berkeley was a snob and a brute, and everything hated by Maginn, and by Dickens himself when he drew such figures as Lord Frederick Verisopht and Sir Mulberry Hawk. Maginn's approach in his review is to seize upon this question of what constitutes a gentleman, and in the light of all that Dickens was to face over the subsequent six months in setting up *Bentley's Miscellany* and writing *Oliver Twist* it is of interest to dwell on Maginn's treatment of a topic that was always to be controversial in Dickens's own vocabulary.

Maginn, as we have seen, was a harsh reviewer of Colburn's silver-fork literature of the 1820s. What so irritated Maginn was that the slang talk of this "club-haunting gang" (243) should carry any cachet in the literary world:

We do not know one of these fellows who, when he comes forward from the circle in which he is a "gentlemanly man," does not prove himself to be a blockhead, and something worse. When he takes a pen in his hand, he not only displays a dire ignorance and stupidity, but, in nine cases out of ten, an utter meanness of thought and manners, and a crawling vulgarity of soul.
(*Fraser's* 14 no. 80 Aug. 1836: 242)

The question of what constitutes vulgarity is what Maginn, and later what Dickens in all his replies to his critics about the "lowness" of his fictions, were concerned to argue. Maginn maintains that "The slang of the gilded cornices of St. James's is not in essence one whit more dignified than the slang spoken over the beer-washed tables of St. Giles's" (242).

It is in this context that Maginn interjects praise of "Boz the magnificent" and the parenthetical comment about his Whiggish politics. Maginn finds that in writing the slang of the street − this is just at the time when Sam Weller makes his début − Boz writes with more interest and insight than "the most celebrated hero of the Rookery" (242). The irony of Maginn's statement is that "Rookery" can refer both to a set of mean tenements in London and, in military slang, to a barracks of disorderly subalterns, both the St. Giles and the St. James senses of one word. Here, in the very month that Wellerisms begin to make *Pickwick* famous, is the critical argument that will justify Sam Weller, and, more significantly, *Oliver Twist*.

Maginn was always an enemy of silver-fork fiction; Dickens was to write the novels which would supplant it. In both Maginn's criticism and Dickens's fiction, the notion of the "gentleman" was controversial. Dickens's heroes – Mr. Pickwick, Oliver, Nicholas Nickleby – are "born gentlemen," a phrase telling us that their station at birth is not a noble one. They are also uninteresting, compared with their "low" companions and relations; it was a common criticism, especially after *Nicholas Nickleby*, that Dickens knew nothing of the inward life of a gentleman.[9] What he projects onto the character of Sir Mulberry Hawk is not very far off the caricatured Mr. Grantley Berkeley as he appears in Maginn's review.

The notion of the gentleman is a politically divisive one, especially in 1832. In the famous story of how Grantley Berkeley and his brother Craven went to the publisher Fraser's shop in the aftermath of Maginn's review (which according to the practice of the times had been published anonymously) and beat the small man Fraser about the head with a gold-headed riding whip, we can appreciate all that Maginn and Dickens found repugnant about "gentlemanly" behaviour. The "honour" defended by these bullies was completely fraudulent: they were merely a large brood of illegitimate sons who could think only of the title they had been denied. The story recalls all those profligate sons of George III, their morganatic marriages, and the numerous bastard cousins surrounding the young Victoria as she ascended the throne in 1837. This world was accepted as much more commonplace in the England of the 1830s than it would be a decade later, in 1847, when such things are portrayed in *Vanity Fair* in a self-consciously historical way. By then, it was a novel such as *Dombey and Son* which had a more contemporary feeling in its attention to the domestic life of the rising business classes. Dickens's career was to proceed contemporaneously with the emergence of these classes, but in 1836, the year of Dickens's first publication, Maginn's career was virtually to come to an end with this review of *Berkeley Castle*.

IV

Fortunately for *Bentley's Miscellany*, Maginn did not die by Berkeley's duellinr pistols, and he and Dickens shortly went on their separate ways to strike bargains with the publisher of Berkeley's romance. Whatever one might think of losing a magazine contributor by aristocratic forms of violence, the high profile of *Fraser's* was exactly what Bentley craved, and such was the kind of journalistic setting he presented Dickens with in his first editorship.

Dickens may have been chosen as editor of the magazine, but it was Father Prout who wrote the opening verse, "Song of the Month," and Maginn who produced the "Prologue" which set the tone of the magazine for its prospective audience:

"Doctor," said a young gentleman to Dean Swift, "I intend to set up for a wit."

"Then," said the Doctor, "I advise you to sit down again."

With this opening, Maginn produced the desired tone of high jinks and also made a hit at the discarded original title of the magazine.

The prologue in fact would seem to have been written in two parts. The digressions, verbal dartings-about, and latinisms of the section leading up to the words "Bentley's Miscellany," are characteristic of Maginn. The gentler and damper wit of the second half suggests Dickens. It would be hard to imagine Maginn self-consciously celebrating "the soul-touching feeling" of his fellow conspirator at *Blackwood's*, John Wilson, or the tales of Mrs. Hall (particularly, as S. C. Hall, a fellow Irishman, was notoriously an enemy of Maginn's). It is unlike Maginn to wish his periodical rivals "every happiness and success" or to bother himself so awkwardly about taking up with their contributors ("We wish that we could catch them all, to illuminate our pages, without any desire whatever that their rays should be withdrawn from those in which they are at present shining"). After all, Maginn himself had just "illuminated" Bentley's pages for the matter of a fee. There is in all these sentiments a mawkish modesty more proper to a young man than to a professional writer of some years' experience: "We have only one petition to make, which is put in with all due humility; – it is this – that we are not to be prejudged by this our first attempt."

Most of all, one cannot imagine Maginn proclaiming that "we have nothing to do with politics" or asking, "is it a matter of absolute necessity that people's political opinions should be perpetually obtruded upon public notice? Is there not something more in the world to be talked about than Whig and Tory?" This is anomalous in the context of *Fraser's* definition of magazine literature as quintessentially political. Dickens, like Thackeray, came of a generation that saw Fox and Pitt as history, not news. This prologue declares that the contributors to *Bentley's Miscellany* are "so far Conservatives as to wish that all things which are good and honourable for our native country should be preserved with jealous hand" and "so far Reformers as to desire that every weed which defaces our conservatory should be unsparingly plucked up and cast away." Such sentiments smack too much of conciliatory Canningism to come from Maginn, who might write for both sides at once but not for anything in between. Where some might construct a middle path between the two parties, Maginn was not so nice about using such labels as *Conservative* (which really did not come into firm usage till a few years later) and *Reformer*, for both terms diluted the "partyness" of the old allegiances.[10]

The *Bentley's Miscellany* which burst upon the world in January 1837 gives only a diluted impression of Regency rowdiness. The so-called wit includes an "Opening Chaunt," facetious verse, comic narrative verse, Ossian parody, sentimental songs, and choruses of an "Anti-Dry-Rot Song." In fact, the first issue is pretty evenly divided between eleven bits of verse and nine articles, all making up a little over a hundred pages. The "articles" include a biographical sketch of a playwright and theatre manager who had just died, two Irish tales, one naval-ghost tale, Dickens's own Tulrumble tale of village life, a belle-lettristic essay on the beauties of octosyllabic metre, a Fenimore Cooper travelogue of French society, an anecdote of a traveller in Italy, and a comic essay on dentistry.

The second issue contains about six pieces of verse, all comic, and spoofs of society fortune-hunting, American manners, and Gothic romance writing. There is also more theatre history, eighteenth-century gossip, another ghost story, an Irish tale, the comic adventures of a young man getting into debt, some recollections of a childhood, and a romantic tale of a domestic tragedy. Dickens's contribution, "The Progress of a Parish Boy," this time leads the issue. In fact, *Oliver Twist* soon became one of a number of regular features repeated in the *Miscellany*, including: "Nights at Sea; or, Sketches of Naval Life," "Haji Baba" (a series of Persian looks at English life), the *Ingoldsby Legends*, "The Portrait Gallery" (satirical sketches), and *Handy Andy* (Samuel Lover's Irish novel). Most of these date from the same February 1837 issue that began Oliver Twist's "Progress." Thus, there were a fair number of "regulars" interspersed usually with tales, and, less frequently, with travelogues or biographical sketches. Poetry occupied about one tenth of the *Miscellany* pages and came to make up less. There was no "Song of the Month" from January 1838, as Prout, the most regular supplier, left London for an extended Eastern Tour late in 1837. Indeed, it was tales and more tales that came to fill the magazine: Irish, Naval, German and Italian Gothic, sentimental and domestic tragedy, facetious comedy, Parisian manners, military adventures, and pseudo-archaic medieval historical romances.

Perhaps the most ludicrous of a consistently ludicrous collection is "John Ward Gibson," by Charles Whitehead (1804–62), the romantic first-person narrative of an introspective orphan boy growing up by a series of accidents to be a murderer who is never found out. It is in fact among the better written parts of the *Miscellany*, and hence its decline into unintentional risibility is the more noticeable. Its effect is comparable to the effects that Dickens clearly strives after in the melodramatic interpolated tales of *Pickwick* (of which Chesterton remarks, "It required a man with the courage and coarseness of Dickens actually to put tragic episodes into a farce").[11] Dickens evidently valued the production of introspective Gothic effects, and Whitehead was a writer that he brought especially to the *Miscellany* ("a man who has more in him than three parts of the writers alive ... I think I can make him of great use" *Letters* I, 207–08; to Bentley [5 Dec. 1836]). Whitehead himself had solicited contributions from Dickens for Chapman and Hall's *Library of Fiction* (1836) and is usually credited with suggesting to them that Dickens might provide the copy for *Pickwick*.[12] K. J. Fielding has discounted the reliability of this story but even he is not able fully to explain the downfall of a career that started very promisingly but ended in a pauper's grave in Australia. Dickens admired his *Richard Savage* (1842), a romance published by Bentley the same year in the *Miscellany* and later dramatized. Whitehead was later to produce a revised version of Dickens's edition of the *Memoirs of Joseph Grimaldi* in 1846. He worked as a reader for Bentley for a while, and his own life and bearing appear to have been of a kind with the sad romances he produced.

Dickens seems to have had a taste for such macabre tales. His father-in-law, George Hogarth, began supplying a series called "The Poisoners of the Seventeenth Century" from September 1837, and this fits in with a gradual sobering up of the "Wits." In the first issue produced by Dickens after Mary Hogarth's death, there are some "Elegiac Stanzas" by Mrs. Cornwall Baron Wilson – to whom Dickens wrote, "I cannot tell you ... with how much melancholy pleasure I shall insert them in the miscellany" (*Letters* I, 266; [?late May 1837]). And the August 1837 "Song of the Month" begins, "I stood by a young girl's grave."

At the same time, Dickens's incapacitation after Mary's death must have brought Bentley more fully into the editorial proceedings, and by 28 September 1837 there is a new agreement under which Bentley had the power to "originate" three articles in every issue rather than having just the power of veto. It also specified that Bentley do the arranging of payments to contributors. These changes were no more than a reflection of what had been going on in any case. Dickens started deferentially enough, as indeed could only be the case with a young editor of twenty-five, but his objections to Bentley's over-ruling of editorial decisions, mostly without notice to Dickens himself, became increasingly less mild.

Of course, Dickens's relations with Bentley could not be the same after Bentley had first shown himself unwilling in March 1837 to accede to any more than one of four changes Dickens requested in the *Miscellany* agreement, had then muddied the negotiations with Macrone about the *Sketches by Boz* copyright, and throughout the summer of 1837 refused to accept *Oliver Twist* as a second novel in the first contract between them. In August, Dickens declared that any business to be conducted between them should be done through a third person. By September, just before the new agreement, Dickens complained that, while he had been out of town, the whole *Miscellany* as he set it up for September had been altered and papers never seen by him had been inserted. He considered that ''By these proceedings I have been actually superseded in my office as Editor of the Miscellany'' (*Letters* I, 308; 16 Sept. 1837) – and gave a month's notice. The differences were patched up, but by the end of the first year the notion of an Editor's duties had changed greatly. There is no longer the flurry of correspondence to contributors found among Dickens's letters, as he handed this task over to Bentley.

V

To determine in retrospect how much of the *Miscellany* was Bentley's ''child'' and not its editor's is not easy. The correspondence and contract negotiations offer some information, but it is perhaps most helpful to reflect on the significance of the circle gathered round Dickens in his first editorship, something that is not possible to see with *Master Humphrey's Clock*, which was so wholly Dickens's own that there were no other contributors whatsoever. Most of the con-tributors first gathered were of Bentley's generation rather than Dickens's. Theodore Hook (1788–1841), for example, who wrote the opening prose article on the playwright George Colman, was past his prime and seems to have had only this briefest of professional connections with Dickens.[13] He was more a Bentley's author than a *Miscellany* contributor. The Irishman Prout (Francis Mahony [1804–66]), who wrote the ''Song of the Month'' for most of the first year and also much facetious verse, was evidently not an acquaintance of Dickens until Bentley announced him as a contributor (*Letters* I, 192; [?9 Nov. 1836]). Prout, though a Jesuit, was closely associated with Maginn with whom he shared nationality, dazzling linguistic facility, and bohemian tendencies. Like Maginn and Hook, he was not much longer a part of London literary life after 1837, when he went abroad permanently. It is perhaps worth remarking that Dickens remembered him well enough to make him the Rome correspondent for the *Daily News* in 1846.

Yet another Irishman, Samuel Lover (1797–1868), is the author of the second prose piece in the first issue, a comic Irish tale that became a regular feature in the *Miscellany* and was published by Bentley in 1842. He had moved to London in 1835 (after helping found the *Dublin University Magazine* the same year), became like Prout an habitué of Lady Blessington's circle, and had his first novel, *Rory O'Moore, a National Romance*, published in 1837 by Bentley and dramatized very successfully for a run of a hundred nights. He supported himself before 1833 mainly by miniature painting; after the early 1840s, by songwriting and evenings of Irish entertainments in which he toured. His professional "Irishness" seems to have made him popular with Dickens's set: he was invited to the *Pickwick* dinner, Charley's christening, outings with Harrison Ainsworth and Laman Blanchard, and he and Dickens were in social correspondence even after the end of Dickens's connection with the *Miscellany*.[14]

At this time when the jaunts and jollities of London literary life were first opening up to him, these outings were entered into by Dickens with much enthusiasm and facetiousness. It is of incidental interest to note that none of the men at these occasions – Ainsworth, the son of a Manchester solicitor, Lover, son of a Dublin stockbroker, Blanchard, son of a Norwich glazier – had attended university, and all had broken away from the drudgery of office work to go into literature. These, like Forster, plus actors like John Harley, and John Braham, and singers like Dickens's brother-in-law Henry Burnett make up the circle most frequented by Dickens. The singing of songs by Dickens himself and his guests of an evening is often referred to: Bentley writes of a party on 29 April 1837 – "Dickens was in force, and on joining the ladies in drawing room, Dickens sang two or three songs, one the patter song, 'The Dog's Meat Man', & gave several successful imitations of the most distinguished actors of the day" (*Letters* I, 253n). Dickens had less in common with learned men like Maginn, Prout or Thackeray, all of whom had attended university and travelled abroad.

Charles Ollier (1788–1859), author of "A Gossip with Some Old

English Poets'' (January 1837), though older and long a literary adviser to Bentley, was also someone who had started out as a clerk (in a banking house) and then become a literary journeyman. He had the distinction of receiving encouragement from Leigh Hunt and of being the first publisher of Keats. His own work included poems, and prose romances *à la* Ainsworth. If not close to Ollier, Dickens evidently liked and trusted him, and Ollier's son Edmund (1827–86) was later to be associated with the *Daily News*, *Household Words*, and *All the Year Round*. Ollier was one of the few men liked by both Bentley and Dickens. Otherwise, it is noticeable that the "Show of Names" in the first advertisement for the *Miscellany* in 1836 was largely of Bentley's devising, and we might consider in detail what these names would have denoted to a reader of the times. Specifically, the list consists of: Hook, Prout, G. P. R. James, Dickens, Maginn, Captain Chamier, Jerdan, Captain Glascock, the "Author of the 'Munster Festival,'" Dr. Millingen, Mrs. Trollope, J. Hamilton Reynolds, S. Beazley, the author of "Stories of Waterloo," Douglas Jerrold, Major Skinner, "The Old Sailor," Samuel Lover, Lieutenant Conolly, Augustus Wade, W. H. Carleton, and Charles Ollier. Repeated twice and placed at the head of the advertisement are the words "Edited by Boz, and Illustrated by George Cruikshank."

These last words alone would have suggested a compendium of Cockney fun and satire. The names of Hook and Jerrold suggest more of the same. The Irish contingent, Prout, Maginn, Lover, and Carleton,[15] promise another kind of linguistic rowdiness, and so does mention of the author of "Stories of Waterloo," published by Colburn in 1829 and in the *Standard Novels* in 1833. This was William Hamilton Maxwell (1792–1850), a graduate of Trinity College, Dublin, and a former captain in the Peninsular War. He had taken holy orders but was better known for his rollicking sporting and military sketches. Bentley published his book *The Bivouac; or, Stories of the Peninsular War* in 1838. Although Maxwell was to contribute to the *Pic Nic Papers* ("edited" by Dickens and published by Colburn), Dickens objected to nearly everything he contributed to the *Miscellany*.

Mention of Maxwell draws attention to another kind of writing that appeared in every periodical of the time: the military tales of the French wars. The contributions of Captain Chamier (1796–1870) and Captain Glascock (1787?–1847), both commanders in the navy, were of this type. Chamier wrote a series of minor sailor adventure novels after his retirement in 1833 and had just finished revising a naval history published by Bentley and advertised at the same time as the

Miscellany. Bentley also published his *Life of a Sailor* in three volumes in 1832, and *Ben Brace* in three volumes in 1836 (in the *Standard Novels* in 1839). Glascock produced variations of his *Tales of a Tar*, published by Colburn and Bentley in 1830, and his *Naval Sketch-Book* published in 1831, during intervals of leave during the 1820s and 1830s. The *DNB* says of them that as novels they are "stupid enough, and in their historical parts have little value, but are occasionally interesting as social sketches of naval life in the early part of the century." Of Glascock, Dickens wrote, "I never met an officer yet, who didn't seem to think an Epaulette, and a brawling licence, synonymous terms" (*Letters* I, 207).

Dickens was more complimentary about Matthew Henry Barker (1790–1846), whose *Nights at Sea; or, Sketches of Naval Life during the War* illustrated by Cruikshank, an old friend, appeared in the *Miscellany* from May 1837. Bentley published these sketches in collected form in 1852. Major Skinner (1800?–43) was an active army soldier from 1816 until his death, and his only claim to literary fame appears to be two accounts of exotic overland excursions in India published in 1832 and 1836 by Bentley. There is no evidence of his work ever appearing in the *Miscellany*.

John Gideon Millingen (1782–1862) was another contributor whose military experiences rather than literary talents qualified him for a place in the *Miscellany*. He had lived through the Terror in Paris and had been a physician to the British forces in the Peninsular campaign. He left the army in 1823 and afterwards ran a lunatic asylum. He published various dramas, medical writing, and some fiction, but was generally known as "author of *The Bee-Hive*," a libretto produced and published in 1811. His "Portrait Gallery" at the end of the first issue of the *Miscellany* is the anecdote of a professional observer of physiognomy; it has greater curiosity than literary value, and indeed Dickens seems to have had a difficult time bringing it to a finished form. Millingen wrote six more stuffily facetious anecdotes of a middle-class family travelling on the Continent in this series of "The Portrait Gallery" till May 1838. He is notable otherwise only as being the one chosen by Bentley to propose Dickens for election to the Garrick Club.

"Lieutenant Conolly" (1807–42?) refers to one member of a distinguished family, many of whom wrote memoirs of their service in India. There appears to have been a Mr. Conolly on an outing made to Blackwall in July 1838 (when, says the *DNB*, Conolly would have been home on furlough) with a number of Bentley's acquaintances, including Dickens and Forster, who appears to have been memorably rude. Arthur Conolly's memoirs of an Indian expedition were published by Bentley in 1834; he met a horrible death during imprisonment in India in 1842.

In the *Miscellany*'s first "show of names," Samuel Beazley (1786–1851), who combined architecture and playwrighting, is notable for having designed minor London landmarks, including the St. James's theatre, site of Dickens's first produced play. He is said to have written over a hundred dramatic pieces, mostly farces and domestic comedies. Undoubtedly, the reason he appeared in the list of Bentley's "names" was that he had written two novels, one of them, *The Oxonians*, published by Colburn and Bentley. But there is no record of anything he may have written for *Bentley's Miscellany*. Similarly, the only reason for Mrs. Trollope's inclusion in the preliminary *Miscellany* list of authors can be seen in the fact that Bentley had published her *Paris and the Parisians* in 1835, *Life and Adventures of Jonathan Jefferson Whitlaw* in 1836, and the *Vicar of Wrexhill* in 1837. However, there is no record of any contribution she may have submitted to the *Miscellany*.

The correspondence between Boz and potential contributors and promising young writers must necessarily have dwindled when it came down only to a striking of bargains between Bentley and his authors. Of the twenty-two contributors advertised on 1 December 1836 for the first issue, at least seventeen are Bentley authors. Only such men as Maginn, Prout, Jerdan, and Reynolds, who had independent loyalties to other periodicals, are not. Jerrold, in fact, was at this time primarily a playwright who contributed to magazines and seems never to have given any of his work to Bentley or his *Miscellany*.

Among the contributors to the first issue, at least ten of the fifteen are authors published by Bentley. Of the authors not mentioned so far, we have only to note that Edward Howard (d. 1841), author of "The Marine Ghost," was a former shipmate and later co-editor with Marryat on the *Metropolitan Magazine*. Howard's most successful novel, *Rattlin the Reefer* (1836), had just been published by Bentley.[16] There is no record of any further contribution by him to *Bentley's Miscellany*. A similar contributor is Richard Johns (1805–51), who was a lieutenant in the Royal Marines stationed in Chatham in 1837. He contributed at least ten pieces to the *Miscellany* between March 1837 and December 1840, plus a sketch to the *Pic Nic Papers*. Bentley published his *Legend and Romance, African and European* (1838). A letter from Dickens to Johns, on Mary Hogarth's death, suggests that he and Dickens had become friendly for a short while as well.

The name of Thomas Love Peacock in this list is intriguing, but there is no record of his work in the *Miscellany*. The presence of his name may be accounted for by the fact that *Crochet Castle, Maid Marian, Nightmare Abbey*, and *Headlong Hall* had all been published in the *Standard Novels* series in 1837.

Finally, the Reverend Richard Harris Barham (1788–1845), a quintessentially English writer of facetious verse, had been a friend of Bentley's since schooldays. He contrived to help Bentley out with his *Miscellany* by providing "The 'Monstre' Balloon" and other things for the first issue. His most famous contribution was the *Ingoldsby Legends*, which ran more or less continuously in the *Miscellany* and were published by Bentley in collected form in 1840. They make one of the greatest features of Bentley's catalogue (comparable to *Oliver Twist* and *Jack Sheppard*) and have been a classic of English nonsense verse ever since.

Other contributors of passing interest who appear in the *Miscellany* in its first year are John Harley (1786–1858) the actor (Boz's "Strange Gentleman"); Thomas Haynes Bayly (1797–1839), who contributed five poems and a tale between January and July of 1837 and wrote thirty-six plays between 1831 and 1839 (one of them reviewed by Dickens for the *Morning Chronicle* in January 1836); Gilbert à Beckett (1811–56), who had been editor of *Figaro in London* illustrated by Cruikshank and Seymour, had dramatized *Oliver Twist* in 1838 (Harley played Mr. Bumble) and *The Chimes* (at Dickens's request), and was later part of *Punch*; and James Sheridan Knowles (1787–1862), whom Hazlitt had called the first tragic writer of the time in his *Spirit of the Age* (1825). Knowles's earliest successes featured William Macready, the leading tragic actor of the day, and he was concerned like Macready with the revival of Shakespeare. His romantic tale "Glorvina, the Maid of Perth" ran for a while in the *Miscellany* from June 1837. During the 1840s, Dickens organized amateur theatricals in the effort to raise money to make Knowles curator of the newly established Shakespeare House.

The number of unsolicited contributions accepted is not unusually small, especially given the state of Bentley's publishing list and Dickens's literary acquaintance at this early stage. Dickens was naturally well disposed towards tiros, but there were very few, and among them only Mark Lemon (1809–70), the future founder of *Punch*, became a close friend. He had been trained to the trade of hop-merchant in Kent and was exactly the sort of unknown that the prologue had spoken of bringing forth. His "Passage in the Life of a Disappointed Man" was received anonymously and appeared in the

September 1837 issue. Dickens's personal relations with Thackeray, whose "The Professor," appeared in the same issue as Lemon's "Disappointed Man" (September 1837) were less intimate.

After the agreement of 28 September 1837, Dickens generally avoided dealings with correspondents. It is therefore less easy to assign authorship of articles for 1838. In February 1838, Dickens also became annoyed with Bentley for precipitately sending out advance copies of *Memoirs of Joseph Grimaldi* minus Dickens's preface and Cruikshank's etchings. This led to a sarcastic notice from John Hamilton Reynolds (1796–1852), best known as the friend of Keats and proprietor of the *Athenaeum* until 1831. The *Miscellany* published a light essay by Reynolds on Lady Wortley Montagu in February 1837, but this did not stop him from abusing its publisher and editor. Dickens was only just restrained by friends from publishing a public reply to Reynolds in the *Miscellany*.

This falling out with Bentley was awkward, for at the same time Dickens was eager to have Bentley's co-operation in changing the form of *Barnaby Rudge* from three volumes to monthly numbers in the *Miscellany*. Then in May came the anger at Bentley's meanness with payment for half pages of *Oliver Twist*. Nevertheless, the two of them still made up a sailing party to Blackwall in July. The summer, as we have seen earlier, was full of negotiations and threats, and the fourth *Miscellany* agreement came in September 1838 after Dickens had withheld *Oliver*'s instalment for June. But with the fretting over *Barnaby Rudge* in January 1839, just when Dickens was due to begin work on it, the situation in the *Miscellany* became explosive. He officially resigned as editor on 31 January 1839.

The man picked by Dickens as his editorial successor, apparently against Forster's advice, was a prominent writer whose work had not appeared in the *Miscellany* until surprisingly recently: William Harrison Ainsworth, author of *Rookwood*, and the man who had introduced Dickens to his first publisher, Macrone. Ainsworth's *Crichton*, which was supposed to have been published by Macrone but was published by Bentley after the other's death, had been eulogized in a rather out-of-place article in the *Miscellany* a few months after it had come out in February 1837. The article is more a puff than anything else. But Ainsworth, whether because he was not asked or because he did not wish to write for the *Miscellany*, had not been among Bentley's show of names in the first advertisements. And yet, Ainsworth's portrait had appeared in *Fraser's* "Gallery" in July 1837, and both *Rookwood* (published by Bentley in 1834) and *Crichton* had been popular successes. Bentley was by no means immediately agreeable to the suggestions of Ainsworth as editor but took the advice of Richard Barham, who seems to have been something of a mediator in this affair.[17]

Nominally, Ainsworth was a Fraserian. He is present in the group portrait of the dinner of 1835. Maginn seems to have been friendly towards him until the publication of the sensationalistic *Jack Sheppard* in 1839; considering Maginn's fondness for the slang of St. Giles, his disapproval of a novel imbued with it is perhaps surprising. *Jack Sheppard* was not reviewed by *Fraser's* until 1840. By 1840, Ainsworth was no longer a Fraserian, and neither was Thackeray or Maginn. Ainsworth's biographer, the unreliable Ellis, when writing of Ainsworth's editorship of the *Miscellany*, describes a companionship that existed in the early 1830s but not by 1839, and never convincingly so among Bentley's contributors. Ellis states that Ainsworth knew Maginn by 1827, the time when Ainsworth was setting up as a publisher and making the most of introductions to prominent people such as Scott.[18] It is more nostalgia than fact when Ellis says,

That was essentially a dining age, so, following the example of the Fraserians, the leading literary men connected with *The Miscellany* often met for gastronomic purposes in the Red Room at the publisher's house in New Burlington Street, which in those days had a large garden at the rear.[19]

In the grab-bag of quondam literary celebrities that Bentley simply transferred from his booklist to his *Miscellany*, one begins to see how shallow this aping of *Fraser's* is, and how commercial the principle by which Bentley can be said to have made the *Miscellany* his own. Magazines like the old *Monthly* and *Fraser's*, as well as the great quarterlies, expressed the circumstances of men meeting with like-minded men and exchanging opinions about their society. When the *Edinburgh Review* was formed, most of those who got together were associated with the Speculative Society. They were gifted amateurs rather than Grub Street hacks, Whig lawyers in a city where the political rewards went to Tories. It was they who commissioned the publisher Constable to act for them, and not the other way around.

The establishment of the famous publishers' monthlies later in the nineteenth century is quite different and expresses not so much the clubbiness of writers, or of men who had separate occupations and found that their writing brought them together, as the gathering of a publisher's property, his authors, about him. These men did not converse or debate with one another, and, by extension, with their public; instead, they were paid to purvey the commodity of their own individual talents. They relived the bohemian tavern life of the 1830s at nostalgic second-hand only.

By that time, however, not only had fiction become respectable, it had become the profitable subsistence for writers, so much so that it tended to drive out the demand for other genres. The prologue to *Bentley's Miscellany* still describes the age of literary coteries, but its advertisements, with their lists of names not topics, presages the age of publishing "stables." This is a pushing of commodities, not opinions. And the greatest commodity of them all was fiction. What the readers of magazines wanted was, to extend Chesterton's phrase, "simply lengths cut from the flowing and mixed substance called Dickens"[20] – or any of the other popular writers Bentley might have conscripted. Hence, the inevitable development of "continuations" from month to month. These elbowed out the traditional notion of a monthly periodical as a flexible commentator on contemporary affairs.

There is no reason to doubt Dickens's own affection for clubs, but increasingly any semblance of conviviality was lost as the arguments between him and his publisher escalated. It is also notable that when he finally did manage to establish his own club – that of *Master Humphrey's Clock* – it consisted only of himself. The Pickwick Club had under his writing come down really only to Pickwick; so, too, Master Humphrey's club dropped away to the melancholy bachelor Humphrey himself. Thus, given Dickens's lack of school connections and Bentley's commercial attitude towards his *Miscellany* authors, it is not surprising that there is no history of any diners-out called the Bentleians.

6

1838 The writer of parts

I

With the years 1837–38, Dickens entered upon the flood-tide of his early reputation. As well as the editing of *Bentley's Miscellany*, these years brought Dickens a host of publishers' commissions; between the winding up of *Pickwick Papers* and the commencement of *Nicholas Nickleby* there was little relief. Both Bentley and Chapman and Hall were eager to strike the iron of Dickens's popularity while it was hot. Not since Sir Walter Scott had there been such a promising literary property, although there was still some question as to what shape this celebrity might take: Dickens may have decided he wanted to be known as a novelist; his publishers were continuing to promote the humorist.

Throughout this hectic period, when Dickens's work was turning up everywhere, anonymously as well as pseudonymously, in reviews, sketches, editions, and serial fictions, the reading public was living through the serialized narrative of Lockhart's *Life of Sir Walter Scott*, which was published in a series of seven volumes appearing between March 1837 and March 1838. Any account of Dickens's life at this time must include its intersection with the narrative of Scott's career that arched across the literary world during these months. Even if one were not reading either Dickens or Lockhart, their narratives were ubiquitous in the form of lengthy excerpts in the newspapers and magazines. By January 1838, publication of Scott's biography had arrived at the sixth volume, where Scott in his diary records the death of his wife. It inspired Dickens in the same month to commence a diary of his own – beginning with a remembrance of Mary Hogarth's death. The effort to record his introspective moments was not long kept up and was abandoned after Dickens copied out a long extract from the passage in Scott's diary where Scott describes his wife's corpse:

"I have seen her. There is the same symmetry of form, though those limbs are rigid which were once so gracefully elastic – but that yellow masque with pinched features, which seems to mock life rather than emulate it, can it be the face that was once so full of lively expression? I will not look upon it again." *(Letters* I, 632; 14 Jan. 1838)

Dickens copies this and another extract out, and writes: "In Scott's Diary ... there are thoughts which have been mine by day and by night, in good spirits and bad, since Mary died" *(Letters* I, 631; 14 Jan. 1838). With the climax of this Sunday morning entry, Dickens comes to the end of the daily exercise of recording his feelings; the sporadic entries after this record daily engagements only.[1]

A review of the sixth volume of Lockhart's *Life of Scott* appeared in the *Examiner* at this time (no. 1562 7 Jan. 1838: 4–6). We do not know who wrote it; shortly afterwards, Forster's usual schedule was interrupted, and during this time Dickens stepped in to review for him a number of light literary publications and plays, including Macready's *King Lear* (4 Feb. 1838).[2] The main feature of this production was, as Dickens approvingly noted, that after one hundred and fifty years of Tate, Macready had restored the Fool and the deaths of Lear and Cordelia. His review shows that at the same time as he read about Scott's wife and recalled Mary Hogarth, the pathos of Cordelia's death struck Dickens's mind forcibly.

Nevertheless, there was little time for musing. The interval of December to January was a busy time for Dickens. The readers of *Pickwick* might look forward eagerly to the promised new serial of *Nicholas Nickleby* in April, but Dickens had a number of other projects to tackle first. On 8 January, his diary of the New Year records,

I began the Sketches of Young Gentlemen to-day. One hundred and twenty five pounds for such a little book without my name to it, is pretty well. This and the "Sunday," by the bye, are the only two things I have not done as Boz. *(Letters* I, 630; 8 Jan. 1838)

Dickens had also contracted on 29 November 1837 to "edit" the memoirs of the pantomime clown Joseph Grimaldi for Bentley. Grimaldi had died in June 1837; his memoirs had been written and were to have been revised by a journalist named Thomas Egerton Wilks (1815–54), but Bentley bought out Wilks's interest and turned over the commission to Dickens. Dickens finished working on the bulk of the manuscript by early January and struggled with the preface later in the month, when he was also coping with *Sketches of Young Gentlemen, Oliver Twist,* and the reviews for Forster.

Thus, January 1838 was for Dickens a month of miscellaneous literary journalism. By 25 January he had finished off all his various

tasks, including his work for the *Miscellany*. Then in a letter to
Ainsworth on this date, he speaks of plans to research Yorkshire
boarding schools, and also of a projected collection of tales about
old and new London to be written with Ainsworth and published in
monthly parts. Ainsworth himself spoke of them as appearing "in
a Pickwick form," but it is of interest to note that, in the earliest
projection of this periodical, Ainsworth had described them as "an
alternation of comedy and tragedy" that he hoped would *not* be
compared to *Pickwick* (*Letters* I, 358n). The periodical was originally
advertised for January 1837 by Macrone, but by 1838 Ainsworth and
Dickens were thinking of doing it for Chapman and Hall. The celebration of London was something for which Ainsworth had often
praised Dickens; however, Dickens's relationship with Ainsworth
seems always to have been equivocal, and this project never came to
fruition. Subsequently, Cruikshank's cover design for their "Lions of
London" was used by Ainsworth for the monthly cover of his own
Old St. Paul's, a serial published from January to December of 1841.
The opening, too, of Dickens's *Master Humphrey's Clock*, in 1840,
with its tales of Gog and Magog, seems very close to the "Lions of
London." Indeed, one of the reasons Dickens eventually set up *Master
Humphrey's Clock* was to lighten his monthly load by bringing in
other contributors, and the scheme with Ainsworth may have
suggested the format by which he hoped to do this.

Meanwhile, readers of his present periodical, the *Miscellany*, were
complaining of a lack of variety: there is a letter from Dickens to a
would-be contributor to the *Miscellany* in which he notes that subscribers had lately "complained bitterly of our numerous continuations" (*Letters* I, 364; 29 Jan. 1838). *Oliver* was not one of the serials
generally complained of, but there is none the less a tone of weariness
in the reviews greeting it for the months of January and February
1838. Although *Oliver* is singled out as usual from the other contributions in the *Miscellany*, the terms of praise are no more than trite.
Only appreciation of the comic scene of lovemaking between Mr.
Bumble and the workhouse matron seems animated. The *Morning
Advertiser* speaks for many of the commentators when it says of the
February instalment: "Its interest is only moderate, and but that it
proceeds from the pen of Boz, would not excite any great attention"
(5 Feb. 1838).

The *Memoirs of Joseph Grimaldi* received similarly lukewarm
applause. The *Life* itself had already passed through so many hands
that Dickens could be congratulated merely on having made it tidy
and presentable. The *Weekly Dispatch* called it mere "book-making"

(no. 1899 11 Mar. 1838: 118). *Sketches of Young Gentlemen*, appearing on 10 February 1838 without the benefit of Dickens's name, also received noticeably fewer reviews. The *Morning Post* of 10 February 1838 gave merely excerpts, while the *Examiner* gave a facetiously jocular review (no. 1566 4 Feb. 1838: 68–69). It would be surprising, did we not know of Forster's interest, that the *Examiner* should praise this anonymous production at all; even though its notice consists basically of a few introductory words and long extracts, they occupy nearly two columns. A rather ironic illustration of how far Dickens had come from his earlier anonymity is shown by a complaint made about these sketches by the less intimate *Bell's New Weekly Messenger*: "The author attempts to imitate 'Boz,' but his exertions are frequently distressing" (8 no. 325 11 Mar. 1838).

II

In startling contrast, then, is the warmth that was to greet the commencement of *Nicholas Nickleby* a month later in April 1838. *Oliver Twist* might have won respect from the reviewers for its greater power, but respect was inevitably qualified by dislike of its low characters and setting, over which even the loyal Forster was defensive. *Pickwick*, simplistic as it might have been, was still the true favourite; nothing Dickens had done for the flash Bentley so far drew as much loyalty.

Thus, where Dickens himself was eager to show the advancement in technique that *Nickleby* represented over *Pickwick*, the reviewers preferred to point out the resemblances between the familiar periodical and the new one. Under the heading "Boz's New Work," *Bell's Life in London* wrote that *Nickleby* "promises to be as humorous and amusing as its great predecessor" (1 Apr. 1838). *Bell's New Weekly Messenger* hailed "another comic romance of real life" and looked forward to the twelve months' "intimate" acquaintance with a new set of characters (8 no. 328 1 Apr. 1838). This way of speaking about Dickens's work – the assumption of joviality and intimacy, the arrogating of the author and character as friends – is well enough known as a cliché of Dickens criticism. None the less, the emphasis on amusement over art, the complete identification of Dickens as a writer of "entertainments" rather than as a writer of novels is still surprising. Other papers also singled out his powers of "observation" and drollery.[3] In these remarks, neither Dickens nor his reviewers seem to have come very far from *Sketches by Boz* two years earlier. The renewed enthusiasm for long and numerous extracts which is immediately noticeable about the *Nickleby* reviews would also suggest that the favourite sketch-writer is being welcomed back. Even more than *Pickwick*, *Nickleby*'s course of publication is notable for widespread extracting. The effect of a few favourable reviews is nothing compared to the phenomenon of seeing everywhere the same extracts, with the same titles assigned in some sort of invisible accord by sub-editors of the newspapers and magazines – "Golden Square," "London Gardens," "The Yorkshire Schoolmaster." It would be easy to mistake *Nickleby* for another series of Boz's "Sketches of London," especially after the false start of the Yorkshire scenes (and, as the common reviewers saw it, the misguided effort of "fine" writing) had been left behind.

Yet we know that Dickens worked much harder in preparing *Nickleby* and did not particularly wish to repeat the experience of hot-to-the-press improvisation. What Forster wrote in the *Examiner* may give the clue to Dickens's hopes for his new periodical. As before, the publishing information about the book being reviewed tells us that *Nickleby* was "Edited by Boz." Forster, like his less literary brethren, receives the new work with a figurative embrace of "heartiest welcome," and detailed remarks are suspended for a few moments of uncritic-like handshaking. The young Nicholas has come to visit and passes along the greetings of the absent Pickwick. None the less, *Oliver Twist* has interposed itself in the meantime, and Forster is too sophisticated a critic not to measure the difference it has made. *Nickleby*, he hopes, will have the Pickwickian warmth – "the same affectionate heartiness of tone; the same liberal, exuberant, unrestrained vein of humour" – but also, he pointedly anticipates, better design of character and plot (no. 1574 1 Apr. 1838: 195).

The reviewer for *Bell's New Weekly Messenger* evidently agreed with this perception that Boz was showing more art, but how differently his judgement was slanted. This reviewer disliked the new pretensions to art:

"Boz" has been puffed into the belief that he ought to occupy a much higher station in our literature than he does; he has been classed with Fielding and Smollett, and, no doubt, in consequence, believes that he is equal to those great novelists; but in endeavouring to "be like" them, he will ruin himself. "Nickleby" is an effort at the "Tom Jones" and "Joseph Andrews" style, and a very respectable effort truly; but, still, only an effort; there are one or two touches of great truth and beauty in the first number, but "one swallow does not make a summer."

(*Bell's New Weekly Messenger* 8 no. 329 8 Apr. 1838: 6)

Thus, both friends and enemies early on recognized the models Dickens was setting up for himself. The *Morning Advertiser*'s review, too, expresses the sense of a novelist who has not yet written a novel (6 Apr. 1838).

The very feature for which the *Sun* commended Dickens in its review of 2 April 1838 – that of getting right into the characterization as in a novel – suggests Dickens's intentions. The opening of the Pickwick Club's proceedings had been slow, and this time Dickens saved his Muffin Joint-Stock Company spoof for the second chapter. In this way the lovers of both *Tom Jones* and Sam Weller got what they wanted. Our taste may have predisposed us to prefer Dickens's attempts at Fieldingesque effects, but we should not ignore the pressures to feed the appetite for amusement which were exerted on Dickens by critics who also held Fielding in high esteem.

The review by the *Sunday Times* provides a final example of the concerns animating contemporary criticism. Under the general heading of "Magazine Day," the *Sunday Times* criticized the *Oliver Twist* serial for being "out of place in a magazine that started, professing to dedicate its space to wit and humour" (no. 807 8 Apr. 1838). And in the review immediately following, of *Nickleby*'s first number, the reviewer noted that, although Dickens's fame rested on his humour, he seemed fonder of his pathetic effects: "we feel assured that Boz would feel prouder of his dissection of the depravity of Sikes, and his miserable companion, than of twenty 'Pickwicks'" (no. 807 8 Apr. 1838). This debate over what constituted Dickens's "real" talent and subject was one that had been going on since the publication of *Sketches by Boz*, when the *Spectator* professed to see something more in these comic sallies and remarked that Dickens's "strength lies in pathos" (9 no. 399 20 Feb. 1836: 182).

By 1838, however, papers such as *Bell's New Weekly Messenger* were positively complaining of Boz's inclination to the artistic and serious (8 no. 333 6 May 1838). This review (reprinted in the *Magnet*) goes on to complain of the incongruities set up by the shifts between the Bozian and the Fieldingesque modes of writing. Obviously, all Dickens's commentators felt they could see the aesthetic tugs-of-war in Dickens's mind and felt no hesitation in expressing their own preferences, be it for "fine" writing or broad comedy. It appears that most reviewers found Dickens's "fine" writing a bit tame.

They preferred the familiar comic effects of both the May and June numbers of *Nickleby*. The Yorkshire scenes were to continue for another number (July 1838), until finally Nicholas thrashes Squeers and sets out for London. The Kenwigses' anniversary party ends the number with a return to Dickens's best "Bloomsbury Christening" style. Still, the *Magnet* professed to find this number "rambling" and remarked that the humour of the Squeers-thrashing "is destroyed by the high tragedy tone of the hero" (2 no. 69 9 July 1838). Most critics' comments, even those of the *Examiner*, are similarly frivolous.

In fact, what is striking at this point in *Nickleby*'s progress is that there are very few critical comments at all, although there are more notices than ever. A place for *Nickleby* and *Bentley's Miscellany* in the "Magazine Day" column of all the papers had become a matter of course. But no longer is Boz an "emerging" genius, nor has *Nickleby* the novelty of *Pickwick*. Nicholas may have been more literarily respectable than the Pickwickians, but he was certainly no more interesting. The most notable aspect of these months is a lack of serious criticism, paradoxically set alongside the very proliferation of extracts from *Nickleby*. A comment from the *Mirror* of 21 July 1838 about *Nickleby* describes exactly what one observes in all the papers: "As we do not follow the narrative of the work, our plan is to detach sketches and artificial *bits*, with which Mr. Dickens's writing generally abounds" (32 no. 904 21 July 1838: 60). And here follow two extracts entitled "London Lodgings," and "A Party in Lodgings."

Again and again it is these detachable "bits" of Dickens that present the reading experience of his works. Extracting was far commoner then than now, but the sheer volume everywhere of these peripatetic paragraphs, identical from paper to paper, each with its distinctive title as if a story or essay on its own, begins to take cumulative effect. The reader repeatedly comes across paragraphs called "A Member of the Reformed House of Commons" (Part V), "Making Love at a Milliner's," "A Serious Scene" (Part VI), "Beauties from Boz" (Part V), and so on. Chesterton aptly catches the spirit of this when he says, "It would be easy enough for Dickens, instead of publishing *Nicholas Nickleby*, to have published a book of sketches, one of which was called 'A Yorkshire School,' another called 'A Provincial Theatre,' and another called 'Sir Mulberry Hawk or High Life Revealed,' another called 'Mrs. Nickleby or a Lady's Monologue.'"[4]

As the fact of such copious extracting suggests, the reviews of the summer months are unremarkable. Predictably, those with an appetite for extractable "bits" were glad to see Boz back in London again in both serials: the August number of *Oliver* concentrates on Fagin, and in the same month Nicholas returns from Yorkshire and falls almost immediately into an entertaining episode of satire on members of Parliament that was widely reprinted. The sketch-writer had not deserted his public.

III

If Dickens's writing at this time is not at its most memorable, it may have been because he was more concerned with its professional aspects. The August number of *Oliver* officially began the third volume of the "novel" promised Bentley. It was well past mid-summer, and yet *Oliver* was still appearing in the *Miscellany*; to judge by some of the reviews, its continuation was carrying the magazine. Dickens was still trying to get the promised novel out of the way as late as the end of July. By the end of the month, he was asking Bentley for a month's break from *Oliver*'s appearance in the *Miscellany* so that he might get on with the writing of it as a book. In compensation, Dickens proposed to allow the *Miscellany* to announce the impending commencement of a new tale (*Letters* I, 421; [?26 July 1838]). Whatever some reviewers thought of "continuations," clearly Dickens and Bentley thought them a good thing for the *Miscellany*.

Meanwhile the October deadline for delivering the whole of *Barnaby Rudge* was coming up. Dickens had already put off this deadline from 1 March and at the same time proposed that *Barnaby Rudge* be written in monthly instalments, not volumes:

If I sat down to Barnaby Rudge, writing a little of it when I could (and with all my other engagements it would necessarily be a very long time before I could hope to finish it in that way) it would be clearly impossible for me to begin a new *series* of papers in the Miscellany. The conduct of three different stories at the same time, and the production of a large portion of each, every month, would have been beyond Scott himself.

(*Letters* I, 370; to Bentley, 10 Feb. 1838)

And Lockhart's account of Scott's breakdown published at the end of March 1838, in the seventh and last volume of the *Life*, begins: "Sir Walter was now to pay the penalty of his unparalleled toils."[5]

The change in format of *Barnaby Rudge* was formalized in the agreement of 22 September 1838. Bentley agreed that *Barnaby Rudge* should appear in the *Miscellany* after *Oliver* (which was to be delivered complete by 21 October). In the case of *Oliver*, it was spoken of as a series of "Original Articles," of which Bentley had sole copyright for three years. After that time Dickens shared the copyright with Bentley and they could print "the same Original Articles, or a selection thereof, in a collected form" (*Letters* I, 668). There was a separate clause (Fifteen) on the disposal of and payment for "the entire work called 'Oliver Twist'" (*Letters* I, 669). It also prohibited publication of this work "or any of the series of papers of which it shall be composed in the 'Standard Novels,' or in numbers or in parts, or in any other manner or form than that of Post Octavo" (*Letters* I, 669–70).

Quite differently, *Barnaby Rudge* was spoken of as "an original novel" (which would appear "in the same manner as the original papers under the title of 'Oliver Twist' have heretofore done": *Letters* I, 670). It was to appear in eighteen monthly parts, with the remaining manuscript to be delivered separately as a whole. In one clause (Nineteen) it is alternately spoken of as a "novel," an "entire work," and as a "series of papers" (*Letters* I, 671). Whatever happened to the work in its "collected" form, three years from its completion Bentley could "reprint, publish, and sell for his own benefit any number or numbers of the said 'Miscellany' containing any one of the series of papers entitled 'Barnaby Rudge'" (*Letters* I, 671). This was also the case with *Oliver Twist*. But for all the careful calculations of this new contract, relations between Bentley and Dickens continued to deteriorate.

IV

The reviews of *Bentley's Miscellany* were not as kind as they once had been, and it is notable how often the reviewers exempt all contributors but Dickens from praise (see *Bell's New Weekly Messenger* 8 no. 353 23 Sept. 1838). We may no longer find September's satire of the British Association for the Advancement of Science (the "Mudfog Association") funny, but the general opinion of it at the time was high. The praise for *Nickleby* is not notably more enthusiastic.

Dickens seems to have lost nothing by putting off *Oliver* for a month, but the story itself shows signs of Dickens's eagerness to get through to the end. The dramatic high point of the number is a meeting between the whore Nancy and the maiden Rose, which the *Sun* compared in interest and vividness to Scott. It praised the scene's "air of reality" (2 Oct. 1838); the only other commentator on this scene, the *Sunday Times*, however, thought the portrayal of Nancy not realistic enough, inasmuch as she was "made to employ language utterly at variance with her manners and education, and quite out of keeping with that quoted in former numbers" (no. 833 7 Oct. 1838). Finally, the *Morning Advertiser* opined that *Oliver* was a "miserable failure" and the *Miscellany* fit only for the "trunk-maker" (11 Oct. 1838).

Dickens may have felt he need not bother about what the dailies or weeklies said, for it was at this time that the venerable *Edinburgh Review* came out with its first review of his work, and the verdict was highly favourable. As in earlier quarterly articles, the attention paid to Dickens is justified on the grounds of his unique reputation as "the most popular writer of his day." The reviewer points out that "Since the publication of the poems and novels of Sir Walter Scott, there has been no work the circulation of which has approached that of the Pickwick Papers" (68 no. 137 Oct. 1838: 75).

Most of the reviewer's comments, favourable though they are, none the less largely suggest that Dickens is still a sketch-writer, an observer, a teller of tales (the running head of the article is "Dickens's *Tales*"). The reviewer says of his works, "the most popular among them owed its success, certainly not to its merits as a whole, but to the attractiveness of detached passages" (86). The reviewer notes Dickens's own admission of this problem in his preface to *Pickwick*, and the effort being put forward in *Nickleby* to change. Devoting most of the remaining discussion to outlining the action of *Oliver*, the review concludes that it proves that Dickens is a fine novelist – who has yet to write "a good novel" (96). Thus, the *Edinburgh Review* articulates the main challenge facing Dickens at this time. It was precisely in this same month of October, following the drawing up of the new contract with Bentley on 22 September, that Dickens had to prove his boast of *Oliver* as a "prose epic."

The reviewer acknowledges the peculiar risks of writing to a periodical deadline, but like other critics he also notes how indulgent this has made Dickens's public: "he would be subjected to a severer criticism if his fiction could be read continuedly" (96–97). This echoes a remark the *Spectator* had made some months earlier when, upon the appearance of *Nickleby*'s first number, it had shrewdly analysed the "mechanical circumstances" of Dickens's popularity:

Had the *Pickwick* been first published in a volume, it is questionable whether its circulation would have reached one-fifth of its actual extent, or whether the work would have been read through by the multitude. It is a significant fact, that the Sketches of this writer, collected into volumes, have a far less extensive demand, although they are more adapted for connected publication.
(*Spectator* 11 no. 509 31 Mar. 1838: 304)

The reviewers had been indulgent towards a monthly entertainment appearing indefinitely and were indifferent to the sense of an ending. But *Pickwick* and *Oliver*, the one a series of sporting engravings and the other a series of satirical articles, had unexpectedly become more than the sum of their parts. The subsequent researches on the part of Dickens for their successors, *Nicholas Nickleby* and *Barnaby Rudge,* reflect his developing ambitions as an artist.

The last volume of *Oliver,* which covers the instalments from August 1838 on (chs. 38–53), certainly shows the effort to respond to the challenge of constructing a sustained plot. The previous four instalments had all been imbued with that strain of nostalgia about Mary Hogarth that found its way into the story of Rose Maylie on her sickbed. The instalments from August onwards are heavily taken up with the thicket of circumstances surrounding Oliver's birth. Once Oliver was safe with Rose in the country (and it would have been tiresome to lose him a second time, however thrillingly), the narrative moves back to London and to Nancy in particular. Dickens's sacred and profane female figures, Rose and Nancy, meet in the October instalment (ch. 40), and Monks, who had been introduced in the last chapter of the July number, makes his way to London. It is in the conversation between Rose and Nancy that we find out he is the brother of Oliver; and in the next chapter Oliver sees Mr. Brownlow again. With this, the winding up of the story begins. After the delivery of Oliver safely into the care of both Miss Maylie and Mr. Brownlow, the reader may, like the irritated Dr. Losberne, be driven in a moment of exasperation and facetiousness to ask how the story is to conclude: "'Are we to pass a vote of thanks to all these vagabonds, male and female, and beg them to accept a hundred pounds or so apiece as a trifling mark of our esteem, and some slight acknowledgment of their kindness to Oliver?'" (*Bentley's Miscellany* 4 Oct. 1838: 327; *Oliver Twist* ch. 41). Such, indeed, was a possible ending, of the sort that had wrapped up *Pickwick.*

Oliver, however, had only reached to a part of its contracted length; Dickens had over 50,000 words to go if he were to fulfil his contract with Bentley. Mr. Brownlow cautions the irascible doctor to "'proceed gently and with great care'" (327). Of course, if justice and the proper hanging of Fagin and his gang are all that is in view, this seems laughable advice for the winding up of a tale. But Mr. Brownlow has something more in mind – and so has Dickens in the late introduction of the character of Monks – which is, "'the discovery of Oliver's parentage, and regaining for him the inheritance of which, if this story be true, he has been fraudulently deprived'" (327). The change in Oliver's status as an orphan and a pauper – the very features that had started the original Poor Law satire – now becomes the business of the novel which Dickens had been challenged by contract, and subsequently by professional pride, to produce.

Dickens does his best: suddenly in the last volume, all the odd corners of the novel are searched out and a miser's hoard of revelations appears. Noah Claypole, originally left behind in Mudfog, somehow manages to turn up in the very London pub frequented – at that very moment – by Fagin; Mr. Bumble, shorn of all his parochial sublimity, becomes a humble pawn in the schemes of Monks, Oliver's long-lost half-brother, who was completely unheard of at Oliver's birth; and Noah is set to following Nancy, who has become a confidante of Mr. Brownlow and Rose Maylie. The den of Fagin is entirely cleared out, and Fagin himself is hanged for a crime that, as contemporary critics pointed out, is never identified. The last days of both Sikes and Fagin give Dickens the chance to write another Newgate sketch, but these are mere pauses in an unravelling of Justice's purposes that takes seven instalments (chs. 39–53).

This acceleration of the plot's intricacies reaches its climax, or nadir, in the fifty-first chapter, in the interview between Brownlow and Monks at Mudfog, where, in the manner of theatrical last scenes, Oliver's inheritance is set right, Mr. and Mrs. Bumble are punished by becoming inmates of their own workhouse, and Rose accepts Henry Maylie's proposal of marriage. In the revelation of Oliver's near relation to Rose, the narrator writes, "A father, sister, and mother, were gained and lost in that one moment" (*Bentley's Miscellany* 5 Mar. 1839: 286; *Oliver Twist* ch. 51) – and the reader may blink at the railway-like speed with which these familial spectres have been whisked in and out of the novel.

Even with this furious spinning of coincidences and relations in the last volume, however, Dickens did not quite persuade his critics that his intentions had been all so comprehensive when he had first taken up his Poor Law satire back in February 1837. The *Atlas* remarked:

When this story of *Oliver Twist* was commenced the author apparently designed to illustrate the influences of the workhouse system, and the peculiar characteristics of pauperism to which it bears a constant reference. But the subject either wearied him, or was not found to be so productive of materials as he expected ... subsequently [he] expands the narrative into a sort of thieves' romance. (*Atlas* 13 no. 653 17 Nov. 1838: 730)

In the end, the review is critical of the plot's improbabilities, and concludes with advice to the author to consider his next production more carefully from the beginning: "The surpassing excellence of particular parts is not sufficient compensation for want of completeness in the general conception" (731).

This review is entirely typical of what is said about *Oliver* then and since. One wonders why *Oliver* should have been fastened upon as the peculiar test of Dickens's powers, in preference to, say, *Nicholas Nickleby*, which Dickens had begun as much as a year later and in which the attempt at "fine writing" was evident from the start. *Sketches by Boz* and *Pickwick Papers* had obviously been happy accidents, *Nickleby* had not, and the extension of *Oliver*, even though kept apart from the Pickwickian green covers, was itself little more than an accident of another kind.

The *Edinburgh Review*, too, had fastened upon *Oliver* as the crucial demonstration of Dickens's powers. So did the *Spectator*, in the most interesting notice among the weeklies. It chose the occasion of *Oliver* "in a collected shape" to consider two questions:

1. Has the author capacity to construct a story, or, to speak in the language of art, a *fable*? – which point has been raised by the *Edinburgh Review*.
2. Has he the power of sustaining a continuous interest, or in other words, does he tell as effectively in volumes as in numbers?

(*Spectator* 11 no. 543 24 Nov. 1838: 114)

The *Spectator* reviewer admits that he himself has not followed the monthly progress of publication and comes to the story for the first time, in its present form. His opinion on both the questions raised is negative, and the review explains why.

As a reader of volumes, not parts, the *Spectator* finds Dickens "*magazinishly* diffuse, as if spinning paragraphs" (115). In parts or numbers his sketches of low-life London ("the work, in reality, is *a series of sketches* of life amongst paupers and thieves") are remarkable for their vigour, truth, and sympathy. The review repeats the *Quarterly Review*'s comment about Dickens being the first to make the language of the metropolis a literary one. His thieves are "living creatures" (115) beside the posturing and generalized creations of Hook, Ainsworth, or Bulwer, which come out of farce or romance.

The paradox is that, whereas in his narrative he offends in the general category of probability, in his descriptions of individuals Dickens uniquely fulfils the contemporary appetite for realism – the abstract question of the probability of a Fagin, for example, never arises. The explanation of this contradiction comes back to the difference between the story's appearance in volumes and in parts. And it is to the appearance of his works in parts that the *Spectator* attributes the rise of Dickens's fame and the reason that the publication of this novel should receive so much more attention than any other contemporary novel published in three volumes:

Appearing in parts, each of which contained something striking and readable for all ranks, his works were the very thing for "the press" to fasten upon, as furnishing a ready means of filling up blank space, without any trouble on the part of the journalist, beyond a hearty panegyric on the writer who had occupied the "abhorred vacuum;" so that his production really gets a score of "notices," where others, however *taking*, only receive one.

(*Spectator* 11 no. 543 24 Nov. 1838: 115)

Whatever the holier-than-thou tone here, we can recognize the truth of this account. In an age of criticism that had not quite left off the eighteenth-century habit of voluminous extracting, Dickens's monthly stringing together of the sketch-writing he had always done was fortuitously suited to commercial habits. His eye as a reporter had also helped him ride the spume of contemporary life in satirizing the Poor Law.

Forster, in the *Examiner*, took another view of these topicalities. Forster had all along expressed his uneasiness about the story's "lowness," but in his final assessments he provides all the critical ammunition Dickens might need in defence against such complaints. Avoiding overt questions of the plot's probability, he describes the third volume as showing the "tragedy of common life": in this, Forster, unlike the *Spectator*, finds proof of a laudable moral conscientiousness (no. 1607 18 Nov. 1838: 723). This is really Forster's only point, and most of the notice consists of long extracts depicting Nancy's murder, Sikes's guilt-ridden wanderings, and Fagin's trial and last night alive; he extols these scenes over the traditional literary horrors raised by "Romance writers [who] have created fine effects by the howling of wind and the shaking of old tapestry and visions of old skeletons and of blood-rusted daggers" (725). And, from any evidence we have, it seems that these were the scenes over which Dickens himself had taken the most care.

Forster's fuller review of the novel as a whole, a week later (the extended attention for a single novel proving the *Spectator*'s point), continues the picture of Dickens as a writer who depicts evil for the purposes of good. If one should object to having everyday manners depicted, says Forster, Dickens's claim to being a truth-teller will remain: posterity will justify any contemporary indulgences by reading Dickens for "the very *history*, as it were, of the character and moral abuses of our time" (no. 1608 25 Nov. 1838: 740). The italicization of History represents one of the highest claims Forster could have made for Dickens, especially in its connection with Fielding's realism. In fact, all the reviews eventually end with the praise of Dickens's powers of description, his fidelity, and his realism.

The *Dublin University Magazine* is entirely typical when it excuses *Oliver* by saying that it shows Dickens "is endowed in a high degree with that first of qualifications for a writer of fiction – the power of making a faithful transcript upon paper of his own close and accurate observations of nature" (12 no. 72 Dec. 1838: 700).

The publication of *Oliver* in three volumes confirmed Dickens's reputation. Comparisons with Fielding and Scott are commonplace in these reviews. The *Weekly Dispatch*, for example, like most of these notices, complains of many things, but is still emphatic in declaring that *Oliver* "stamps Mr. Dickens as the first author of the age, and in this class of writing equal to Fielding, or to any one that our country has produced" (no. 1936 25 Nov. 1838: 562). Nevertheless, with the next couple of months, Dickens had to decide whether he could continue to work as a journalist and still be considered, at the end of every nineteen months, a novelist.

The *Monthly Review*, like the *Spectator*, challenged him on this score, saying that normally works published in periodicals were disqualified by their format from serious critical attention. Passing remarks under every month's "Magazine Day" were all very well, but final consideration of *Oliver*'s narrative structure found only "a mere string of sketches that might be carried to any length" (1 no. 1 Jan. 1839: 39). For this reason, the reviewer places Dickens among the lower ranks of "moral fictionists" (41), of whom Richardson, Goldsmith, and Sterne are the highest. Dickens is no more than a "sketcher," and his work "mere continuation" (40). The reviewer makes due allowance for the conditions imposed by the necessity of keeping up monthly instalments – but none for the fact that Dickens himself chooses to continue writing this way:

it does not appear from anything that Boz has yet done that he is equal to the demands of a regular novel, or that he is willing to throw himself at once upon a three-volumed production simultaneously published.

(*Monthly Review* 1 no. 1 Jan. 1839: 40)

The *Weekly Dispatch*, reviewing a recent instalment of *Nickleby* (Part VIII) the previous week, had compared Dickens's attenuation of his talents to the tragic case of Sir Walter Scott, who had been driven by just such popularity to write himself seemingly to his death (no. 1935 18 Nov. 1838: 550). And the year 1838 was the year when the final volume of Lockhart's *Life of Scott* appeared. The same readers who relived the extraordinary career of the last literary giant of their age, in the progress of Lockhart's seven volumes published over 1837–38, had also followed the progress of *Oliver Twist* and the rising interest in Dickens himself. Dickens's emergence as "the first author of the age" over the course of *Oliver*'s publication made comparisons of Dickens to Scott inevitable. At the close of 1838, Dickens's readers wondered aloud if they were to witness before very much longer the exhaustion of yet another great talent. Dickens had every cause to take the lesson of Scott's example to heart, as the acceleration of his own writing career marched along in tandem with Lockhart's impressing upon the literary world the gloomy moral of a man overtaken by "his unparalleled toils."

7

1839–1840 The "Man of Feeling": *Nicholas Nickleby* and *Master Humphrey's Clock*

I

Dickens had every reason to take the lesson of Sir Walter Scott's life to heart, as his own writing career proceeded alongside the darkening of Lockhart's narrative. The effort to complete *Oliver Twist* in the latter part of October 1838 had meant an intensification of his usual labours, and in January 1839 the only relief from overwork seemed to lie in resigning from the editorship of *Bentley's Miscellany*. This was perhaps also a tacit signal to the critics who had rebuked him for not yet sitting down to write a novel in three volumes. The reaffirmation of his own ambition to publish a novel is expressed in a letter to Serjeant Talfourd, to whom *Pickwick* had been dedicated in gratitude for his efforts to relieve literary improvidence. Dickens enclosed a bound copy of *Oliver Twist* and rejoiced that his new arrangements with Bentley meant that the long-planned *Barnaby Rudge* would be published "as a Novel, and not in portions" (*Letters* I, 504; 31 Jan. [1839]).

This serves to show that Dickens maintained in his own mind a generic distinction between his work so far and his aspirations: he evidently still did not think of his serial narratives as novels. In some ways it was unfair of the critics to judge *Oliver Twist* by the standards associated with a three-volume publication – after all, it had never been conceived in that way. But as such it had ended, and Dickens's elaborate plot linkings in the last few chapters were the signal that he wished to have its narrative treated as a novel. What aroused carping was that *Oliver* had already achieved its fame in a manner disallowed most three-volume productions, for serial publication led "newspaper and periodical editors to insert such striking individualized pieces as may suit their humour and the vacancies in their columns, and thus to keep the author always and fully before the public" (*Monthly Review* 1 no. 1 Jan. 1839: 40).

As we have seen, the practice of reviewing and excerpting from

130

periodicals had been a significant factor in *Pickwick*'s success. Modern readers ascribe the early fame of Dickens to the vague fact of *Pickwick*'s appearing monthly in the bookshops, being unaware of its unique attraction to magazine readers and reviewers in its capacity for being broken down into "bits." In view of the tendencies of literature in 1839, at least as described by one paper,[1] the episodic nature of *Nickleby* seems perfectly suited to the newspapers in its timeliness and its extractability. The research done for it by Dickens illustrates this. During December 1838, he went on a trip to the industrial Midlands, because he thought it important "to strike the heaviest blow in my power for these unfortunate creatures." Without any fastidiousness about artistic genre, he wrote to a friend, "whether I shall do so in the 'Nickleby', or wait some other opportunity, I have not yet determined" (*Letters* I, 484; 29 Dec. 1838).[2] In a kind of commercial symbiosis, the newspapers cannibalized Dickens's stories to fill up their columns, and Dickens in turn thickened his own narratives with newspaperish daily matter.

The publication of *Oliver* in three volumes had marked a kind of notch in Dickens's progress that was of greater seriousness than the attention given to *Pickwick*'s publication in three volumes. But after the initial recognition of Dickens's imitation of Fielding in its early chapters, *Pickwick*'s Nicklebian successor was never given the same conscientious criticism as *Oliver*. The comparative paucity of Forster's attention to *Nickleby* in the *Examiner* alone would tell us that. If anything, the topics of *Oliver* continued to dominate critical notice. Meanwhile *Nickleby* ambled along amiably enough, with some few carping comments and a great deal of excerpting. "Admirable" was the innocuous praise bestowed by both the *United Services Gazette* (5 Jan. 1839) and the *Examiner* (no. 1614 6 Jan. 1839: 4) on the first number of the new year. Excerpters showed a fondness for Nicholas's "Theatrical Last Appearance" (ch. 30) and for the passage about his arrival in London, "London at Night" (ch. 32). The *Morning Post* spoke scornfully of the improbabilities of the narrative and then proceeded to give it more notice than any other publication gets (nearly two columns of excerpts, out of four devoted to literary news), winding up none the less with the comment "we see nothing in them to entitle the work to take rank much in advance of mediocrity" (14 Jan. 1839). *Bell's New Weekly Messenger* also did not think that Boz's reputation would be much advanced by the February number of *Nickleby*, and then followed up its sniffy remarks with no fewer than eight extracts (9 no. 973 10 Feb. 1839).

In this way we see that Dickens by 1839 had gone beyond serious criticism, just as, when he started out five years before, he had not yet come within its ken. Dickens's serial commonly gets its own heading and is not lumped in with the reviews of all the other periodicals. There is a splendidly graphic image of his popularity at this time offered by the reviewer in the *United Services Gazette*:

As we were passing along the Strand on the last day of the month, the two sides of the street looked almost verdant with the numerous green covers of this popular book, which were waving to and fro in the hands of the passengers along that busy thoroughfare. "This, thought we, is fame!"

(*United Services Gazette* no. 317 9 Feb. 1839)

The *Morning Advertiser* cited the dramatizations of the unfinished *Nickleby* in both Edinburgh and Dublin as well as London as proof of its popularity (9 Feb. 1839). The *Courier*, giving extracts from the May number, observed, "The less we say about our friend Nicholas, and the more we allow him to speak for himself, the better our readers will be pleased" (9 May 1839). The June number was represented in the *Examiner* merely by extracts; there were no comments attached (no. 1635 2 June 1839: 342). In this respect, it is of interest to note here the differences in criteria applied to *Nickleby* and *Oliver*. In the *Morning Advertiser*'s notice of *Bentley's Miscellany* this month, the critic calls it an error in a magazine, which ought to be composed of short self-contained articles, to include "whole novels by piecemeal, which he [Bentley] intends to publish in a separate form at an after period" (9 May 1839). The *Observer*, too, complained of the *Miscellany*'s lack of variety in having "no fewer than four 'continuations' of articles previously commenced." And yet the same reviewer could rather inconsistently praise *Nickleby* in its bits, and observed of the June number that it was "hardly so well sustained as previous numbers; but there are detached scenes of surpassing excellence" (2 June 1839).

In fact, Dickens seemed to have worked particularly hard at plotting the outcome of *Nickleby* from the fourteenth number (May 1839). He had gone out of town for four or five months in order to write the serial, and was making as careful and workmanlike a job of it as he could, freed from the harassments of Bentley and in anticipation of the *Barnaby Rudge* labours to come. In this respect, the notice by the *Sun* of the July number (XVI) must have bolstered all his artistic hopes when it quoted a passage from Mrs. Nickleby's love affair in ch. 49 (where her lover comes down the chimney) and praised Dickens's writing for its truth to nature. The *Sun* declared, "There is nothing in Fielding better than this" (4 July 1839). Dickens received all this (Forster sent him two copies of the review) "with joyfulness" (*Letters* I, 562; [14 July 1839]).

II

The context of Dickens's response to the *Sun*'s enthusiastic notice is important for its hints as to his ambitions at this time. In the same letter Dickens also speaks at some length about proposed negotiations with Chapman and Hall to start a new periodical:

I should be willing to commence on the thirty-first of March, 1840, a new publication consisting entirely of original matter, of which one number price threepence should be published every week, and of which a certain amount of numbers should form a volume, to be published at regular intervals. The best general idea of the plan of the work might be given perhaps by reference to *The Tatler*, *The Spectator*, and Goldsmith's *Bee* ...

(*Letters* I, 563; [14 July 1839])[3]

This describes the venture that came to be known as *Master Humphrey's Clock*. For it, Dickens proposed the format of a club like the one in *The Spectator*, the reintroduction of Sam Weller and Pickwick, an *Arabian Nights* feature of stories about London, a series of satirical papers comparable to *Gulliver's Travels* and *Citizen of the World*, and a set of papers on his possible travels to America or Ireland. Dickens intended to have contributions by other writers as well but entirely subject to his control. His proposal has a strong eighteenth-century flavour and is removed as far as possible from the tone of the faddish *Bentley's*. It allowed for the observation of topicalities, and he hoped it would be easier to produce than the continuous narratives of the past three years – and the novel that he had not yet managed to write.

Forster duly began negotiations with Chapman and Hall, and one notes his own comments in a review he wrote shortly afterwards, for the *Examiner*, of Washington Irving's *Crayon Papers*. In this review, Forster remarks that Irving "has become tired of writing *volumes*" and quotes the author's introduction: "'I have thought, therefore, of securing to myself a snug corner in some periodical work, where I might, as it were, loll at my ease in my elbow chair, and chat socially [sociably] with the public" (*Examiner* [no. 1647 25 Aug. 1839: 532], quoted from *Bentley's Miscellany* 6 July 1839: 24). These comments would have been of more than usual interest to Dickens, for it was at the same time that Lewis Gaylord Clark, editor of the *Knickerbocker*, proposed that there be an exchange of the *Crayon*

Papers, which had originally appeared in the *Knickerbocker*, for *Oliver Twist*. Dickens wrote two letters in reply, saying he would be interested in having the *Papers* appear in *Bentley's Miscellany* but no longer had himself any editorial influence on the *Miscellany* (*Letters* I, 469; 588). The *Miscellany* in fact had announced in the meantime that it would publish the *Crayon Papers* simultaneously with their appearance in the *Knickerbocker*; they published two in 1839. Forster notes in his review that they had fallen behind with this promise, and his review is of the *Knickerbocker* numbers themselves for the months March to July.

The preface to *Nicholas Nickleby* seems to have been written around the same time as Dickens's letter of September 1839 to Clark and echoes much of this romanticism about the periodical format. Here Dickens addresses his readers in terms far warmer than those of the prefaces to *Sketches by Boz* or *Pickwick*, which had concentrated more on making a show of authorial competence. Where the other prefaces cited all the most literary precedents and insisted on the novelistic integrity of his characterizations, the preface to *Nickleby* completely renounces "Horace's rule, of keeping his book nine years in his study." Instead, calling himself a "periodical essayist," Dickens waxes sentimental about the course of *Nickleby*'s serialization:

"The author of a periodical performance," says [Henry] Mackenzie, "has indeed a claim to the attention and regard of his readers, more interesting than that of any other writer ... the periodical essayist commits to his readers the feelings of the day, in the language which those feelings have prompted. As he has delivered himself with the freedom of intimacy and the cordiality of friendship, he will naturally look for the indulgence which those relations may claim; and when he bids his readers adieu, will hope, as well as feel, the regrets of an acquaintance, and the tenderness of a friend."

(*Nicholas Nickleby* [Preface ix–x])

This is obviously less of a preface to a novel than a pitch to set the tone of his presentation of himself in the upcoming *Master Humphrey's Clock*. In its air of intimacy and informality, it uncannily echoes Irving's presentation of himself in "Wolfert's Roost," the first of the *Crayon Papers* (see *Bentley's Miscellany* 6 July 1839: 24).

In fact, when one looks at the programmes which Dickens expounded for his journals, one sees how congenial a figurehead or persona Nicholas Nickleby would have made for any of them: his picaresque adaptability to any number of settings and encounters makes him a usefully transparent medium. *Nickleby* is not generically shaped by didacticism about Yorkshire schools or anything else. It is barely even held together by the identity of the hero. The most obvious thing about Nicholas is his spontaneous disgust at hypocrisy and his good-hearted interest in the downtrodden of this life – qualities always prominent in his author's life. The narrative strings together a whole succession of topics – Yorkshire schools, Parliamentary abuses, Manchester factories, even the dramatizing of unfinished serial fictions – which Dickens felt it necessary to comment on as they caught his attention.

The remarkable fact to be noted is that by this time Dickens had already established his own formula of periodical writing quite outside the standard magazine format: the Pickwickian or Nicklebian progress. Quite apart from the fact that *Bentley's Miscellany* was now full of "continuations" *à la Oliver*, there was openly recognized imitation of the twenty-month serial everywhere. There had always been the publication in parts of things such as encyclopedias and Shakespeare's plays, but now the review columns had also to include notice of what the *Morning Post* had "learned to call the 'Pickwick Periodicals' – we mean the several adventures of 'Michael Armstrong,' 'Valentine Vox,' 'Heads of the People,' 'Mary Ashby,' and 'Will Whim'" (8 Aug. 1839). The *Shipping and Mercantile Gazette*, reviewing one of these, complains of "The innumerable progeny of the Pickwick Papers – or rather the endless list of publications to which those papers have given birth" (27 Aug. 1839). And although Dickens himself may have given birth to the *"great original,"* as the *Gazette* called *Pickwick*, he was now tired of sustaining such a form, and his imitators were in turn tiring the patience of his readers.

III

Since May, the fourteenth number, the narrative of *Nickleby* had been showing – like the last few numbers of *Oliver* – Dickens's efforts to tie up all its threads. The scheme to marry off Madeline Bray to the old usurer Gride, which had begun in June, had been brought to an abrupt close in August, with the death of Madeline's father on the wedding day. Nicholas hears the thump of the old man's body falling on the floor above and cries out at Ralph Nickleby: " 'if this is what I scarcely dare to hope it is, you are caught, villains, in your own toils' " (ch. 54). The penultimate instalment (XVIII), which appeared in September, shows the effort of drawing the serial into novelistic closure. In this number, Madeline convalesces from her own toils in the melodrama, Smike expires (to make way for Frank Cheeryble's wooing of Kate), and Ralph and Gride send the suddenly reappearing Squeers off on a most improbable chase after the papers that show the fortune into which the husband of Miss Bray will come. Ralph is certain (like Dickens's readers) that it will be Nicholas, and the thief is Gride's old housekeeper, who has meanwhile been provoked into jealousy by Gride's plan to marry Madeline. That Squeers should be designated as the bait to seduce these papers out of Peg Sliderskew's possession is the toppling improbability in a gargoylish structure of villainy.

Not surprisingly, the reviewers' comments were few and terse. The *Observer* was comparatively kind − "has fewer humorous scenes than previous numbers" (1 Sept. 1839) − while the *United Services Gazette* was not − "Mr. Dickens appears to have floundered most completely in the later numbers of his work. His love scenes are a dose for a horse" (no. 348 7 Sept. 1839). Most of the papers contented themselves with noting that the work was drawing to a close, and extracts were more popular than critical remarks, which were generally being saved for the appearance of the work as a whole.

Dickens finished *Nickleby* on 20 September, and it was published in volume form a month later. The critics' reaction did not carry the same sense of excitement that had been the case for *Oliver*: none of the main characters including the villain Ralph Nickleby seems to have inspired the same attachment as Fagin or the Artful Dodger. The passages building up to Ralph's suicide are finely written but lack the power of the comparable treatment of Fagin's last moments. The lovemaking between Frank Cheeryble and Kate and between Madeline Bray and Nicholas is conducted offstage, and it is the middle-aged Cheerybles who wind up two courtships that have never properly been commenced. The *United Services Gazette* was reminded of once having read "a folio romance containing the lives and adventures of no fewer than 365 knights-errant, the whole of whom were comfortably married and settled in the last page of the volume" (no. 352 5 Oct. 1839).

The *Sun*, too, however sympathetic, had to admit the lack of a "constructive faculty." *Nickleby* was merely a collection of scenes and characters:

You may commence them [Dickens's works] where you please, in the middle or towards the close; or even begin with the last chapter, and so work your way back, crab-fashion, towards the first. You will lose little by such an irregular process, for any one Number will serve nearly as well as another, to give you an insight into the author's peculiarities ... (*Sun* 4 Oct. 1839)

The *Sun* predicts that, once Dickens becomes more poetically or artistically ambitious, he will leave behind his easy popularity, and it encourages him to do so. However, the *Examiner* still asked the awkward question — "And with all these masterly requisites for his art, is Mr Dickens a perfect novelist?" — and the answer again was, "By no means. He has yet to acquire the faculty of constructing a compact and effective story, without which that rank can never be attained" (no. 1656 27 Oct. 1839: 677). *Tom Jones* set the standard by which this was determined. The other model was historical writing: "The creative powers of the novelist, when properly directed and well sustained, take rank with history itself" (678). A writer such as Dickens, thought Forster, has the power to write of characters bearing in their verisimilitude the authority of History's truth.

However, Dickens for the moment renounced all aspirations to these ideals. Instead, he wrote the preface for *Nickleby*, which is in some ways more remarkable than the novel itself. If the narrative shows little if any advance on what had been achieved in *Pickwick*, the preface signals the professionally innovative step Dickens was to take in *Master Humphrey's Clock*. Dickens preferred at this point to appeal to the sympathies of someone like the *Sunday Times* reviewer, who wrote of *Nickleby*'s end, "At the conclusion of a day's pleasure, there is always a regret that it is gone — we wish to pass the day over again, to re-enjoy its delights" (13 Oct. 1839). To such readers, Dickens was a hearty friend, not a master of abstruse art. The fact that Dickens was now no longer advertised as Boz but actually had his portrait as the frontispiece to the volume publication of *Nickleby* gives some idea of how far the cult of a Dickensian personality or sensibility had gone. The *Town*, that model of decorum among newspapers, protested the vulgarity of such self-advertisement:

While Scott remained as the "Author of Waverley," his unrivalled productions were eagerly sought after, and as eagerly read; but, when the charm of mystery was broken, and it was known to be Walter Scott, what a palpable falling off followed. So, we fear, it will be with Charles Dickens.

(*Town* no. 123 5 Oct. 1839: 983)

With Scott the acknowledgement of his literary identity had been resisted for as long as possible, out of his belief in its essential ungentlemanliness. Although there was little more than twelve years between the revelation of Scott's authorship and Dickens's own, there was not only a gap of generation but of class between the two careers, which made comparisons rather misleading. Scott had depicted nostalgically a conservative feudal relationship between classes, or more properly, ranks. This was no longer possible without self-consciousness, but Dickens showed how dialogue and feeling could still be exchanged amid London's urban jostle. He reassured his middle-class readers that the labouring poor were not monsters of Radical dissent. His critics praised him for a sense of "humanity," in a society that had just come through a period of mutual accusation and readjustment between classes: "He is, like Scott, an advocate for fair play between rich and poor, the peer and the plebeian," says the *Sun* (4 Oct. 1839).[4]

Unlike Scott, though, Dickens had no other profession. Dickens needed his literary fame, and the persona was an essential part of this. Essential, too, to the method of his art was the confirmation that there was a real person behind it. The *Nickleby* preface and portrait were an important preparation for the initial success of *Master Humphrey's Clock*. Whatever the fictional elements of the persona of "Charles Dickens" which speaks in these prefaces, Dickens came to understand that the trappings of reality surrounding his own identity and the values associated with it — most succinctly described as the "Christmas philosophy" — lent reinforcement to the imaginative world of the books which were introduced by remarks in that identity. "Boz" had already implied the spirit that would lie behind Master Humphrey's conception, but "Charles Dickens" is the bridge between these two pseudonyms. It is *Oliver Twist*, the most powerful of all his works so far, which is really the anomaly in the line that goes from the "Boz" of *Pickwick* to the "Charles Dickens" of *Nickleby* to the "Master Humphrey" of the *Clock*.

The faceless Boz, Mr. Pickwick, Nicholas Nickleby, and Master Humphrey all typify to some extent the Mackenzian observer who continually finds "the romantic enthusiasm rising within him" in his eccentric journeyings, and who stops at the first place "in which he saw a face he liked."[5] The "editor" of the "bundle of papers" collected under *The Man of Feeling* complains that "I could never find the author in one strain for two chapters together: and I don't believe there's a single syllogism from beginning to end"[6] — and so might the critic of *Pickwick*. The only principle to be discerned is that of a miscellany: the variety of life registered in the annals of tremulous moral sensibility. This was not exactly consistent with the narrative of a novel as Dickens still conceived it. He was to become famous for the serial publication of his novels, but at this stage the Pickwickian sense of life, its spontaneous and improvisational quality, was at least as suitable for another sort of periodical narrative. Its versatility was troublesome: both novels and magazines were apparently compatible with Dickens's peculiar qualities as a writer but he continued to search for the format which by its very principle of organization would positively establish the nature of his narrative genius.

Master Humphrey's Clock, and eventually the Christmas stories, typify the vehicle by which Dickens sought to achieve his power, and the establishment of the public "philosophy" which is termed "Dickensian" – a rhetoric which argued against the Benthamite and Malthusian reduction of human happiness to a statistical science and in favour of the importance of individual intuition and charity. Unlike the rhetoric against which it inveighed, the "Christmas philosophy" does not translate very happily from the narratives in which it is evoked into specifiable dicta, and this is an important fact about Dickens's writing as a social commentator. During the same years as he was publishing these stories, and throughout most of his career, he was incompletely successful in his attempt to speak from an officially influential position.

The earlier transition from a mere transcriber of news to "Boz" had been much smoother, perhaps because in coming to narrative writing he had quickly found his most pragmatic medium: the spirit of a Nicklebian progress was quite as consistent and substantial as any editorial page he might have produced. Apart from any ambitions to be a novelist, Dickens needed the tools provided by narrative; and serially published narrative, however fortuitously it came to him, ensured the possibility of response and thus a sense of the social effectiveness of his thought. The Christmas stories were to be a spectacular confirmation of this; so in a less happy way was the failure of *Master Humphrey's Clock*. The name of "Boz" or "Charles Dickens" was finally the institution he would succeed in "founding." He was to do this through the discipline of his imaginative life, and in the end it was the philosophy of this discipline – "the Romance of everyday life" – that became his most successful editorial position.

IV

"Our Lucubrations," the famous substance of Richard Steele's *Tatler*, would seem to typify the difference between Richard Bentley's conception of a miscellany and one Dickens would truly call his own. In the substantial outline of the proposed magazine enclosed in the letter to Forster on the eve of negotiations with Chapman and Hall about his literary property, Dickens invokes the *Tatler* and *Spectator*, and one thinks of a small boy sitting on his bed at twilight, "reading as if for life" these books from another era. These dreams eventually led to the image of Master Humphrey whiling away the night hours from ten to two with stories and reminiscences. The conception of Humphrey as a solitary but observant man also recaptures another aspect of Dickens's early adolescence, when he wandered homeless round London, fascinated by its street life in spite of his loneliness.

Completely unlike the faddish Bentley, Dickens was not apprehensive about reverting to a format of the previous century, and seemed to feel that cultivation of an *eidolon* personality would be as attractive to readers of the 1840s as it was to those of the eighteenth century or an unworldly boy in the 1820s. We may summarize something of what the boy had admired and the hopeful editor remembered when he thought of Master Humphrey.

The name of Isaac Bickerstaff had preceded that of the *Tatler* and helped to draw attention to its incorporation, but the paper had substantiated Bickerstaff's personality and deepened the attraction. Although solitary, an old bachelor disappointed long ago in love, he obviously likes people, watching them talk and meet in the various coffee- and chocolate-houses which make up his news headings. None the less, he generally indulges a personal streak of whimsicality and also sets up a heading outside the domains of politics, fashion and the arts, called "From my Own Apartment." He combines a personal eccentric attractiveness with an unforced curiosity about others. The length of the numbers moved from being organized in the departmental sections of between three and eight hundred words each, to single papers of fourteen hundred words, suggesting that Steele discovered that length was congenial to his purposes. Within the length of one essay might be included exemplary tales and allusions, reported dialogue, and "correspondence."

As well as these casual correspondents, other characters appeared as authors of several papers, and these contributions soon acquired a distinctive tone and place. The writings and matrimonial adventures of Jenny Distaff, the sister of Bickerstaff, soon became valuable inclusions; and, in the light of later developments, we may wonder why the "club" of Bickerstaff's friends introduced in No. 132 did not become a regular feature also. Certainly Bickerstaff seems to set them up as being a habit with him, meeting from six every evening till ten at the same fireside for many years; and he emphasizes in his description of their intercourse the philosophical pleasure which old men derive from the discursive recital of events and observations. There is a mood over this whole number of almost elegiac tranquillity. But very unlike what Dickens was to do, Steele does not flatter or

140

sentimentalize the group of old worthies, and, in fact, their conversation is made out to be repetitious and dull, fit only for the hours before bed – thereby accounting perhaps for the absence of further appearances. Bickerstaff's own thoughts and activities in his daytime rounds are felt to be more valuable as entertainment and philosophy.

All these aspects of an *eidolon* figure which Steele learned in writing the *Tatler* were revived when he collaborated more closely with Addison in the *Spectator*. Steele never extended the conceit of No. 132; Addison, writing the first number of its successor, commits the entire serial to this format. In No. 132 of the *Tatler* Bickerstaff preens himself on being the wit of the old men's group, whereas Mr. Spectator is said to live his days in silence, even sullenness, though known by others for his learning. Again, like the Tatler, he easily frequents the various public houses of refreshment, but the Spectator speaks publicly only within his own club. There are no headings derived from the public houses, and it may be noted with reference to Master Humphrey that, even though Mr. Spectator is eager finally to communicate his thoughts to his contemporaries for philanthropic reasons, he refuses to reveal his age or address and instead cultivates obscurity.

Steele's tastes perhaps show up more in the description of Sir Roger de Coverley, who exhibits the temperament of the hearty country gentleman, benevolent and comfortably old-fashioned; as with later portrayals of this type by Sterne and Goldsmith, his eccentricities proceed from an inherent unworldliness. The most striking feature of his description is how lively and appealing Steele has made this second depiction of an intimate club; excepting Sir Roger, they may turn out to make little impact on the periodical as a whole, but one is still surprised by the enthusiastic revival here in the *Spectator* of an idea which seemed so unpersuasive earlier in the *Tatler*.

Such are some of the associations and roots in literary history of *Master Humphrey's Clock*. When Dickens explains what he sees as the resemblances between the *Spectator* and his proposed magazine, he refers to this introductory fiction of a small club, the history and transactions of which will become a motif in his paper, and we may note the similarities between the clubs of Mr. Spectator and Master Humphrey. Dickens has the indulgence of greater length, making his description of the club rather more a narrative of how he first became acquainted with these people. In the emphasis upon the age and retiring tendencies of its characters, Master Humphrey's club resembles the dullness rather of Bickerstaff's than Mr. Spectator's group, and the hours from ten to two push their lucubrations virtually into the realm of sleep rather than just post-prandial relaxation, and the placid routine of the day into the frenzied activity of the dream world. Gentle and sentimental as Master Humphrey may be (and Dickens probably emphasized these qualities in order to attract the reader who would feel uncomfortable with the flashy glancing wit of a magazine like *Bentley's Miscellany*) but Steele was intuitively correct in leaving the peculiar pleasures of old men to themselves, and in merely summarizing their dullness.

Two other eighteenth-century models for *Master Humphrey's Clock* were *Gulliver's Travels* and *Citizen of the World*, particularly for that section of the magazine that was to include "a series of satirical papers purporting to be translated from some Savage Chronicles, and to describe the administration of justice in some country that never existed, and record the proceedings of its wise men" (*Letters* I, 564; [14 July 1839]). Typically, the didacticism is made palatable by an exotically removed setting. The sub-title of the satiric papers called *Citizen of the World*, which were written by Oliver Goldsmith during the years 1760–61, is "Letters from a Chinese Philosopher Residing in London to his Friends in the East." Dickens never got around to writing such papers, but to any reader of *Household Words* or *All the Year Round*, the similarities to Goldsmith in choice of topic are noticeable. One feels the links between Goldsmith and Dickens, not only in the topics chosen but also in satirical mannerisms: the usual format of the *Citizen* is to describe in ironic terms the custom singled out by the Chinaman till a pitch is reached in the final paragraph where an aphorism or fable by the philosopher neatly makes Goldsmith's polemical point. Neither Goldsmith nor Dickens achieved the graceful amplitude of the *Spectator* in this vein. Goldsmith had attempted a less satirical manner in his periodical *The Bee*, also mentioned by Dickens in the letter quoted above, which consisted rather nondescriptly of general essays, short fables, and lively comment on topical doings, but it was sustained for only eight issues, from October to November 1759.

A final eighteenth-century model for *Master Humphrey's Clock* is Samuel Johnson's *Idler*, which ran from 15 April 1758 to 5 April 1760; it is cited by Forster in that list of Dickens's early reading where the *Tatler*, *Spectator*, and *Citizen of the World* also appear (*Life* I, i, 11). Here again the periodical writer strives for an easy tone when soliciting readers:

The Idler has no rivals or enemies. The man of business forgets him; the man of enterprize despises him; and though such as tread the same track of life, fall commonly into jealousy and discord, Idlers are always found to associate in peace, and he who is most famed for doing nothing, is glad to meet another as idle as himself.   (*Idler* no. 1 15 Apr. 1758)[7]

Despite this Humphreyish sounding address, the *Idler* was at first untypical of Johnson in its topicality and attempt to emulate the lightness of the *Spectator*, but after the first twenty numbers the characteristic Johnsonian preoccupations reasserted themselves; and, when reading even this casually projected work, we realize that it is the ability to sustain mood and depth of insight, instead of flitting over a number of verbal conceits – the hold on a subject which is thought of indeed as essentially "Johnsonian" – which one misses in Goldsmith, and in Dickens, when he attempts the same ephemeral format. Perhaps the significant fact is that both authors came nearer to such an achievement in their novel writing.

Actually, however deliberately Dickens may have intended Master Humphrey's Club to recall Mr. Spectator's, he has come closer to that of Mr. Bickerstaff; and it is another periodical publication – "THE PICKWICK CLUB, so renowned in the annals of Huggin-lane, and so closely entwined with the thousand interesting associations connected with Lothbury and Cateaton-street" (advertisement, *Athenaeum* 26 Mar. 1836) – which more nearly captures the attractive spirit of the *Spectator* model. And, in the case of both *Pickwick* and *Master Humphrey's Clock*, the "miscellaneous collection of tales, anecdotes, etc., collected and arranged by Boz" eventually gave way to the organizational demands of a novel – and, thus, a different principle of length. The miscellany *eidolon* becomes more fertile as a novelistic character: Master Humphrey gives way to Little Nell.

The necessity of a familiar persona is also suggested by the fate of *Sketches of Young Couples*, Dickens's only publication between the end of *Nicholas Nickleby* in October 1839 and the first appearance of *Master Humphrey's Clock* in April 1840. *Sketches of Young Couples* was published anonymously because of Bentley's contractual stipulation that Dickens work on nothing else except *Barnaby Rudge* after *Nickleby* was finished. This and *Sketches of Young Gentlemen* were Dickens's only anonymous publications since *Sketches by Boz* and *Sunday under Three Heads* in 1836.

Sketches by Boz, it is more accurate to say, was not quite anonymous, since the public for it had been prepared by two years' worth of appearances by "Boz" in the *Monthly Magazine* and the two *Chronicle* papers. The sketches in *Young Gentlemen* and *Young*

Couples, on the other hand, appeared only once. As critics had already commented, most books, making a fleetingly single appearance, never got the repeated regular attention that Dickens's works got week after week, month after month. In this case Dickens underwent the more usual experience of an author of entertainments. The publication of *Sketches of Young Couples* was scheduled to coincide with the marriage of Victoria and Albert on 10 February 1840, and seems to have cost Dickens very little effort. In any case, he was no longer the tremulous beginner of six or even four years earlier. He knew what he was about, and what his public worth as a sketch-writer was. None the less, the paucity and nature of the reviews of this work – produced on the eve of his most characteristic and self-directed project so far, *Master Humphrey's Clock* – are intriguing.

As part of the general hysteria surrounding the royal wedding, such sketches were hardly worth noticing. As the Pilgrim editors note, " 'Sketches' were so common at the time that CD's hand was not recognized" (*Letters* II, 1n). The *Sunday Times* blandly called it "a pleasant, chatty book" and ascribed it to Hook (no. 851 10 Feb. 1840). The *Literary Gazette* called it a *"jeu d'esprit"* and printed copious excerpts (24 no. 1204 15 Feb. 1840: 98–100). The *Atlas* complained that "The descriptions are humorous enough, but are a little spoiled by an air of Cockneyism" (15 no. 720 29 Feb. 1840: 139). What ought to have given the game away was the fact that the *Examiner* noticed it at all – "A most agreeable and well-timed little book" (no. 1672 16 Feb. 1840: 100–01) – since such fillips did not normally appear in its columns. But, apart from this, Dickens generally received criticism essentially no different from that given the début of the collected Boz in February 1836.

This fact – that in anonymity the peculiar quality of his work could still be passed over – seems not to have bothered Dickens. What concerned him more at the time was quite the opposite. He was sensitive to the way in which the monthly number in green covers was being trivialized by some rival writers' use of the same format. He had objected privately to Colburn's advertisements of *Michael Armstrong*; in January 1840, he wrote to Longman's (unlike Colburn they could be reasoned with), objecting to their misleading use of an *Examiner* review of *Poor Jack* in a *Morning Chronicle* advertisement (8 Jan. 1840). Whereas the review clearly elevated Dickens above his imitators, the advertisement had talked about "those shoals of trash which we owe to Pickwick and Nicholas Nickleby" (*Letters* II, 6; 11 Jan. 1840). Perhaps it was with this in mind that he wrote to Cattermole a couple of days later that *Master Humphrey's Clock* would be published in weekly rather than monthly parts, "my object being to baffle the imitators and make it as novel as possible" (*Letters* II, 7; 13 Jan. 1840). Four years after *Pickwick* broke upon the literary scene, Chapman and Hall and Dickens now set out to astonish the publishing world this time in high deliberation. The result was to be equally, if less pleasantly, surprising to themselves.

V

Dickens's career is reviewed by *Fraser's* on the eve of *Master Humphrey's Clock*'s publication. In telling how Boz began, the article (the leading one for April 1840) assumes that the popularity of the Bozian sketches "suggested the idea of weaving similar papers into a connected series" (21 no. 124 Apr. 1840: 381). This review, unlike most, thought it important to quote at length from Dickens's account of how *Pickwick* took shape and, in doing so, went on to query Dickens's notion of characterization and the novel form. Briefly, the thesis of the article is that Dickens had not yet depicted a realistic character: his *"come-and-go"* characters were fine; *"standing"* ones he had not (382). In the preface to *Pickwick*, Dickens had attempted both to explain the deficiencies in his characterization and at the same time to deny that there were any. In other words, Dickens tries to pass off his "flat" characters as "round" ones. The pressure was on Dickens to demonstrate that he had written a novel rather than just a serial. *Fraser's* was not having any of it, however. The article shows cogently and not vindictively just how unconvincing is the transformation of Pickwick from "a mere ass" of a burlesque antiquarian (383) to a man "who acts with decision, and speaks with sense and propriety" (388): "In the hands of Boz, he commences as a butt and ends as a hero" (391). It was equally inconsistent that Winkle and Snodgrass, too, should go from being unprepossessing poltroons to gentle lovers.

Dickens, in his preface, had pointed out that "some of the greatest novelists in the English language" had to face similar objections. *Fraser's*, responding to Dickens's nudges about the "great novelists," then compares Pickwick to Dr. Primrose in the *Vicar of Wakefield* and to Parson Adams in *Joseph Andrews* – and finally declines to find any similarities. There is every possibility that Dickens may well have intended to make Pickwick into a Dr. Primrose as the nineteen months of serial wore on, but the decision to emulate Goldsmith's work clearly comes after the satire on the British Association is already in the text. Although one could say Goldsmith was never far away from Dickens's mind, in this case the original commission from Chapman and Hall had been something quite different from whatever Dickens's own favourite reading was and more akin to the writing demanded of a literary hack in the 1820s and 1830s.

The reviewer finally comes back, as had Dickens himself in the *Pickwick* preface, to the fact of periodical publication, which necessarily demands the filling up of vacant space:

In short, the habits of the reporter break out – the copy is to be given in – and what shall we write of but what we know? How fill the paper, but by reports of debates, meetings, societies, police-offices, courts of justice, vestry-rooms, and so forth, spun out as amusingly and as lengthily as possible, all with a view to the foreman's bill at the end?

(*Fraser's* 21 no. 124 Apr. 1840: 400)

Hence the writer concludes by warning Dickens against falling into the example of Pierce Egan and literary hackdom, that is, of writing too much too fast merely to fill up the dreaded void: "talking of literature in any other light than that of a hack trade, we do not like this novel-writing by scraps against time," and concludes, "we trust that, since *Master Humphry* [*sic*] has set up *a clock*, he will henceforward take *time*" (400).

Convincing as this may be, *Fraser's* colleagues on the other London papers did not necessarily agree. The *Sun*, generally one of the most acute, allowed all of *Fraser's* criticism but preferred finally to find the inconsistencies in characterization trivial and the hastiness of the original *Pickwick* commission excusable. The *Sun* reviewer is quite emphatic about the greater importance of characterization over plot – even in romance, where plot has always held pride of place. The *Sun* preferred Dickens's characters to those of Ainsworth, who is recognized to be writing in the mould of the romances of Scott, and *Guy Fawkes* is compared directly to *Woodstock*. In the claim to the mantle of Scott, who was still the prose colossus of the nineteenth-century critical world, Ainsworth had taken his place before Dickens, and Ainsworth's works bore a much closer resemblance to the Waverley tales than did *Pickwick*, *Nickleby*, or *Oliver*. Strictly speaking, Dickens had yet to write a romance and had no reason in critical terms to be proud of his accidental generic innovation. It is telling that, in the same columns, the *Sun* cursorily notices "Paul Periwinkle" as "One of the almost countless works of fiction which the popularity of the 'Pickwick Papers,' 'Nicholas Nickleby,' and 'Jack Sheppard' has called into a questionable existence" (1 Apr. 1840).

Other papers, the *Morning Herald* (3 Apr. 1840) and *Bell's Weekly Messenger* (4 Apr. 1840), also admitted the deficiencies of the original machinery of these serials but found such problems inconsequential. The defence of *Pickwick* by *Bell's Weekly Messenger* in particular is interesting: if Fielding's characters were the measure against which Dickens was found wanting by *Fraser's*, it was by reference to a great eighteenth-century periodical that *Bell's* found his rebuttal:

> It is indeed true that the "Pickwick" towards the end of the volume is nothing like the "Pickwick" at the beginning; but is Sir Roger de Coverley in the Spectator at all like the moon-struck and dumb-foundered idiot who is introduced to us in the first Number? Of what consequence is this inconsistency of character in a work of mere humour?
>
> (*Bell's Weekly Messenger* no. 2294 4 Apr. 1840: 110)

If Dickens had been content to let *Pickwick* go as a work of "mere humour," he might have thought of just such an argument when composing his preface, but at that time he was more concerned to prove his ability as an incipient novelist and therefore to show *Pickwick* as a novel. Given his new project, *Master Humphrey's Clock*, and the models cited for it, however, the comparison of Pickwick to Sir Roger could hardly have been more convenient. Mr. Pickwick was duly to reappear, between the covers of *Master Humphrey's Clock*, and the welcome given him in the form of renewed excerpting, shows that he had a fictional life separate from his story.

Still, even the admirers of *Pickwick* found it hard to welcome *Master Humphrey's Clock*. The *Sun* found its "machinery" cumbersome and put it down as "merely a vehicle for introducing a variety of odd stories, serious and comic, legends, sketches from life, &c. &c." (14 Apr. 1840). It expected that Dickens would discard the framework as quickly as he had that of *Pickwick*. The *Sun* thought Dickens had given in too much to the pressure of novelty and enjoyed the tales but not the device for their introduction.

What Dickens wanted in this case was a vehicle for incorporating a variety of tales and sketches. To *Fraser's* criticism that his works so far had lacked the constructive ability of Fielding, Dickens replied, no longer in the equivocating terms of the *Pickwick* preface of 1838, but in the announcement of intentions given in the autumn of 1839 in the *Nickleby* preface. Nor were the papers slow to notice that the models for *Master Humphrey's Clock* were not Fieldingesque. The *Spectator* noted the resemblance to Irving's Sketch-Book (no. 614 4 Apr. 1840: 331). The *Sun* discerned the influence of both Irving and

Sterne, and disapproved, "There is too much of the imitative" (20 Apr. 1840).[8] The conception of *Master Humphrey's Clock* had been a very self-consciously literary one. But however fondly Dickens may have summoned up his childhood reading of the eighteenth-century authors, the reading public of 1840 wanted a nineteenth-century periodical.

Both the *Sun*'s and the *Monthly Review*'s articles on *Master Humphrey's Clock*'s first two numbers take to the expedient of italicizing single sentences which they found as isolated specimens of the Dickens they knew − "we occasionally recognize a faint glimmering of the wit which gave such celebrity to the *Pickwick Papers*" (*Monthly Review* 2 no. 1 May 1840: 38). In this, the *Monthly Review* is grasping at favourable straws; most of its review seems written in a tone of disbelief: "How Dickens, with his talents and experience, could have suffered such a *thing* to go forth under the sanction of his name, is to us a matter of unfeigned marvel" (41). The final judgement is a harsh one, "If the reputation of even Charles Dickens can obtain purchasers for such rubbish as this, we are grievously mistaken" (43). The *Sunday Times*, too, felt the difference from previous productions but was kinder: "It is the curse of reputation that an author is expected, in each new work, to improve according to geometrical ratio" (no. 914 3 May 1840). The reviewer thought that the excursion into pathos would disappoint those who depended upon Boz's comedy but claimed to prefer the new pathetic vein. The review includes a long excerpt, "Christmas Day in a Tavern," that rather anticipates the *Christmas Carol* of a few years later.

However, by June, the *Monthly Review* and the *Sunday Times* were in unhappy agreement. The first had begun its May review by indeed allowing the right of an author to attempt a pathetic tale, but questioning "whether it were a prudent step for the works of Charles Dickens to be issued in any other form than in the monthly parts" (35). The difficulties of stringing together a number of tales, if the teller were not Scheherazade, are acknowledged but without giving much credit to the device of the old man and his clock. The *Sunday Times* in June came to the same conclusion: "The further this work proceeds the more evident it becomes that a collection of short stories from the pen of Boz, is what the public neither expected nor desired" (28 June 1840).

Dickens himself had apparently perceived this, for the *Old Curiosity Shop*, which had begun as a tale in the fourth number, was now continued uninterrupted. Dickens wrote to Forster, saying that he would "run it on now for four whole numbers together, to give it a fair chance" (*Letters* II, 70; [?May 1840]), but in fact it continued for the remaining seventy-six numbers to the end. He had already put an announcement in the ninth number (30 May) saying there were no plans to include contributions by other writers.

Despite the *Old Curiosity Shop*'s subsequent reputation as a signpost to the readiness of Victorian tears, the response at this time was decidedly dry. The *Morning Advertiser* wrote on 9 July: "there is nothing in it, which were it written by an unknown or unpopular author, would excite attention, much less elicit admiration." The *Age* of 9 August 1840 thought the anonymous set of illustrations of *Master Humphrey's Clock* "likely to advance the reputation of 'Master Humphrey's Clock' to a greater extent than its own unaided merits can ever attain." In fact, it could be argued that these illustrations by P. Sibson received more notices than the serial itself. The other signs of lack of interest were a paucity of widespread excerpting and of *Examiner* notices. Whatever Forster was advising Dickens privately at this time, he said little publicly to guide his readers to an appreciation of the *Old Curiosity Shop*.

In terms of artistic direction, perhaps the most interesting fact about this summer of 1840 concerns Dickens's new agreement with Chapman and Hall: it provided for the delivery of *Barnaby Rudge*, no longer in three volumes, but in "matter sufficient for ten monthly numbers of the size of 'Pickwick' and 'Nickleby' " (*Letters* II, 93; 2 July 1840) which might also be published in fifteen monthly numbers. In the letter announcing this, Dickens makes no comment on the fact that a three-volume novel was to appear nowhere in his foreseeable future. Presumably the contract largely reflected the wishes of Chapman and Hall, for they were rescuing Dickens from his "Bentleian bonds" in buying up the rights to *Sketches by Boz*, and *Oliver Twist*, and the unsold stock of the latter. Dickens had both Forster and Talfourd (to whom in 1839 he had so triumphantly announced the projected publication of *Barnaby Rudge* in three volumes) look over the contract.

The number of monthly numbers projected, ten or fifteen, suggests however that twenty had not yet emerged as the talismanic Dickensian number it was to become. Dickens himself had certainly tired of that length in writing *Nicholas Nickleby* and *Pickwick*. He may have established a "school" of writing, but that did not exempt him from the reviewers' scorn for the form sullied by imitation. The *Monthly Review* of July 1840 had words of praise for one of these imitations and abuse for Dickens's own serials:

... "Master Humphrey's Clock" is dragging along its weary length in a fashion that can not do otherwise than diminish the number of its readers every week, – while Boz is absolutely working his imagination thread-bare, a task that is apparently by no means a difficult one ... he is compelled to introduce some of the leading characters of the "Pickwick Papers" into his new work in order to save that new work from absolute ruin, it having been pronounced a complete failure not only by the majority of the public press, but also by the subscribers to the circulating library and the news-room ...

(Monthly Review 2 no. 3 July 1840: 398–99)

The *Morning Post*, too, runs through the progress of a number of samples of what it calls "the French system of publishing books in monthly parts," *Valentine Vox, Paul Periwinkle, Poor Jack, Tower of London*, and speaks of the comparative lack of interest in the serial by the man who himself had started all these progresses (12 Oct. 1840). And finally, the *Morning Advertiser* recommended (in a review, it should be noted, of the anonymous illustrations that had been dogging the serial almost since the beginning – there is no review of the *Clock* itself) that "Boz should retire for some months, and gain fresh life from new scenes and more extensive observations" (22 Oct. 1840).

VI

The meanderings of the nostalgic old man of *Master Humphrey's Clock* did finally yield to the young orphan child and sustained narrative of the *Old Curiosity Shop*. What are seen by a Humphreyish old man as the minutely observed eccentricities and the manners of the workaday world are, to a child, the bewildering irrationalities of adults – and because inherent in this format is the child's peculiar sensitivity to power, the irrationalities amusing to a philosophic old man and the adult reader become a sustained critical vision of society. One recalls George Orwell's remark about the Murdstones in *David Copperfield* and how they hold, simultaneously, the potential of terror for the child reader and satire for the adult reader – two contrasting but coeval perceptions of these characters. The key difference is that the adult perceives immediately what the child takes the whole of a progress to discover. This is the difference between fable and fiction: between a symbolic illustration whose final intention is continuously self-evident at every stage, and a narrative which begins in order to discover its ending and cannot discriminate between its purposeful and its contingent elements.

The extended tale of the sensitive girl making her way among grotesque figures and scenes has the advantage of greater length in which to work its persuasion. The old schoolmaster under whose care Nell spends her last days listens to her adventures in a spirit that belongs to the sentimental tradition of the "Man of Feeling" and of Wordsworth. The account he hears is the novel the reader holds. Master Humphrey is explained to be the "single gentleman" who afterwards has spent his days retracing Nell's wanderings in order to reproduce them emotionally for himself also.

This is no more than the general principle by which *Master Humphrey's Clock* was originally supposed to proceed when amassing its tales. However, it was only when the miscellany was revised as a continuous tale that Master Humphrey is shown to be the projector of Nell's adventures. Ironically, once the decision to organize the *Clock* differently had been made, the most notable change was the disappearance of Master Humphrey himself. His essential characteristics are still recognizable in the single gentleman, the Bachelor, and the schoolmaster, and the realization of the significance of Nell's story is shared among these three men, but the actual essence of its meaning is conveyed throughout the book by an unpersonified narrator, not by any of their tellings, which are only assumed or summarized.

The end of Master Humphrey and the first-person voice meant, in fact, that the range and variety of scenes shown could be much greater. This did not mean any great dissipation of effect. Dickens had taken on the idea of Master Humphrey partly in order to avoid the exertion of continuous plot constructions, in the hope that the unity lent by the subsuming identity of a single narrator would give another type of coherence to the variety of topics brought to the notice of the reader. But his artistic mistake lay in constructing a narrator whose character was unequal to his own narrative talents: as he was gradually to discover, the *eidolon* of "Charles Dickens" carried its own very recognizable identity and attraction. All that caught his notice – the very breadth of his attention – coalesces in the keenness of a "Man of Feeling," and the very immediacy of his sympathies and fears furnishes its own consistency of tone and style. As well as this, continuity is provided in working out the speculations attached to these passing phenomena through the progress of a central fantasy. Similarly, in *Bentley's Miscellany* the one sheet of "original matter," initially called the Mudfog papers, had been superseded by a "Progress." This goes beyond the interest of the reporter: by coming under comment, the public scene becomes part of a personal idea developed by the commentator. Thus far in Dickens's experience it seemed that only fiction serially published could begin to handle this significant personal translation of public life successfully.

8

1839–1841 The historical novelist: *Jack Sheppard* and *Barnaby Rudge*

I

The failure of *Master Humphrey's Clock* in the spring of 1840 put a momentary end to Dickens's ambitions as a magazine editor. Over the course of his career as a fiction-writer, he persisted in setting up several periodicals and was eventually to become a successful editor. But, at this point, the "editing" of a periodical had turned out to be very much like the writing of *Pickwick* and *Nickleby*, and did not give Dickens the income and leisure he had hoped for. If the business of correspondence with contributors had been a problem with *Bentley's Miscellany*, the work involved in editing a weekly magazine without contributions was no solution. Dickens was not able to provide all the wealth of tales demanded, nor did his readers seem to want a series of short goes at piquant narrative. His recreation of eighteenth-century serial writing, however fondly undertaken, was unappealing to a post-Reform-Bill society. Still, he managed to rescue the serial by writing the *Old Curiosity Shop*, and, following it, *Barnaby Rudge*. What his readers were not to know was that this salvage effort meant an end to his ambitions as a three-volume novelist.

When Dickens had first pictured to himself the shape of his future as a writer of fiction, it was as a successor to Sir Walter Scott. The example of Scott was so compelling that Dickens and many other young writers necessarily saw their fortunes in historical fiction, at that time considered to be the most respectable form of novel-writing. Thus, in 1833, Dickens envisaged for himself a novel about the anti-Catholic Gordon Riots of 1780 with scenes comparable to those in *The Heart of Mid-Lothian*; and in 1836 when Bentley asked Dickens for a novel, his thoughts immediately flew to the effort at research it would demand. However, this grand project receded as he became an increasingly busy supplier of monthly parts.

One temporary solution had been to announce that *Barnaby Rudge* would follow *Oliver Twist* in *Bentley's Miscellany*. This was in January 1839, when Dickens was in the middle of journalistic fact-finding on Yorkshire schools for *Nicholas Nickleby*, due to begin serialization for Chapman and Hall three months later, and he could not see where he was to get the time to begin researches on his historical novel. Whether Dickens knew it or not, his work as a novelist of contemporary life had already put an end to historical novel-writing. Bentley grudgingly gave his assent to the new arrangement of having *Barnaby Rudge* appear in his *Miscellany* and not in his fiction list, but this lasted only a short while before Dickens then decided that the problem lay in his duties for the *Miscellany* and not in the contract for the novel. So, in the same month, January 1839, he resigned from the *Miscellany* and revived plans for his historical novel. He wrote to Harrison Ainsworth, coincidentally, the historical romancer touted as Scott's successor, to ask if he would become the new editor of the magazine.

At that time there were natural reasons for thinking of Ainsworth: both he and Dickens had recently been celebrated as guests of honour at a dinner in Manchester on 14 January, and the publication in parts of Ainsworth's *Jack Sheppard* had begun that very month in the *Miscellany*. After *Oliver Twist* (there were four overlapping instalments between the two serials), it became the centrepiece of the magazine. Both featured Hogarthian depictions of London low-life, and the momentum already achieved by *Oliver* fuelled an even greater conflagration of *Jack Sheppard* mania. Bentley's puff of the *Miscellany* for January 1839, ostensibly a review taken from the *Sunday Times* (31 Dec. 1838), gave pride of place to the new Ainsworth serial (see *St. James's Chronicle* 17 Jan. 1839). Another puff in the *Sun* (14 Jan. 1839) spoke of the rivalry between the serials as one of the attractions of the *Miscellany*. *The Sun* itself had already praised *Jack Sheppard* but also mildly complained that, with all these stories of notorious criminals, the *Miscellany* was beginning to appear something of a Newgate Calendar (4 Jan. 1839). And by that spring, when a third serial, *Colin Clink*, joined the other two, the magazine also became notorious for its "continuations." Still, if we are to believe the *United Services Gazette* of 5 January, the *Miscellany* was doing very well: "The aid of Mr. Dickens has, we are told, effected all that was anticipated of it for this publication. It enjoys the largest circulation, with the exception of *Blackwood*, of any magazine of the day."

Under Ainsworth, the circulation climbed even higher. *Jack Sheppard* may now be a forgotten book, but in 1839 it inspired a mania that went beyond the literary pages of the newspapers. Had Dickens known how successful it was to become, he might not have resigned. Chapman and Hall were issuing the serial parts of *Nicholas Nickleby* at the same time, but *Nickleby*, however enthusiastically welcomed because of its resemblance to the wildly popular *Pickwick*, received very little critical attention and earned its value simply by being mindlessly excerptible. *Jack Sheppard* not only provoked innumerable theatrical adaptations in the London theatres (*Nickleby* had one) but also a flood of controversial reviews. What is more, these reviews led to editorials on nothing less than the contemporary state of literature and morality in England. *Pickwick* may have been responsible for a prodigious traffic in Wellerisms; *Jack Sheppard* came to be held culpable for an increase in vandalism. In its resemblances to *Oliver*, which in fact amounted to little more than the coincidence of both being located in *Bentley's Miscellany*, *Jack Sheppard* caused a retrospective reclassification of Boz and his own "Newgate" novel. The effect on Dickens himself can be seen in the first preface to *Oliver Twist*, which was not written until three years after the serial's end, and which makes sense only when one realizes that Dickens wrote it in self-righteous indignation at the effect the *Jack Sheppard* mania was having on his own reputation in 1841.

Jack Sheppard (1702–24) was a notorious London thief and jailbreaker, whose career was all the more spectacular for its being ended by his hanging at Tyburn at the age of twenty-one. The son of a carpenter, he had been brought up in a workhouse and was made famous by his superhuman feats of escape through the manacles, iron bars, bolted doors, and twenty-foot-high walls of various London prisons. His badness and boldness were immortalized while he was still alive by portraits, pamphlets, ballads, and plays. Defoe wrote a pamphlet on him, and preachers everywhere declaimed on his career. His execution was witnessed by over two hundred thousand people and occasioned a riot afterwards.

Sheppard was hunted down by Jonathan Wild (?1682–1725), a receiver of stolen goods and infamous "thief-taker-general." Wild ran a complete corporation of thieves and informers, and kept premises for storing and altering stolen goods; part of his income came from selling such property back to its owners. He had a number of criminals and officials submissive to his direction for a good many years but was finally also hanged at Tyburn in 1725, six months after Sheppard. Wild is best known through the Newgate Calendar and Fielding's satiric *Life* of him (1743). There, Fielding introduces him as a "Great Man," taking care to distinguish "Greatness" from "Goodness." Wild is said to be as great as Caesar or Alexander, inasmuch as "Greatness consists in bringing all Manner of Mischief on Mankind, and Goodness in removing it from them."[1] Fielding says that his purpose is not to present flawless virtue but to "induce our Reader with us to lament the Frailty of human Nature, and to convince him that no Mortal, after a thorough Scrutiny, can be a proper Object of our Adoration."[2] In this satire on "Greatness," Fielding partly intended a hit at Sir Robert Walpole, who as Prime Minister of the past twenty years was commonly styled the "Great Man."

It was to Fielding's example above all that contemporary critics of *Jack Sheppard* looked when analysing what Ainsworth had done. A large part of their analysis, however, consists in reflecting on the contrast between the society that had produced *Jonathan Wild* and that which produced *Jack Sheppard*. The *Athenaeum*'s review is portentous with the decline of civilization and what *Jack Sheppard* foretells about the nineteenth century. For, indeed, the critic ascribes such controversial significance to Ainsworth's book, explicitly remarking that he takes notice of this magazine serial only because of its great sociological interest (no. 626 26 Oct. 1839: 803–05). As Keith Hollingsworth says in *The Newgate Novel*, these commentators "never doubted that the art of literature was an art of power."[3]

In this light, the *Athenaeum*'s description of moral causes and effects is of interest for the specific way in which it shows the society of 1839 oscillating between greed and guilt, between the increase in industrial money-making and the accompanying rise of religious enthusiasm. According to this analysis, men, beset by the uncertainties of making a living and crowded together into cities, resort to the extremes of indulgence and fanaticism. Both contribute to a debased literary appetite. The thirty years following the French Revolution have been culturally barren: "Under that stimulation a miraculous harvest of intellect was produced; and a corresponding poverty of the exhausted soil may be but a natural consequence" (804). The result, following out this analogy, is that literature itself has become an industry and a trade. It deals in "fanatical theology, or fashionable novels; in parliamentary sketches, or annals of Newgate; in the pencillings of a Brougham, or an Ainsworth" (803). Despite the familiarity of this charge, it is notable here because it is connected in the writer's mind with fears of political incendiarism. The *Athenaeum* itself may have appealed to a broader circulation eight

years earlier by lowering its price from 8d to 4d, but the phenomenon
of Jack Sheppardism was not confined to those who could read. It
was not merely the increase in sales of *Bentley's Miscellany* during
the run of *Jack Sheppard* that had alerted commentators to its
popularity. As the *Examiner* of 3 November 1839 enumerates, there
were adaptations of the story appearing in at least seven theatres
simultaneously; and the book was but a single ingredient in the larger
phenomenon. The perspective of the late 1830s on democracy was
significantly different from that of the early 1830s. Chartism did not
evoke the same hopefulness as the call to Reform had done, and there
was no cachet attached to the title of Chartist. According to the
Athenaeum, it was no longer a question of too little democracy but
of too much. The problem was not to assert the essential humanity
of people in poor clothes – but to find it at all in a society polarized
between useful knowledge and silver-fork fiction. The eighteenth-
century's idealism preferred to see social distinctions as no more than
accidents attending a common humanity; nineteenth-century materialism was forced to acknowledge that humanity had been overwhelmed
by substantive circumstances.

The *Examiner* objected not to the inclusion of thieves in a fictional
narrative (as is proven by its laudatory references to *Gil Blas*, *The
Beggar's Opera*, and *Jonathan Wild*), but the rhetorical uses to which
this is put. In these eighteenth-century works, it stressed in italics, *"The
vulgarity of vice was the object at which they drove, and not its false
pretensions to heroism or its vile cravings for sympathy"* (691). The
Examiner's arguments about the disguising of vice in *Jack Sheppard*
suggest that in fact the mistaken lurchings of the masses were being
fed, not by simple sensationalization of their own crimes and manners,
but by the confounding of them with upper-class manners. The
appetites for Newgate novels and for silver-fork novels were comple-
mentary aspects of a society's continued cringing to St. James.
Ainsworth's novel portrays in morbid detail the blood indulgences
of crime in all cheerfulness and ease, and then, what is worse, excuses
these by throwing over its actors the *haute couture* of high birth. Thus,
Jack Sheppard's mother acquires an air of refinement previously
"unnoticed," and Sheppard comes to repentance and right conduct
– when he discovers that he by birth is the son not of a carpenter
but of a nobleman: " *'Thank Heaven! I'm not basely born!'*" Forster
is disdainful of this all too traditional sycophancy: "He now feels that
if he had only known of his high birth he'd not have been a
housebreaker. And this, if there is any moral in it, is the moral of
the book!" (no. 1657 3 Nov. 1839: 693; "Jack Sheppard" *Bentley's*

Miscellany 6 Aug. 1839: 118; Epoch the third, ch. 5). And, indeed, Ainsworth's notions of characterization seem laughable when we read that

Ever since the discovery of his relationship to the Trenchard family a marked change had taken place in Jack's demeanour and looks, which were so much refined and improved that he could scarcely be recognized as the same person. (*Examiner* no. 1657 3 Nov. 1839: 693 ["Jack Sheppard" *Bentley's Miscellany* 6 Oct. 1839: 330; Epoch the third, ch. 13]) (Forster's italics)

As Forster points out, even the execution of Sheppard by hanging comes to seem vulgar, and "The gentility of a bullet is therefore called in aid" (693).

Thus, where the *Athenaeum* sees *Jack Sheppard* as a vision of England delivered up to the Mob, the *Examiner* sees *Jack Sheppard* as the unfortunate revival of hero-worship, where, in a reassuringly English way, gentility is the sufficient sign of morality. Whichever Ainsworth has done, he has not pointed out "the vulgarity of vice." He is merely giving the public what it wants and pays for; literature is a trade and the poor author must live by it.[4]

This refrain is echoed in the *Monthly Review* which spends the first five pages of its leading article for December 1839 (a review of two plays) on *Jack Sheppard*. The immediate relevance of this to the works in hand is that there can be no chance for legitimate drama when seven theatres at once find it profitable to put on *Jack Sheppard* in preference to anything else: " 'Jack Sheppard,' – have you been to see 'Jack Sheppard,' striking the ear in every quarter and almost in every assemblage" (3 no. 4 Dec. 1839: 460). And, once again, we find a literary review discussing politics and the condition of England. The first premise of its argument is matter-of-factly stated: that "Authorship has become a profession, and like other trades it is greatly overcrowded" (459–60). Given, too, the premise that the trades must cater to tastes, "What prospect is there for the literature of England, when such are the gross and violent excitements that the public seems at present chiefly to relish, as those we have been speaking of?" (461).

The necessarily brief analysis offered by this writer is hardly profound, but the similarity of the explanations offered – the growth among the masses of industrialism and religion – is noteworthy. It is quite certain that the working classes did not buy *Jack Sheppard* as it appeared in *Bentley's Miscellany* at 1s a month. The writers for such reviews need never have bothered to do more than give Ainsworth's work the usual notices and extracts. It was through the visual media – Cruikshank's etchings and the romance's dramatization at the minor theatres – that *Jack Sheppard* became a phenomenon of mass consumption. Only then did it become a matter of interest to the journalistic world and the literary journeymen of whom Ainsworth was one. The deplorable state of the drama, and, by extension, of poetry and fiction, was already one of the recurrent topics of the age. Dickens's cheering of Macready's efforts to revive Shakespeare is only typical of the professional moralizing on this topic that went on in all the "Theatricals" columns of the papers.

Thus, the leading article of the *Monthly Magazine* for March 1840 is headed "The Age of Jack Sheppardism" and begins: "The present state of literature is of a nature to produce the utmost amount of alarm in the well-constituted mind ... The times are out of joint, and Chartism rages while Jack Sheppard *reads*" (3 no. 15 Mar. 1840: 229). The alarm is raised for the downfall of order and reason, and the state of literature, Jack Sheppardism, is looked to as its weathervane. Interestingly, the writer calls for a return to aristocratic patronage of the writer as a release from the crass calculations of publishers. The aristocracy, having given up the support of literature, finds itself "undefended by the most influential writers" (230); democracy, in the form of public trade, is the more powerful voice. One feels here how much things had changed in a decade and how far we have come from the cry of "Rotten Boroughs" of 1830, when the Tories were not perceived as deserving much of a defence. By 1840 the Highland robbers of Scott and Wordsworth were safely quaint, and the greater proximity of Ainsworth's London felons made their crimes more objectionable. Scott's Highland thieves had lost their place in their society, and their very "romance" consists in nostalgia for something that never can be again, while the outlaws of Ainsworth's romance, however historical, presented a palpable threat. The element of society they represent was still a power to be reckoned with, and the title of the *Monthly*'s review affirms their predominance.

This review ends with an appeal to the aristocracy and Prince Albert to save the country's literature, a call that would have sounded strange only ten years previously, when critics gagged on a diet of silver-fork novels. In the alarm over Chartism, some thought history could be reversed. One recalls that by 1840 Carlyle is rereading the lessons of the French Revolution: "we cannot do without Great Men!"[5] In the *Monthly*'s review of Jack Sheppardism, Carlyle (with whom the *Monthly*'s editor Heraud shared a reverence for things German) and the Great Man are near at hand. In such articles we see the final bankruptcy of the eighteenth-century's democratic spirit.

Amid this general fear of society's being overrun by the Vandals and the Goths, *Fraser's* remained notably calm. *Fraser's* was a good deal behind everyone else in taking notice of *Jack Sheppard*, and in the article which finally appeared in February 1840 its reviewer expresses little surprise or horror at the Sheppard mania. The review refers the reader back to the notice written in *Fraser's* six years earlier, of Charles Whitehead's *Lives and Exploits of English Highwaymen, Pirates, and Robbers* (March 1834). That notice had been written by the same man who writes this one – William Makepeace Thackeray. The reference to Whitehead's book is perhaps a gentle way of avoiding notice of the book in hand, for in fact very little of the review deals directly with Ainsworth's work. Most of the excerpts are from the earlier review or are passages showing Ainsworth's research. It is noticeable that Thackeray is at pains to be gentle with Ainsworth, preferring like other reviewers to discuss the phenomenon more than this particular execution of it. He acknowledges merely that the "avowedly fictitious part" (228) of the story (the introduction of Sir Rowland Trenchard) is "agreeably written" (228).

Thackeray has other things on his critical mind. This, as in other reviews, specifically concerns the portrayal of evil. To this end, *Fraser's*, like the *Examiner*, invokes Fielding and *Jonathan Wild*. The interest of Fielding's story lies in its rhetoric of irony on Greatness; the interest of Ainsworth's consists in the secret of Sheppard's noble birth. The one lampooned the "greatness" of society's heroes such as Walpole; the other raises up the station of an ordinary thief to equality with Walpole. Both strategies may seem "democratic," but Thackeray finds Ainsworth's notion "droll" (237). It is Fielding's realism to show that Walpole is little better, morally speaking, than a receiver of stolen goods; it is moral romanticism on Ainsworth's part to redeem that thief by giving him a Walpoleian genealogy. Such faith in genealogies is both laughable and sad – and the effect of Fielding's characteristic irony should have been to make Ainsworth's romanticism untenable.

Thus far, Thackeray's review makes the same point as Forster's in the *Examiner*, without being quite so indignant about the story's unthinking reverence for Sheppard's aristocratic birth. Forster and Thackeray came from different classes, and the critical perspective they share is more the circumstance of moving in the same bohemian circles of 1830s journalism. By the end of the 1840s, Thackeray was extricating himself from the low-life to return to Vanity Fair, while Forster was taking up the effort to transform that literary life into a middle-class profession. Thackeray is more concerned to show, not that English society is too vulnerable to mass rule or aristocratic despotism, but that there is something called "Society" which should look to its responsibilities rather than its power. Thackeray seems very little amazed or upset that youths in the street will take to aping thieves' manners, and he finds their aping of the aristocracy equally laughable. For he does not see, like his fellow-commentators, that the balance of power is about to be radically shifted, nor does he argue that it ought. What he sees is perhaps larger and more generalized than class antagonism. Ainsworth's reverence for a Sir Rowland Trenchard points to a common perception that the accident of birth holds an impregnable position in the English mind, where it arbitrarily endows anything and everything with moral worth. The alarm would not be raised about contemporary youths pretending to be Jack Sheppard had not those youths in the first place fallen for the meretricious glamour of nobility. Both the would-be Sheppards and their judges are implicitly agreed in that.

As such, therefore, society and its belief in an inherited power are the real villains. This is an argument Thackeray had made as early as 1834 and reiterates here: " 'Can we single out the solitary culprit for condemnation, without even a passing censure on those who pampered the vanity which perpetuated his determination to crime?' " (228). It was not Jonathan Wild who hanged Jack Sheppard − it was society: "He was hanged because it was in accordance with what is called 'general opinion,' 'the spirit of the times,' 'the good of society,' 'the protection of capital,' or whatever is the appropriate scoundrel phrase" (237). Society thus bands together to protect the rights attached to property, and "the tenpoundery of the day" (237) are as retributive in this as any feudal landowner.

Thackeray's argument reaches its most eloquent pitch in comparing Ainsworth's Jack Sheppard to the records found not in Fielding or any other fictionist but in the courts. From those, we discover that Jack Sheppard was in fact hanged on conviction of stealing 108 yards of woollen cloth and two silver teaspoons − not, as Ainsworth would have it, because Jonathan Wild wanted to revenge himself for Sheppard's father's wooing of a nobleborn woman. It is "Society" which ought to have been found guilty: " 'Society' was far the greater culprit than the boy housebreaker; but, then, 'society,' like the House of Commons, is irresponsible, − not to be caught in any defined shape, and ready to plead privilege on all occasions" (21 no. 122 Feb. 1840: 238). The real "poetry" of the story of Jack Sheppard, according to Thackeray, lies in the sacrifice of a lad unknowingly marked out from his birth by society's duplicity.

Society offers him hope in the glamorous shape of the highwayman's cavalier brim – and then society itself dons the judge's black cap. A small fraction of the same close attention and sympathy that caused people to come to his execution or pay admission to his cell might have made him a good instead of a vain man. But his energy and courage were remarked only when they had been put to bad uses: "The honest carpenter's boy, displaying industry and ingenuity, would have no chance of their notice" (243).

Society, however, sees its duty to lie elsewhere: the protection of property. Thackeray's scorn becomes more and more scalding as he piles up cumulative indictment of this term *Duty*. For it is under this blanket-term that Sheppard's end is justified. The professional duties of the informer, the police, the gaoler, the crown solicitor, the Newgate attorney, the jury, the judge, and the chaplain suggest a moral duty justified by a God-given order of things: "From his original lapse, in all probability a trivial one, he was marked out for inevitable destruction" (242).

Thackeray's argument, based as it is on the Old Bailey's records, implies that there has been no change in society in the hundred years since the real Jack Sheppard's career. It also implies that all classes, from the tenpounders to the king, from the informer to the chaplain, are as one in their attitude towards a Jack Sheppard. There is no alarm about the rise of the masses or the decline of literature in this account. Instead Thackeray laments the fate of the individual: he is entrapped by vanity and duty, the twin pulleys of this society's mechanism. This is the same anonymous society, the rising metropolis of London, which Fielding had rebuked in his preface to *Joseph Andrews*: these people take up the habit of affectation or vanity and pretend to be what they are not, on the road to respectability.

The vanity is what Thackeray would purge from society – and here is where literature plays its part. He says of the Newgate account, "The author of the Newgate history is (because he followed the truth) a more real poet" (240). In preferring Newgate chroniclers to romantic novelists, Thackeray makes reference to his own serial *Catherine: A Story*, the tale of a cockney prostitute. This satire of Newgate fiction had been appearing intermittently in *Fraser's* since May 1839 and had been wound up after fifteen chapters in the issue for February 1840 with some remarks about the romanticization of crime. The "*Catherine* cathartic" (*Fraser's* 21 no. 122 Feb. 1840: 210) had been administered by Thackeray as a dose of literary salts against sympathy with crime, such that he claims pleasure at seeing his own narrative abused as dull, vulgar, and immoral. The readers' nausea at seeing unadorned crime is a healthier sign than its tears for Ainsworth's Sheppard or Dickens's Nancy. *Oliver Twist*'s literary rhetoric is so poisonous that "All these heroes stepped from the novel on to the stage; and the whole London public, from peers to chimney-sweeps, were interested about a set of ruffians whose occupations are thievery, murder, and prostitution" (211). To this extent, we see the power that Thackeray ascribes to literature, a power both moral and political. His disgust for Nancy or Sheppard in these books does not contradict sympathy expressed for the real Jack Sheppard of the Old Bailey records: it is the latter who is the victim of a misplaced admiration for the former, inasmuch as literature's glorification of crime is a powerful force in the society that produces real criminals.

II

The consequences of the fictional Jack Sheppard did not end with its serialization, and Thackeray found himself reflecting on this question again, not many months later, when he wrote "Going to See a Man Hanged" for *Fraser's* (22 no. 128 Aug. 1840: 150−58). This is an account of the execution of François Benjamin Courvoisier, the French valet who had cut the throat of a member of the government, Lord William Russell, uncle of Lord John Russell, one morning as he lay in bed, on 6 May 1840. Courvoisier was apprehended immediately, the trial began on 18 June, and he was hanged on 6 July. His trial and execution attracted widespread newspaper coverage and packed the London streets just as the Sheppard hanging had done. Much of the sensationalism surrounding this event came from the fact that Courvoisier claimed he had got the idea for his crime from *Jack Sheppard*.

Thackeray's article is largely taken up with a description of the crowd that watches. It is a mob, and yet he finds the good manners and intelligence of these common people impressive; by contrast, the behaviour of the oligarchy that rules them is chaotic: a young nobleman − "Honest gentleman! high-bred aristocrat! genuine lover of humour and wit!" − is seen among the crowd squirting brandy-and-water over them all (155). To this the crowd makes little response and offers the general observation " 'So-and-so is a lord, and they'll let him off' " (155). From this account, it would seem that Ainsworth's unthinking exemption of a thief nobly born is confirmed by common practice.

If the lower classes seem to have no serious quarrel with exemptions from morality accorded to their "betters," neither are they concerned about the party politicking that so engrosses the upper classes. Thackeray observes, "that I have never been in a great London crowd without thinking of what they call the two 'great' parties in England with wonder. For which of the two great leaders do these people care, I pray you?" (152). To the ordinary man in the crowd, the practice of conducting the country's business on the basis of some division between Whig and Tory is "a silly mummery of dividing and debating, which does not in the least, however it may turn, affect his condition" (152). "Populus" is a great deal wiser than his "guardians," and the glorious causes of Conservatism and Reform are irrelevant to a democrat.

Thackeray professes here to be taken aback by the spontaneity of his own "republican tirade" (153) in this passage and asks himself why such thoughts occur to him in the course of a hanging. Quite simply, these "republican" musings seem to have arisen from the effect of being in a crowd and admiring the conduct of these common people. The intelligence of various conversations overheard has impressed Thackeray:

> I have met with many a country gentleman who had not read half as many books as this honest fellow, this shrewd *prolétaire* in a black shirt. The people about him took up and carried on the conversation very knowingly, and were very little behind him in point of information. It was just as good a company as one meets on common occasions. I was in a genteel crowd in one of the galleries at the queen's coronation; indeed in point of intelligence, the democrats were quite equal to the aristocrats.
>
> (*Fraser's* 22 no. 128 Aug. 1840: 153)

This is indeed the rhetoric of republicanism.

None the less, for all Thackeray's disgust at the aristocrats and admiration of these proletarians, the piece does finally turn against the crowd. The description of the crowd before the execution is an argument for democracy; the account of them afterwards is imbued with horror and shame at the spectacle. He himself notes that his reporter's "we" has changed to "I"; it is one sign of his dissociation from the crowd. True, he was only an observer before, but after the execution there is a positive urgency to separate himself from them, for "It seems to me that I have been abetting an act of frightful wickedness and violence performed by a set of men against one of their fellows" (156). And he imagines the single figure alone against his society, beset by preachers of all sorts to repent: all this glorified and excused by the reasoning that the answering of murder with murder is "*natural*" (157). The witnessing of this murder induces in Thackeray a sense of guilt, personal and collective, and thus, by the end of his article, the good-natured democracy of the crowd seems to have turned to brutishness again. Where earlier he was at pains to specify that one man is as good as another, now he is spontaneously filled with disgust at the whole race of man; he exempts no one, neither pickpocket nor peer, from the act of blood-lust.

Dickens, who was also present, appears to have been disgusted throughout by the proceedings at Courvoisier's execution. He published no such detailed account of the hanging; what we have instead is a series of letters he wrote a few years later to the *Daily News* (1846) on the topic of capital punishment. It is in the first of these, the only one uncollected, that he describes his experience of attending the hanging. Unlike Thackeray, he had no intention beforehand of watching, but, having gone out about midnight to see the preparations, was excited enough to stay. He, Daniel Maclise, and Henry Burnett hired a second-floor room; from this perspective they found the crowd "a rocking surging sea of degradation."[6] They were not placed as Thackeray was to have any kind of personal intercourse with the crowd, and so Dickens sees only "ribaldry, debauchery, levity, drunkenness, and flaunting vice in fifty other shapes."[7]

The Courvoisier hanging was the first execution either Dickens or Thackeray had ever seen. Whatever their repugnance at the crowd, their disapproval of a law that staged such a public debauch under the guise of Christian principles was stronger. The sympathy Thackeray felt for the criminal was felt by all his journalistic colleagues. As Dickens says, "if any one among us could have saved the man (we said so, afterwards, with one accord), he would have done it."[8] He wrote in a letter to Macvey Napier on the topic that the criminal potential was brought fully out in those so disposed by the meretricious spectacle, which set up "a diseased sympathy – morbid and bad, but natural and often irresistible – among the well-conducted and gentle" (*Letters* IV, 340; 28 July 1845).

Philip Collins remarks that, in fact, during the 1840s to oppose the death penalty "was the expected thing, in literary and journalistic circles."[9] The year 1846 was to mark the high-water point of abolitionist campaigning. As early as 1830, in *Paul Clifford*, Bulwer had appended two epigrams that encapsulated the topic. He quoted from the Duke of Wellington's speech, for the 1829 Metropolitan Police Bill, about the common danger of highwaymen, and from *Jonathan Wild*: "Can any man doubt whether it is better to be a great statesman, or a common thief?" The novel ends with a sentiment somewhat less lighthearted – "The very worst use to which you can put a man is to hang him!'' But it was ten years before the abolitionist campaign got under way − set off by the report that Courvoisier had read *Jack Sheppard*.

Scott, in writing of eighteenth-century Highland outlaws, had infused the realistic novel with renewed poetry. People like Ainsworth and Bulwer had followed this up with their Corsairs: Paul Clifford, Eugene Aram, and Dick Turpin. *Jack Sheppard* was in the same tradition but moved out of it into an inflammatory contemporary relevance. Even the thieves' gang of *Oliver Twist* was no match for the immediate sensation of Sheppardism. It was in this context that Bentley in 1841 took advantage of the *Jack Sheppard* fad to reissue *Oliver Twist*, the shape of which had now been distorted in the public mind to make it part of the same phenomenon. Thus, unlike his usual practice, Dickens wrote his first preface to the novel a full two years after the serial publication had finished, four years after it had begun. It therefore contains his reply to Thackeray and all the other reviewers who had lamented the sensationalism of the intervening years.

Oliver Twist was being condemned in retrospect by the critical quarterlies as part of the seditious trend that had led to Jack Sheppardism, and there is a significant change in the conceptualization of *Barnaby Rudge* between the historically researched novel that Bentley contracted for in 1836 and the novel that came to be written after *Jack Sheppard* had appeared. By 1841, Dickens could no longer write about Newgate or mass uprisings in the Sir Walter Scott mode of nostalgia. Somehow his literary career had got tangled up with the alarm raised over Courvoisier and Chartism and mobs in the streets. Thackeray, in *Catherine*, had criticized both Dickens and Ainsworth for leaving out the truth about their London thieves and prostitutes. Dickens makes it the business of the *Oliver Twist* preface to answer this charge, saying that he has in fact dispelled the glamour surrounding the traditional romantic thief: he has shown ''no jack-boots, no crimson coats and ruffles'' but instead ''The cold, wet, shelterless midnight streets of London'' (lxiii).[10] He also specifically claims to have told the truth about Nancy and her kind. He concludes his argument by comparing himself to no less than Cervantes, Fielding, Defoe, Goldsmith, Hogarth, Smollett, Mackenzie − and even Richardson − all the great debunkers of vanity, who defied ''the insects of the hour'' (lxiv) to bring truth into their fiction. His testiness on the topic knew no graceful bounds.

This is a debate that had more to do with the sentencing of criminals in the 1840s than with Scott's Highland Jacobites. As well, behind all this is the unspoken fact that Scott was a gentleman; Dickens was not. Scott dabbled in fiction as a respite from his historical researches; Dickens was a professional journalist trying to make an income from serialized stories. It was largely as a result of the democratic hysteria in which a second-rate historical novel and Chartism could be conflated that Dickens was forced to realize that his literary career did not lie in becoming the second Sir Walter Scott. By the time of the *Oliver Twist* preface, Dickens could no longer write about Newgate or mass uprisings in the Scott mode; the novel he had so proudly planned in the early 1830s could not be written in the 1840s. Unlike Ainsworth, who continued the tradition of Scott romances, Dickens was to become a Victorian novelist, or in other words, a novelist of contemporary life.

III

Dickens made an abortive start to *Barnaby Rudge* in January 1839, the same month that *Jack Sheppard* began in *Bentley's Miscellany*. This, as we have seen, led to the break with Bentley and the postponement of *Barnaby Rudge*'s delivery date. He next sat down to the writing of it in October and November of that same year. By this time, the *Old Curiosity Shop* was well under way, and *Jack Sheppard* had finished. In the meantime, the novel had been signed over to Chapman and Hall, and the first two chapters were given to them as a token of their contract, eventually to be published in numbers like *Pickwick* and *Nickleby*. The only point of difference was that there were to be no more than ten or fifteen numbers − the figure of twenty was not a permanent feature of Dickens's writing even yet. By January 1841, however, he had redivided the first two chapters and, with the addition of new material, made them into the three chapters that comprise the first two numbers of *Barnaby Rudge* so that they would fit the divisions of *Master Humphrey's Clock*. The announcement of this change had been made on 9 January 1841 (no. 41) in *Master Humphrey's Clock* (four months before the end of the *Old Curiosity Shop*), saying that "Barnaby Rudge, though originally projected with a view to its separate publication in another and much more expensive form, will be, like its predecessor, written by Mr. Dickens expressly for these pages" (*Letters* II, 167n).

The action of *Barnaby Rudge*'s first two chapters and their illustrations, an old Gothic mansion and Maypole customers in period costume, announce the traditional historical quality of its narrative − "In the year 1775," it begins. The description of the Maypole launches energetically into the picturesque and the nostalgic: "It was a hale and hearty age though, still.'' Into the homely company of the Maypole regulars come two strangers – one ''a gallant gentleman'' and the other, a hardened and grizzled man of sixty. '' 'A highwayman!' '' whispers one old village regular to another, and one of the local worthies launches into a mystery story of gravediggers and unsolved murder. The number ends with the revelation that this very day of the story's telling marks the twenty-second anniversary of the murder.

Thus, Dickens manages to make his narrative resemble those of both Sir Walter Scott and *Master Humphrey's Clock*. The Pilgrim editors tell us that alteration of the first two chapters of *Barnaby Rudge* for publication in the *Clock* was made mostly by inserting the Maypole conversation, and this conversation echoes the beginning of *Master Humphrey's Clock* (*Letters* II, 191n). The narrative of the second number, however, quickly discards the gentleness of humble men's clubs to launch into an Ainsworthian highway adventure. There is a nod to Scott in the inclusion of some magisterially historical remarks about the badness of the roads at this time. Unspeakable crimes are mooted by the morose traveller, who is clearly a highwayman staying his hand for the moment (''his firmly closed jaws, his puckered mouth, and more than all a certain stealthy motion of the hand within his breast, seemed to announce a desperate purpose'' [*Master Humphrey's Clock* II, 245; no. 1; ch. 2]).

Having supplied the mandatory highwayman excitement in these first two numbers, Dickens turns, in the first number written fresh for the *Master Humphrey's Clock* serial, to the London working classes and domestic comedy again. Shades of *Jack Sheppard* rise, with the introduction of the widow mother, Mrs. Rudge (not unlike Mrs. Sheppard in the traces of both former beauty and past affliction), the characterization of Gabriel Varden as an honest locksmith with a shrewish wife (thus resembling the honest draper who takes up Jack Sheppard), and finally the early incident in ch. 5 (no. 48) where the widow recognizes from her past the face of the highwayman whom Varden has encountered the night before. She refuses to divulge her knowledge of the man but it is evidently intimate. Mr. Varden, who is himself an old suitor and protector of Mrs. Rudge (as the draper's wife suspects her husband to be, of Mrs. Sheppard), is unable to pry the secret from her. Where the parallel with *Jack Sheppard* breaks down is in Barnaby Rudge's idiocy, which is enough to distinguish him from the intentionally bad behaviour of Mrs. Sheppard's outcast son.

The incipient threat posed by Jack Sheppard and his cohorts in

Ainsworth's tale is in fact entirely diffused in Dickens, by the comic tone given to Simon Tappertit's doings. The secret society of 'Prentice Knights plans vengeance on one of its members' masters for poor cheese, little beer, and ear-pulling; it speaks of burning down his home and carrying off his daughter. The reader very quickly sees that the Society is out to avenge personal insults only, and its Chartist features, in this period of Chartist agitation, are superficial. A member who is asked "do you love the Constitution" affirms that he loves "The Church, the State, and everything established – but the masters" (*Master Humphrey's Clock* II, 281; no. 50; ch. 8). Contemporary readers made sensitive to talk of sedition by Jack Sheppardism and other -isms of populist societies, would see all danger defused here by humour. In fact, Dickens treats the 'Prentice Knights and their pretension much as he had treated the Pickwickians. The Knights' notion of reformation seems, like that of the Young England movement, to depend on a notion of merrie old England's inherently populistic temper. Dickens was always scornful of naive believers in the goodness of feudal times gone by, and in his hands it comes off as sounding little better than a theory of tittlebats.[11]

In reading this satire on the apprentices, one is reminded of a squib published by Dickens in the *Examiner* in August 1841, "The Fine Old English Gentleman," in which he is harshly satiric about the law and order kept in nostalgic Tory times: "The good old laws were garnished well with gibbets, whips, and chains ... Those were the days for taxes and for war's infernal din; / For scarcity of bread, that fine old dowagers might win." The press was "seldom known to snarl or bark," and "not a man in twenty score knew how to make his mark." The refrain to this ballad runs,

> Oh the fine old English Tory times;
> Soon may they come again!
>
> (*Examiner* no. 1749 7 Aug. 1841: 500)

Such a refrain had particular point, in that the Tories under Peel had just come back into office in the election of 1841, after being in opposition since 1832. According to Forster, Dickens wrote at this time, "By Jove how radical I am getting! I wax stronger and stronger in the true principles every day" (*Letters* II, 357; [13 Aug. 1841]).

One aspect of this radicalism allowed Dickens to take a hit at the government's punitory practices: "it's a blessed thing to think how many people are hung in batches every six weeks for that [the passing of bad notes], and such like offences, as showing how wide awake our government is" (*Master Humphrey's Clock* II, 298; no. 51;

ch. 11). The common dread of London's streets at night is attributed as much to the vices of the upper classes as to those of the lower street life, for gaming indoors created mischief among the servants waiting out of doors. It is about the same time (no. 54; ch. 15) that Mr. Chester, the gentleman of the book, turns out also to be its villain.

Unlike the wilful cruelty of the aristocrat, the villainy of the lower-class criminal (the stranger in the Maypole, shown haunting the London streets) is depicted as a force beyond the criminal's moral control. It may be outwardly more repulsive and bestial but it is rendered the compliment of greater psychological detail:

"I, that in the form of a man live the life of a hunted beast; that in the body am a spirit, a ghost upon the earth, a thing from which all creatures shrink, save those curst beings of another world, who will not leave me; – I am, in my desperation of this night, past all fear but that of the hell in which I exist from day to day."

(*Master Humphrey's Clock* III, 25–26; no. 55; ch. 17)

In this attribution of Byronic or Faustian consciousness to a lower-class criminal, Dickens is as democratic, so to speak, as Ainsworth is in bestowing noble birth on Jack Sheppard. Dickens invokes sympathy for the man's solitary wanderings in the London streets in a way that he never does for Chester: "to have nothing in common with the slumbering world around, not even sleep ... is a kind of suffering, on which the rivers of great cities close full many a time" (*Master Humphrey's Clock* III, 33; no. 55; ch. 18).

The contrast in evils is most present in the encounter between Chester and Hugh. The lower-class brute who performs Chester's will may be neither attractive nor sympathetic, but the gentleman spouter of Chesterfieldian maxims is portrayed as the greater villain because of his manipulation of someone lower in class than himself. Chester's very mode of address quells the brutish Hugh's criminality:

Hard words he [Hugh] could have returned, violence he would have repaid with interest; but this cool, complacent, contemptuous, self-possessed reception, caused him to feel his inferiority more completely than the most elaborate arguments. (*Master Humphrey's Clock* III, 63; no. 58; ch. 23)

Hugh knows that Chester's station as a gentleman will always excuse his crimes, whereas even a hint of insolence on Hugh's part would bring him up before a magistrate for any number of putative crimes. The law which was merely farcical in *Pickwick* and "an ass" in *Oliver* is seen in *Barnaby Rudge* to be a blunt political instrument in the battle between the classes. The point is that neither Hugh nor Chester questions this disposition of justice – whereas Dickens and his readers certainly did. Dickens's Hugh is as helpless as Thackeray's Jack Sheppard before a justice that veils its double standard under Chesterfieldian manners.

It was in this spring of 1841, during the writing of *Barnaby Rudge*, that the nature of Dickens's political beliefs became explicit. Serjeant Talfourd the Liberal member for Reading was retiring, and a party agent approached Dickens through Talfourd about standing for a seat in Parliament. Dickens replied, saying that if he could afford the expense he would act "instantly" (*Letters* II, 288; 31 May 1841). How long Dickens considered this proposal is not known. Members of Parliament received no salary at this time (one of the Chartist points of agitation, along with those for the open ballot, end of the property qualification and annual sittings of Parliament). Forster states that Dickens did not immediately turn down the invitation; he had a great desire to speak on the Poor Law Bill and his ideas at the time were "extremely radical" (*Life* II, x, 147). In any case financial considerations would have been against it. Declining the chance to run for a seat, Dickens spoke, however, of wishing to preserve an "honourable independence" (*Letters* II, 301; 10 June 1841).

The nature of that independence from party and an awareness of where his own "constituency" lay, is symbolized by the great public dinner held for Dickens in June 1841 in Edinburgh. It was the most spectacular display of recognition yet accorded to Dickens and marks the culmination of the early years of his career. On 25 June 1841 over two hundred and fifty men convened to honour Dickens. As such, it was virtually a city and a country which united in the ceremony.

However, even on this occasion, politics undercut the feelings of goodwill. Dickens told Forster,

It will give you a good notion of *party* to hear that the solicitor-general and lord-advocate refused to go, though they had previously engaged, *unless* the croupier or the chairman were a whig. Both (Wilson and Robertson) were tories, simply because, Jeffrey excepted, no whig could be found who was adapted to the office. The solicitor laid strict injunctions on Napier not to go if a whig were not in office. No whig was, and he stayed away.

(*Letters* II, 315; [30 June 1841])

Dickens added, however, that although the Whigs "feared some tory demonstration" there had been nothing of the sort and, "ever since, these men have been the loudest in their praises of the whole affair" (*Letters* II, 315). Dickens, by the tone of this account, seems to have regarded it all as a little humorous and exotic; Edinburgh society may have been so far removed from him that he found it a kind of quaint provincial lark. At a time when he was congratulating himself on being increasingly radical, it is certainly odd that he should sit among so many Tories without remark.

The difference in age and nationality between himself and his hosts may have made these political differences less inflammatory and, in any case, the rhetoric of the evening's speeches dwelt strongly on Dickens's writings as examples of the conciliation between parties and classes. Professor Wilson ("Christopher North"), who presided and gave the main address, stressed that the dinner was composed of men of all professional pursuits and degrees and that Scots of all ranks were reading Dickens's work. His speech portrays Dickens as a genuine force for democracy and patriotism. His works are "popular on just and right grounds, because they appeal to feelings implanted in human nature, and find a universal response returned all over the land."

Wilson's remarks and Dickens's own about the nature of his achievement in fact come together in Dickens's astute quoting of Burns:

> The rank is but the guinea stamp,
> The man's the goud for a' that.

Both speakers hearken back to the spring of democratic idealism as it might validly be invoked in the setting of the eighteenth-century Athens of the North. It had perhaps the air of deliberate nostalgia for an idealism that is pre-French Revolution and certainly pre-Chartist. These are not sentiments that could comfortably have been mooted in London or Glasgow during the 1840s, where too much democracy seems to have fostered only a tendency to mass rule and agitation. And yet it is in the context of such contemporary uneasiness that this vision of Dickens's importance becomes especially meaningful. Wilson states that his contribution to mankind has been to show the good in things ordinary and even low. Even so, Wilson qualifies this by adding, "He does not wish to pull down what is high, into the neighbourhood of what is low" and "he exposes, in a hideous light that principle which, when acted upon, gives a power to men in the lowest grades to carry on a more terrific tyranny than if placed upon thrones" (*Sun* 1 July 1841). In this fear are conflated the national anxiety of the 1790s, and a generation later, of the 1840s, the two generations symbolized in the conjunction of all the grey heads of Scotland's great men and the "brown flowing locks" of the young London author − a juxtaposition much noted (*Letters* II, 315; [30 June 1841]).

In these remarks, we read too, the caution of someone who had lived through the French Revolution and the Napoleonic Wars. What Wilson could not have foreseen was the correspondence of his point with the thesis of the *Barnaby Rudge* chapters on the Gordon Riots that Dickens was to write during and just after this Scottish trip. The description of the riots takes up an extended portion of the book's last third, and involves all the main characters, thereby showing the great store Dickens set upon it as a feature of his narrative. He seems from his scattered notes to Forster to have composed it fluently, and with confidence about its effect, as a kind of massive historical canvas such as his friend Daniel Maclise was to become famous for: "Thus – a vision of coarse faces, with here and there a blot of flaring, smoky light; a dream of demon heads and savage eyes, and sticks and iron bars uplifted in the air, and whirled about" (*Master Humphrey's Clock* III, 228; no. 71; ch. 50).

What is surprising is to see the rather small part of the narrative that Lord Gordon finally occupies. Introduced when the narrative has already run about twenty numbers, this central character is summarized rather than dramatized. Dickens tells us that he was deluded and is to be pitied rather than abhorred. So it is not a new analysis, an original perspective or a bringing forth of new materials that we are offered in this account. Dickens offers a hurried account of Gordon's rise to attention which is psychologically rather than factually slanted. He disposes of a whole historical subject in a page by reference to "human nature being what it is."

The *Tablet*, a Catholic paper which reviewed *Barnaby Rudge*, makes the point that, by ignoring the causes of the Riots, Dickens made an analytic mistake: "the tumults of 1780 were set on foot to procure the repeal of a relief bill that had passed some time before; not to prevent the passing of such a bill" (no. 76 23 Oct. 1841: 693). Violence was employed because it had proved effective in Scotland in preventing the extension of relief to Catholics there. Keeping the actual terms of the religious debate in the background as much as he had done, Dickens in fact weakened the logic of his whole narrative, because there is no clear chain of motivation.

This criticism confirms the feeling that Dickens is indeed emphasizing the irrationality of the Riots' occurrence. By not fulfilling the historian's commission to trace causes and effects, Dickens thereby highlights the psychology of mob behaviour and, by displaying it as irrational, persuades us of his judgement that it is to be condemned. He is more than willing to provide some sociological justification – poor living conditions and a vicious officialdom – but he denies these

crowds the dignity of an ideology. Where the *Tablet*'s more historically responsible account remarks, "There is no doubt that the basis
of these ferocious proceedings was a very intelligible religious
fanaticism" (694), there is no moral context for the mob's behaviour
as it is described by Dickens.

Nor is there any moral dimension allowed to Gordon; the *Tablet*
remarks, "It is easy to set down a man like this as mad, and to take
no further pains about his character" (693). Thus, Dickens's theory
of history, such as it is, does not appear to be interested in the notion
of the Great Man, who in this case is a fool and a pawn. The involve-
ment of the mentally deficient Barnaby in the cause of the mad
Gordon is Dickens's heavyhanded satire on this great historical movement. He has the Caliban-like Hugh enthusiastically mistake the
cause's anti-popery cry as "No Property, brother!" Barnaby's fall
from the grace conferred by his congenital idiocy occurs when he joins
the mob's cause. Barnaby is of course a ready symbol of the
feeblemindedness of the whole venture. But again Dickens seems more
interested in analysing the mind of the masses than that of any hero.
Strangely enough, both Barnaby and Gordon, the most obvious
candidates for the story's heroes, do not seem to interest even Dickens
himself long enough to make them significant figures.

It is the crowd who holds centre stage through the long middle
section of the book. Dickens calls the group that enters the walls of
Parliament "the very scum and refuse of London" and yet immediately qualifies this by saying their very multiplication had been
"fostered by bad criminal laws, bad prison regulations, and the worst
conceivable police" (*Master Humphrey's Clock* III, 220; no. 71;
ch. 49). The difference between their peaceful daily intercourse with
their Catholic neighbours and their feverish anti-popery assemblies
is ascribed to the machinations of Gashford, Tappertit, Hugh, and
Dennis. Yet none of these characters dominates the action, nor are
we ever permitted any glimpses of their attraction. There are no great
men among Dickens's villains, who are generally invisible in the
crowd. It is never quite clear how they work their mischief. The
repeated analogy of the crowd's movement to the sea suggests its
impersonality and spontaneity. The reasons for their persistence in
outlawry are not profound: "poverty ... ignorance ... love of mischief
... hope of plunder" (*Master Humphrey's Clock* III, 241; no. 73;
ch. 53). Their feeling of invulnerability from the law's revenge is based
on a sense of strength in numbers rather than of self-righteousness.
All of this magisterially hands down a picture of morally stunted
children. Dickens's gentlemen are deliberate villains; his proletariats,

their unknowing victims. He preaches a reverence for authority and yet criticizes the historical government that constitutes that authority.

It is at this point that Joe Willet and Edward Chester reappear to save Mr. Haredale, virtually the only Catholic distinguished as an individual. But by this time the two young men have been too long out of the narrative to take it over convincingly. Edward Chester's reconciliation with Mr. Haredale does not carry the weight it might have possessed had it occurred earlier, and the romantic reconciliations are hurried, as so much stage business at the end of a farce where couples are brought out from their hiding places to join hands for the final curtain.

One of the most gratuitous touches of Dickens's attempt to gather together the shards of the book's original plot is worth remarking — the discovery of Hugh's filial relation to Sir John Chester. This occurs notwithstanding all the scorn heaped on Sir John for his gentlemanliness and all Forster's jeers at the false moral of *Jack Sheppard* that a high-born man will instinctively show honour. And Hugh's translation into a gentleman occurs despite the fact that Dickens himself has earlier treated the notion of the "discovery" of a gentleman with irony and scorn, in the passage where Joe Willet, the publican's son, is approached by a recruiting sergeant: " 'You're a gentleman, by G – – !' was his first remark, as he slapped him on the back. 'You're a gentleman in disguise. So am I. Let's swear a friendship' " (*Master Humphrey's Clock* III, 112; no. 62; ch. 31). Willet is indeed an estimable young man, but to apply the term "gentleman" in the sense used here — with a meretricious assumption of immediate bonhomie — is a crass insult. It is a bankrupt formula, and Joe's reply, " 'For bread and meat!' " neatly encapsulates the novel's "radicalism" in suggesting that the lower classes are justifiably sceptical of their governing classes' rhetoric. But from the moment of the discovery of his gentlemanly birth, Hugh is a reformed and eloquent character. He may earlier have had no very clear idea of whether he should yell "No Property" or "No Popery," but he can deliver a speech worthy of the pulpit before he dies. It is not clear if Dickens recognizes the sleight of hand effected, and yet the description of Jack Sheppard that Forster so scorned is exactly applicable here.

Whatever the interest attached to Hugh's newfound social status or Barnaby's moral elevation at the novel's conclusion, their emergence into moral complexity is unconvincing after the portrayal of them as animals. The two romantic leads, Joe Willet and Edward Chester, are absent from most of the novel so long that interest in them is only artificially revived. Thus, between the two unacknowledged sons and the two rebellious sons, Dickens fails to come up with a hero for his novel. Gordon is the obvious figure for this purpose and Dickens virtually throws away the psychological materials offered by him. The commonplace opinion that Gordon was mad is plumped for immediately, and Dickens misses the play that even Scott might have made with the question.

Dickens seems more interested in the question of how far the lower classes are justified in criticizing and challenging the government of their state and to what extent they are qualified to take action. This is not a historical question. In addressing these questions fictionally, Dickens was also telling his readers in 1841 whether or not they had mob rule to fear. In the context of the Chartists and an election, he analysed what features go to create an uprising and an overthrow of existing government. By his own account a blossoming Radical and a man who could not tolerate the Tories, Dickens none the less chooses to depict the nightmarish side of the People.

Whatever kind of social analysis this interesting question makes for, it did not produce a novel that the people would buy. In fiction, especially of the middle-class variety, a Great Man was wanted. A reviewer of the inevitable stage adaptation of *Barnaby Rudge* put on at the English Opera House remarks that the novel, like *Nickleby* and *Oliver*, is

one of forced interest in regard to its main character. The sympathies are enlisted on account of the afflictions endured by the momentary hero. And thus *Barnaby Rudge* is of the same class of interest as *Oliver*, *Smike*, *Nelly*, and the other persecuted creations of Mr. Dickens's muse.

(Courier 14 July 1841)

Smike is not the main hero of *Nickleby*, but in all other respects this complaint has truth in it.

Dickens himself had said to his Edinburgh audience only a fortnight earlier that it was the sufferings of his characters which created the bond between him and his readers: "I feel as if the deaths of the fictitious creatures, in which you have been kind enough to express an interest, had endeared us to each other, as real afflictions deepen friendships in actual life" (*Sun* 1 July 1841). To judge from general comment, this certainly seems to have been true; the difference with *Barnaby Rudge* perhaps was that Barnaby's mind is virtually closed – his suffering opens up no moral dimension in his story. Nor are the inner sufferings of Emma, Mr. Haredale, Joe Willet or Edward Chester fully visualized. The possibilities are quite numerous, but the canvas is almost too large to permit sustained attention to a single character. One might wonder why readers of fiction should need heroes, since history has learned to do without them.

The reasons for the comparative failure of *Barnaby Rudge* are hardly raised in contemporary reviews of the novel – indeed, what is more shocking, it is barely reviewed at all. Some of the most pertinent remarks about the novel are tucked away in the more numerous theatrical reviews of the stage version. It is not too harsh to summarize the gist of these by citing the *Observer*'s recommendation, that the piece will amuse those "who have not had an opportunity of reading the original in Humphrey's Clock, and will save much time and trouble in poring over the volume, which may perhaps be more advantageously employed" (26 Dec. 1841).

Meanwhile, weekly sales declined from 70,000 to 30,000. Correspondingly, the incidence of notices declined 40 percent from 1839, the days of *Nickleby*. Most of the notices, such as they are, are extracts. The very banality of the remarks appended betrays the literary world's yawning indifference: "Barnaby Rudge continues his amusing adventures" (*Bell's Life in London* 9 May 1841). Upon the announcement that the magazine was to be brought to an end along with the serial (no. 80; 9 Oct. 1841), there occurs an outbreak of advice to Dickens. The *Tablet* commented that it had been "ridiculous and offensive" to see "a man of genius winding himself up like a three years' clock, and when so wound up letting himself out to hire to the public, or to a bookseller." The reviewer did not necessarily condemn the expediency of periodical work for an interval, only the constant "profanation" of genius and the industrialization of a mind (no. 76 23 Oct. 1841: 693).

The confounding of the novel and periodical genres with which Dickens had dazzled his critics for the past few years seemed exploded. Instead, he was now part of the "book-manufacturing system," "the trade of authorship," and the producer of a commodity that might have come from the factories of Manchester (*Morning Post* [13 Oct. 1841]). Even if he himself had cut the pattern, he was now merely one of his own imitators: the editor of a *Pic Nic Papers* was little better than an author of a *Colin Clink* or *Valentine Vox*.

Such comments only confirmed Dickens's personal gloominess about matters. He told Mitton in August 1841:

I remembered that Scott failed in the sale of his very best works, and never recovered his old circulation (though he wrote fifty times better than at first) *because he never left off*. I thought about how I had spoilt the novel sale – in the cases of Bulwer, Marryatt [*sic*], and the best people – by my great success, and how my great success was, in a manner, spoiling itself, by being run to death and deluging the town with every description of trash and rot ... if I go to the monthly parts next March, I do so at a great hazard. Scott's life warns me ...

(Letters II, 365; 23 Aug. 1841 – italics in original)

His solution was to propose a year's silence "and then to come out with a complete story in three volumes – and with no cuts or any expense but of printing – and put the town in a blaze again" (*Letters* II, 365). As long ago as Macrone and 1836, this had been the original shape of *Gabriel Vardon*, but the contract with Bentley for three volumes had unfortunately been signed in August 1836, the fateful point at which Sam Wellerisms had sucked *Pickwick* into the vortex of popularity. Dickens had never been out of the public attention from then on, and a story written entire in three volumes was something that he was never to do.

Conclusion

Barnaby Rudge was published simultaneously in two forms, weekly and monthly parts in *Master Humphrey's Clock* and, at the end of its periodical run, in three bound volumes of the complete *Clock*. To say which is the first edition of this novel is even more difficult than usual with Dickens's works; in this case, collectors value the least permanent form, the weekly part, most highly. In any case, the volumes of *Master Humphrey's Clock*, despite the embossed gold design of the *Clock* motif on the cloth cover, are not particularly remarkable examples of bookmaking. As we have seen with *Pickwick*, cloth binding was barely one step up from paper boards, for it still suggested impermanence.

None the less, the fact that Dickens's part-issues, a form generally associated with the servants' hall, should appear between hard covers implies a seeking after permanence. A contemporary reader would have had to shift his way of referring to *Barnaby Rudge* over the course of its publication or juggled the vocabulary of both serial and novel, whereas we, seeing only a single volume called *Barnaby Rudge*, call it a novel. The genre of Dickens's work has settled down by virtue of retrospective cataloguing. We would probably not think to look under "Magazine Day" to find a review of *Barnaby Rudge*. The irony is that, by the time it did appear in three volumes, a review of the book as a whole would have been awkward to find, so drastically had the enthusiasm first greeting *Master Humphrey's Clock* as a new Dickens periodical dwindled.

The question of volumes or permanence is an important one in talking about Dickens's work as Literature. In 1833, when Dickens was about to launch into authorship, Thomas Carlyle, as we have seen, was only one of many literary men who bemoaned the stale state of literature in England. He declared the impossibility of living by it: the only alternative, he said, was periodical writing, which was "below street sweeping as a trade."[1] It took Carlyle years of discouragement to yield to the idea of breaking down his book *Sartor Resartus* into "stripes" in order to publish it in a magazine.[2]

Conclusion

There is, of course, a gulf in intellect and training between Carlyle and Dickens. One can look down upon Dickens's seemingly instantaneous celebrity at twenty-four as merely popular by comparison to the reputation so grudgingly won from the world by Carlyle in his middle age. None the less, Dickens and Carlyle moved as professional equals in the same London literary world, neither one more anomalous in it than the other. Dickens by all rights should have been little more than a daily newspaper hack; Carlyle, a fusty professor in Edinburgh. Both these possibilities – a place in the ranks of anonymous journalism, a chair in a Scottish university – are equally remote from London literary circles, although Carlyle as such would have carried the edge in respectability. However, it is Dickens who has the more secure place in the literary canon and Carlyle's writings which are only recently being moved again into the academic curriculum. Their positions from 1833 have been reversed: Dickens is "Literature," while Carlyle is merely "literary."

The difference resides partly in the meaning of the term *Literature* itself. In an essay called "What is Literature," René Wellek tells us that historically this word's etymological and cultural derivation "has been used to define writings of some significance, to books of whatever subject which made an impact."[3] Wellek regards the eighteenth century as bringing a change in definition, from the word's sense of culture implied by a knowledge of classical languages to a body of writing merely. He notes that the first book in English called *A History of Language and Literature* by Robert Chambers appears in 1836, what might be regarded as a surprisingly late crystallization of this shift in thinking. And indeed in most of the reviewing seen here, it is particularly striking that "Literature" signifies a much more inclusive body of work than it would now:

It refers to all kinds of writing, including those of erudite nature, history, theology, philosophy, and even natural science. Only very slowly was the term narrowed down to what we today call "imaginative literature": the poem, the tale, the play in particular.[4]

We call the making of literature "creative writing"; readers for centuries before us called it "significant writing."[5] Still, whatever the histories that may be traced out to explain this change – the rise in an idea of aestheticism connected with the plastic arts, the growing distaste for classical rhetoric – the key virtue ascribed to "Literature" remains the same: permanence. The only difference is that two centuries of romantic criticism have led us to prefer mythology, folklore, anthropology – the structuralist disciplines, in other words

– to the historical ones. We prefer to read literature out of its rhetorical context and see it instead as a synchronic record of the human mind. Imagination, not information, has become the term carrying the cachet of permanence. The structuralists have even gone to the antipode of declaring that criticism is itself a branch of fiction; in the 1830s, this would have been considered a degradation of criticism, which had always boasted a much longer pedigree than the novel.

W. W. Robson, in *The Definition of Literature*, challenges this idea of fiction used exclusively in "apposition" to imagination: "imagination, whether or not it has anything particular to do with literature, has nothing particular to do with fiction."[6] He finds the current way of thinking about literature an example of "historical parochialism." What he does not dispute is the sense of permanence that adheres to our use of the word "Literature" or what he terms "the transcendence of occasions."[7] However, because of this notion of transcendence, Robson discounts the reactions of a writer's first audiences; he points out that various works once enormously popular have not remained in the canon. So, instead, he prefers to base his judgement of what is called literature on some notion of the author's sincerity.[8]

The determining of intention or sincerity has been a particular thorn in the side of twentieth-century criticism, and Robson reflects the preoccupations of his era in referring to this criterion. Dickens, however, turns Robson's notion on its head: Dickens is a writer whose intentions towards "Literature" were certainly not "sincere" when he took on the *Pickwick* commission, but ponderously so when he planned *Barnaby Rudge*. And his popularity as a writer of periodicals in the nineteenth century has somehow found him a permanent place on twentieth-century shelves as a writer of volumes. By looking at the reactions of his reviewers, this study probes Dickens's "sincerity" or literary aspirations from a materialist perspective.

What did these now neglected arbiters think Dickens was contributing to the canon of "Literature"? For the period 1833–41, the years up to *Barnaby Rudge*, his first novel consciously planned as a literary artifact, the answer could only have been: very little. The reviewers of the time were surprised to find themselves even acknowledging "so anonymous a publication" as *Pickwick* and, when they did acknowledge the element of "transcendence," they found it more in promise than achievement. Looking back from 1841 over the first seven years of Dickens's career as a published author, an incipient feeling of disgruntlement is discernible. The "Phenomenon" was no longer an infant in 1841. The apathy that greets *Barnaby Rudge*, the novel Dickens had written as his first venture into the Sir Walter Scott stakes of literature, is not pleasant to relive. Dickens was certainly right to take a sabbatical after it and to worry that Scott's fate might be reserved for him – without his having ever written a Scott novel. For both authors, seriality became a source not only of riches but of weariness. The first pull of *Pickwick* had been un-expectedly strong enough to make a man such as Carlyle read it against all the violence of his Presbyterian disapproval; however, by December 1840, despite his great personal respect for Dickens, he was to say of *Nickleby*, that he never read it "except pieces of it in newspapers"[9] – one sign of how the Pickwickian brand of popularity could work against itself when it became too easily available. And *Fraser's*, in an article on "The Present State of Literary Criticism in England," thought to wonder in 1840, "Are we become a mere novel and romance-reading people? or rather a people only reading monthly scraps of the *Nickleby* School?" (21 no. 122 Feb. 1840: 200). The *"Nickleby* School" was evidently not to be considered "Literature."

This is, critically speaking, all water under the bridge now. Dickens is Literature. But an inquiry into the perspective of the 1830s may accomplish the revision of our own historically parochial reading of Dickens. In raising the part-issue of the servants' hall to the eye-level of the quarterly reviewers, Dickens changed the shape of the novel, and with it the literary canon. We have inherited this resultant canon, and our own necessary work of revision may be done by getting under the romantic formalist tradition that now overlies our reading of Dickens. There is ample proof that Dickens himself saw his work as rhetorical in nature, and that the persuasion he practised on his readers was considered politically important. He was not naive in thinking that the novel, written as he wrote it – that is to say, as a periodical – had enormous power in the world of the 1830s. His triumphant trampling of Bulwer's silver-fork school demonstrated that.

During the 1830s, Bulwer himself had moved on from *Pelham* to politics. Dickens could never have afforded to do the same thing, much as he might have wished to do so; he had neither the background nor training to go the gentlemanly route to power. Instead, by dint of talent and Copperfieldian earnestness, he forced the quarterly reviewers and the parliamentarians to acknowledge his political presence. We remember Serjeant Talfourd, for example, not as a member of Parliament, but as the man whom *Pickwick*'s dedication and preface honoured for raising the profession of authorship. This issue − authorship as a political force − was a significant one for Dickens, and it has consequences for the modern definition of literature. The canon of which the Dickens mind forms such a substantial part is now what we think of as literary. The meaning of "Literature" is not to be understood until we have felt its meaning for the author who wanted to be part of it.

Notes

1 1828–1833 The parliamentary reporter

1 William Makepeace Thackeray, *The History of Pendennis* (London: Bradbury & Evans, 1850) I, 271–72. Hereafter cited in parentheses.

2 Henry Vizetelly says of the literary generation of which Shandon was part: "Five-and-fifty years ago literature was either a more precarious pursuit than it is at present, or else literary men were more improvident. I can recall a string of names – half of them still remembered by the public, the other half forgotten – of journalists and magazine writers who were accustomed to spend a fair portion of their lives within the high walls of the Fleet or King's Bench prisons" (*Glances Back through Seventy Years*, 2 vols. [London: Kegan Paul, Trench, Trübner & Co. Ltd., 1893] I, 110).

   See also, R. P. Gillies's *Memoirs of a Literary Veteran*, 3 vols. (London: Richard Bentley, 1851), which seems to have been written from prison. Nigel Cross's *The Royal Literary Fund 1790–1918* (Cambridge: Cambridge University Press, 1984) confirms Vizetelly's and Gillies's perceptions, using statistics from the period. Cross places the change in the general fortunes of literary men at around 1840.

3 The fullest history of Thomas Miller can be found in Nigel Cross, *The Common Writer: Life in Nineteenth-Century Grub Street* (Cambridge: Cambridge University Press, 1985).

4 Thomas Miller, *Godfrey Malvern; or The Life of an Author* (London: Thomas Miller, 1842) I, 194. Hereafter cited in parentheses.

5 John O. Hayden, Introduction to *British Literary Magazines: The Romantic Age 1788–1836*, ed. A. Sullivan (Connecticut: Greenwood Press, 1983) xxi–xxiii.

6 Norman Gash, the pre-eminent historian of Peel and this period, emphasizes that more disciplined systems of opposition shadow executives came only later in the century, and that Peel inherited from the long years of the Napoleonic wars a system in which the Cabinet held the real power. By the 1830s, "The whigs in fact were in the anomalous position of forming a party in a non-party political system" (*Mr. Secretary Peel: The Life of Sir Robert Peel to 1830* [London: Longmans, 1961] 9). Gash interprets Peel's splitting of the party in 1829 and 1846 not as "betrayal" of party loyalties but as the continuation of a coalition statesman's

concern for national safety. Victorian politicians, looking back from the vantage point of peaceful prosperity, could not appreciate the meaning of such conservatism to a generation formed by the fear of national invasion and upheaval.

7 George Henry Lewes, *Ranthorpe* (London: Chapman & Hall, 1847) 24. Hereafter cited in parentheses.

8 See Gillies's *Memoirs*, for a parallel account of retreat to Germany.

9 Charles Dickens, *The Letters of Charles Dickens*, eds. Graham Storey and K. J. Fielding (Oxford: Clarendon Press, 1981) V, 190n. This, and other volumes of the Pilgrim edition of Dickens's letters, are hereafter cited in parentheses.

10 The disagreements between Dickens and Thackeray on the subject of the social position of literary men have been chronicled in: K. J. Fielding, "Thackeray and the 'Dignity of Literature'" *T.L.S.* 19 & 26 Sept. 1958, and "Dickens and the Royal Literary Fund" *T.L.S.* 15 & 22 Oct. 1954; Gordon N. Ray, "Dickens versus Thackeray: The Garrick Club Affair" *P.M.L.A.* 69 Sept. 1954: 815—32, and *Thackeray: The Age of Wisdom* (Oxford: Oxford University Press, 1958) ch. 5. Compare also, Thackeray on "A Brother of the Press on the History of a Literary Man, Laman Blanchard, and the Chances of the Literary Profession" *Fraser's Magazine* 33 no. 195 Mar. 1846: 332—42; and Edward Bulwer-Lytton, "Memoir of Laman Blanchard," introduction to Samuel Laman Blanchard, *Sketches from Life* (1846). Dickens endorsed Bulwer-Lytton's position on the plight of the literary man as represented by his unfortunate colleague Blanchard; Thackeray did not.

11 Charles Dickens, *David Copperfield*, ed. Nina Burgis (1849—50; Oxford: Clarendon Press, 1981) 450. Hereafter cited in parentheses.

12 All emphasis in quotations throughout appears in the original works.

13 See Michael MacDonagh, *The Reporters' Gallery* (London: Hodder & Stoughton, 1913) ch. 41, "The First Reporters' Galleries."

14 John Forster, *The Life of Charles Dickens* (1872—74), ed. A. J. Hoppé (London: Dent, 1966; rpt. 1969) I, iv, 52. Hereafter cited as *Life*, in parentheses. Also quoted, in slightly different form, in Charles Dickens, *The Speeches of Charles Dickens*, ed. K. J. Fielding (Oxford: Clarendon Press, 1960) 347.

15 [James Grant], *The Great Metropolis* (London: Saunders & Otley, 1836) II, 226.

16 James Grant, *The Newspaper Press* (London: Tinsley Brothers, 1871—72) I, 298.

17 See William Jerdan, *The Autobiography of William Jerdan* (London: Arthur Hall, 1852), on the life of a parliamentary reporter: "At first the occupation is exciting, and always improving, and I know no better preparatory school for the bar, or almost any description of public life, than the training of a session or two in parliamentary drudgery. It is like reviewing, and by forcing the mind to consider many interesting and important questions, it creates a sort of universality of talent, not always

superficial but always ready ... In a little time, however, the sameness of the work, notwithstanding its varieties, becomes exceedingly unsatisfactory and irksome" (I, 88–89).

18 In his biography of Thomas Barnes, the editor of *The Times*, Derek Hudson writes: "The word 'journalist' (far from signifying, as it now does, membership of an established profession) was in the eighteenth century only a scornful term for one who wrote under political dictation" (*Thomas Barnes of "The Times"* [Cambridge: Cambridge University Press, 1943] 24). Hudson sees a change dating from the famous dinner held by the Duke of Wellington for Barnes in 1834, when the Tories were attempting to form a government: "In the history of English journalism, this dinner to Barnes stands out like the capture of a stronghold in a military campaign" (82).

19 William Makepeace Thackeray, *The Adventures of Philip* (London: Smith, Elder, 1862) III, 30–31.

20 John Manning, *Dickens on Education* (Toronto: University of Toronto Press, 1959) 40–41.

21 Arthur Aspinall, "The Social Status of Journalists at the Beginning of the Nineteenth Century" *Review of English Studies* 21 no. 83 July 1945: 230.

22 *Parliamentary Debates* 16 23 Mar. 1810: col. 29**. Note: the Gallery was cleared for this debate; no source is given for this report.

23 *Parliamentary Debates* 16 23 Mar. 1810: col. 37. Jerdan remarks in his *Autobiography* (1852) that reporters as a "class ought to have taken a higher stand in literature and general estimation than they appear to have done" (I, 88). That they did not, he ascribed to the fact that their necessarily late hours kept them apart from the professional life of the daytime and also led them to tavern-clubs, and hence into drunkenness.

24 *Parliamentary Debates* 3s 20 29 July 1833: cols. 69, 86. Peel's speech was given in defence of the reporters against the prominent Irish member O'Connell's complaint that they ought to be brought to the Bar for not reporting his speeches. The decision not to report O'Connell's speeches had been a deliberately provocative action on the part of the reporters, for, as they well knew, the House could hardly rebuke them for *not* violating the privilege of being admitted – a privilege traditionally granted by the House, which thereby waived the law forbidding reporting of its proceedings. This in itself would have made the affair a joke; and, if O'Connell complained of the newspapers' monopoly and power in regulating the country's opinions, other members could equally express their gratitude that not all was reported. One member, Daniel Whittle Harvey, related how the reporters remarked, "'If we stated to the public one-half the nonsense ... which is spoken in that House, we should soon write ourselves out of existence'" (*Parliamentary Debates* 3s 20 29 July 1833: col. 80).

25 F. J. Harvey Darton, "Dickens the Beginner" *Quarterly Review* 262 (1934): 61.

26 *Ibid.* 63.

2 Literature in 1833

1 Sir Walter Scott, *The Letters of Sir Walter Scott, Centenary Edition*, ed. H. J. Grierson (London: Constable, 1935) IX, 250; to John Murray [9 Oct. 1825].

William Wright (1787–1856), a friend of Scott's and the solicitor who went between Murray and Lockhart, wrote: "though my rank in life was different to your own, having no relations whose feelings could be wounded by my accepting any honest employment, I should not receive an offer of the editorship of a newspaper as a compliment to my feelings as a barrister and a gentleman, however complimentary it might be as to my talents ... An editor of a Review like the *Quarterly* is the office of a scholar and a gentleman; but that of a newspaper is *not*, for a newspaper is merely stock-in-trade, to be used as it can be turned to most profit" (quoted in Andrew Lang, *The Life and Letters of John Gibson Lockhart* [1897] I, 367; 3 Oct. 1825).

When declining the offer, Lockhart told Murray that he was "neither young nor poor enough" to take it up, in effect declaring that he was not a literary hack writer; and, indeed, it was William Maginn to whom Murray finally turned (Samuel Smiles, *A Publisher and his Friends: Memoir and Correspondence of the Late John Murray* [London: John Murray, 1891] II, 196; 7 Oct. 1825).

2 See John Gibson Lockhart, *Memoirs of the Life of Sir Walter Scott, Bart.* (Edinburgh: Robert Cadell, 1837–38): "Literary fame, he [Scott] always said, was a bright feather in the cap, but not the substantial cover of a well-protected head" (II, 185); and "he was all along sincere in the opinion that literature ought never to be ranked on the same scale of importance with the conduct of business in any of the great departments of public life" (II, 338).

3 Scott, *Letters* IX, 253–54. To Lockhart, 16 Oct. [1825]. The prominent editor of the *Edinburgh Review*, Jeffrey himself, had doubts about his own success in combining the two. See Lord Cockburn, *The Life of Lord Jeffrey* (1852) I, 280. In a letter of 1 Nov. 1827 to Cockburn, Jeffrey wrote: "I was always aware that the political character of the work [editing the *Edinburgh Review*], its *party* principles, and occasional party violence, *might*, when concentrated on the head of the only ostensible party, raise an objection of moment; and for this and its consequences I should not care much. But it has occurred to me, I confess for the first time, that the objection may be rested on the notion that the *Editor of a periodical work*, whatever its political character might be, and even if it were purely literary, and without any politics, had derogated from the personal dignity required in a judge, and ought not to presume so high. From the very first I have been anxious to keep clear of any tradesman-like concern in the Review, and to confine myself pretty strictly to intercourse with *gentlemen* only, even as contributors."

4 Robert Blake, *Disraeli* (London: Eyre & Spottiswoode, 1966) 80. Bulwer

professed to have taken on the editorship of the *New Monthly Magazine* to show that a gentleman could do it; in *England and the English* (London: Richard Bentley, 1833), he says of the status of authorship: "A literary man with us is often forced to be proud of something else than talent – proud of fortune, of connexion, or of birth – in order not to be looked down upon" (I, 164).

5 Arthur Aspinall, *Politics and the Press c. 1780–1850* (London: Home & Van Thal, 1949): "Why were the Tories without a single newspaper on which they could confidently rely when they left office in November 1830?" (381). See also Blake, "Disraeli's great object was to get in, and the tide was obviously flowing fast against the Tories. No one who was ambitious would commit himself to the losers" (85). See *Coningsby* (1844), Disraeli's own fictionalized account of politics during the 1830s.

6 Blake, *Disraeli* 82.

7 "Mr. Colburn's List" *Athenaeum* I no. 47 17 Sept. 1828: 735. Novels "in which there was a great infusion of poetry" are defined as novels "in which incident, if not predominant over character, at least possessed a dangerous importance"; and typical poems "in which there was a great infusion of novel-writing" are given as "The Corsairs and the Giaours, the Marmions and the Ladies of the Lake, and the Lalla Rookhs" (735). Scott was said to have written both.

8 [John Fullarton], "Progress of Misgovernment" *Quarterly Review* 46 no. 92 Jan. 1832: 544–622. Scott, a Tory, found his allies guilty of spinelessness: they "reply by a reference to the *spirit of the people* – intimating a passive, though apparently unwilling resignation to the will of the *multitude*. When you bring them to the point, they grant all the dangers you state, and then comes their melancholy – *What can we do?*" (*Life* VII, 254; to Henry Francis Scott, 10 Jan. 1831).

9 See also Thomas Carlyle, "James Carlyle" (dated 29 Jan. 1832) in his *Reminiscences*, ed. C. E. Norton (London: Macmillan, 1887) I, 48: "My Father had seen the American War, the French Revolution, the rise and fall of Napoleon. The last arrested him strongly: in the Russian Campaign we bought a London Newspaper, which I read aloud to a little circle thrice weekly ... For the rest, he never meddled with Politics." And George Steiner writes in "The Great 'Ennui'" *In Bluebeard's Castle* (London: Faber & Faber, 1971): "No string of quotations, no statistics, can recapture for us what must have been the inner excitement, the passionate adventure of spirit and emotion unleashed by the events of 1789 and sustained, at a fantastic tempo, until 1815 ... we do have reliable evidence that those who lived through the 1790s and the first decade and a half of the nineteenth century, and who could recall the tenor of life under the old dispensation, felt that time itself and the whole enterprise of consciousness had formidably accelerated" (18).

Steiner's thesis is that a "great ennui" set in for the next century after 1815: "The generation of 1830 was damned by memories of events, of hopes, in which it had taken no personal part ... The romantic generation was jealous of its fathers" (22).

10 Lockhart, *Life of Scott* VI, 30, 31.
11 *Ibid.* VI, 31—32.
12 *Ibid.* VI, 28.
13 *Ibid.* VI, 28.
14 Royal Gettmann, *A Victorian Publisher: A Study of the Bentley Papers* (Cambridge: Cambridge University Press, 1960) 45.
15 Lockhart, *Life of Scott* VII, 196.
16 Gettmann, *Victorian Publisher* 46.
17 Michael Sadleir says that this series' "importance in English publishing history is hard to exaggerate" (*XIX Century Fiction* [London: Constable, 1951] II, 99). The irony of Bentley's *Standard Novels* series is that in intending simply to do what was perfectly commonplace — the reissue of dead authors in volumes — it made bibliographical history. As Michael Sadleir remarks, "a definite part of the importance of Bentley's Standard Novel Series to students of publishing history is that it represented (in subsequent fact, if not in original intention) the first sustained attempt by a publisher to exploit a cheaper market for his successful novels" (*XIX Century Fiction* [1951] II, 94—95).

The series up till 1836 consisted mainly of romances interspersed with the novels of manners of Austen and Galt. Sadleir also points out the fact, important to bibliographic critics, that the series offered "*the texts finally approved by their authors*" (II, 95). This was because, in order to secure the English copyrights of James Fenimore Cooper, Colburn and Bentley commissioned prefatorial material from Cooper (whose works comprise ten of the forty-nine published up to 1836) and then for consistency's sake continued this feature of authorial prefaces. Thus, a point of textual concern hangs on a decision made in the interests of commerce. What is far from being disguised, despite Sadleir's bibliomaniacal excitement, is the fact that the otherwise forgettable novels published in this series have acquired interest only because of their part in a publishing experiment. Neither the Rev. Gleis's *Country Curate* nor Mr. Banim's *Smuggler* has been remembered for its text — and Dickens would have known this when he later refused to allow *Oliver Twist* and *Barnaby Rudge* to appear in the series: "By the time the publishers' determination to provide special features had faded, the series had become frankly a cheap-edition series of their own best-sellers" (Sadleir, *XIX Century Fiction* II, 95). Sadleir notes that another fiction reprint series begun at the same time, *Roscoe's Novelist's Library* (May 1831—33), is traditionally more sought after by collectors, not because it published the eighteenth-century authors, but because it soon acquired Cruikshank to provide three plates per volume.
18 See Samuel Taylor Coleridge, *Biographia Literaria*, eds. James Engell and Walter Jackson Bate (Princeton: Princeton University Press, 1983): "For as to the devotees of the circulating libraries, I dare not compliment

their *pass-time*, or rather *kill-time*, with the name of *reading*. Call it rather a sort of beggarly daydreaming" (VII, 48n).

19 Charles Cavendish Fulke Greville, *The Greville Memoirs*, ed. R. Fulford (New York: Macmillan, 1963) 63.

20 Greville, *Memoirs* 64 (7 Mar. 1831).

21 G. Kitson Clark, *Peel and the Conservative Party: A Study in Party Politics 1832–41* (1929; London: Frank Cass, 1964) 152. A contemporary source, Henry Vizetelly, writes in his *Glances Back Through Seventy Years* (1893) that cholera appeared "when the Reform excitement was at its zenith, causing almost as much alarm as though the city was about to be decimated by a second plague. Howling mobs paraded the streets, and conflicts with the police were incessant. I remember the gates of Temple Bar being repeatedly shut to keep Westminster and Covent-garden roughs from joining forces with the noisy rabble swarming in Fleet-street" (I, 80).

The excitement in the city came after a rash of rick-burnings in the countryside during 1830–31. It was noted that the Duke of Wellington caused iron shutters to be put up at his London residence.

22 Thomas Carlyle, *The Collected Letters of Thomas and Jane Welsh Carlyle, Duke-Edinburgh Edition*, eds. C. R. Sanders, K. J. Fielding (Durham: Duke University Press, 1977) VI, 74. To Alexander Carlyle, 21 Dec. 1831. Hereafter cited in parentheses.

23 Mary Shelley, *The Letters of Mary W. Shelley*, ed. Betty T. Bennett (Baltimore: Johns Hopkins Press, 1983) II, 160; to John Murray, 4 May 1832.

24 Greville, *Memoirs* 102 (3 Sept. 1833).

25 Marilyn Butler, *Romantics, Rebels and Reactionaries: English Literature and its Background 1760–1830* (Oxford: Oxford University Press, 1981). Bulwer, in *England and the English* (London: Richard Bentley, 1833) asserted, "Wordsworth is German from his singular householdness of feeling" (II, 97) and argued against seeing Germanism as consisting of things Gothic and extravagant.

26 Aspinall, *Politics and the Press*, 380.

27 Allan Cunningham, "Biographical and Critical History of the Last Fifty Years" *Athenaeum* 6 nos. 313, 316, 318, 320, 322, published from 26 October to 28 December 1833. The authors included (in order) are:

Poetry William Cowper, Robert Burns, George Crabbe, Samuel Rogers, Walter Scott, William Wordsworth, Robert Southey, James Montgomery, James Grahame, James Hogg, Samuel Taylor Coleridge, John Leyden, Charles Lamb, Thomas Campbell, Thomas Moore, John Wilson, Henry Kirke White, Robert Bloomfield, Lord Byron, Percy Bysshe Shelley, John Keats, William Lisle Bowles, William Sotheby, William Cary, Walter Savage Landor, Henry Hart Milman, William Tennant, Leigh Hunt, Bryan Waller Procter, Thomas Hood, William Motherwell, Alexander Alaric Watts, Thomas Pringle, William Kennedy, Robert Montgomery, Alfred Tennyson, Ebenezer Elliot, George Darley, George Croly,

John Clare, David Moir, John Malcolm, Joanna Baillie, Felicia Hemans, Letitia Elizabeth Landon, Mary Howitt.

Novels and romances   Anne Radcliffe, Monk Lewis, William Godwin, Madame D'Arblay, Elizabeth Hamilton, Henry Mackenzie, Susan Ferrier, Maria Edgeworth, Jane Porter, Anna Maria Porter, Walter Scott, R. C. Maturin, Lady Morgan, Hannah More, Elizabeth Inchbald, Jane Austen, Mary Russell Mitford, Theodore Hook, James Hogg, Thomas Hope, William Beckford, John Galt, John Wilson, Horace Smith, John Banim, Edward Lytton Bulwer, John Gibson Lockhart, Benjamin Disraeli, G. P. R. James, George Croly, Mrs. S. C. Hall, Robert Plumer Ward, Lord Mulgrave, Thomas Henry Lister, Catherine Gore, James Fraser, Thomas Grattan, James Morier, Leitch Ritchie, Gerald Griffin, Thomas Gaspey, Thomas Crofton Croker, Captain Marryat, Captain Glascock, Captain Chamier, Basil Hall.

History   John Lingard, Robert Southey, George Chalmers, Sharon Turner, James Mackintosh, Walter Scott, William Roscoe, John Malcolm, Henry Hallam, Isaac D'Israeli.

Biography   James Currie, William Hayley, William Gifford, William Godwin, Malcolm Laing, Walter Scott, Robert Southey, John Gibson Lockhart, Patrick Fraser Tytler, Leigh Hunt, John Galt, Thomas Moore.

Drama   Richard Brinsley Sheridan, Joanna Baillie, Walter Scott, Samuel Taylor Coleridge, Lord Byron, R. C. Maturin, Henry Hart Milman, Bryan Waller Procter, George Croly, Mary Russell Mitford, Richard Shiel, James Sheridan Knowles.

Criticism   Francis Jeffrey, William Gifford, Henry Brougham, Sydney Smith, James Mackintosh, William Hazlitt, Thomas Babington Macaulay, John Wilson Croker, Walter Scott, Robert Southey, John Gibson Lockhart, John Wilson, Edward Lytton Bulwer, Anna Jameson.

From my own reading in the press of the time, this appears to be representative of the names that recur. The purpose in printing it here is to give quickly some notion of how contemporary letters appeared *at the time* and how much is left out from our own anthologies. The other point to notice is the domination of Scott, who appears everywhere.

28 Bulwer, *England and the English* II, 52−53.
29 *Ibid*. II, 61.
30 *Ibid*. II, 61.
31 *Ibid*. II, 62. See Isobel Armstrong, *Victorian Scrutinies: Reviews of Poetry 1830−1870* (London: Athlone Press, 1972) on the notion of sympathy in Victorian literary criticism and the "refusal" of such criticism "to regard the poem as a self-contained, sealed-off entity on which moral and social questions external to it do not impinge" (4). Bulwer's criticism demonstrates a tendency to consider the poet in his social and political context that only grew stronger as the decade progressed. Armstrong points out that early criticism of Tennyson is harsh on this score;

it grew kinder as he was perceived to demonstrate more "sympathy" and less "drapery" (23—27).

32 Bulwer, *England and the English* II, 62.
33 *Ibid.* II, 69.
34 *Ibid.* II, 97.
35 *Ibid.* II, 100.
36 *Ibid.* II, 105—06.
37 *Ibid.* II, 106—07.
38 *Ibid.* II, 107—08.
39 Alison Adburgham, *Silver Fork Society: Fashionable Life and Literature from 1814 to 1840* (London: Constable, 1983) 2.
40 Adburgham, *Silver Fork Society* 218.
41 Bulwer, *England and the English* II, 141.
42 William Jerdan (1782—1869), editor of the *Literary Gazette*, writes in his *Autobiography* that many editors of provincial newspapers lived in London (with sub-editors living in the towns themselves) because the main concern was to get the London political news. For him, as for many other literary men, this was an extra source of income (I, 110).

3 1833—1836 The sketch writer

1 There is a falling-off in interest from the genuine political idealism of the first part of the 1830s. The Whig Parliament produced by the Reformed electorate soon became an object of derision: "It would be unprofitable to enter in detail into the history of Melbourne's mediocre Government between the years 1835 and 1841" (Derek Hudson, *Thomas Barnes of "The Times"* [Cambridge: Cambridge University Press, 1943] 106). There were some important measures passed — the Factory Act, abolition of slavery, and the first education grant — but Barnes's dislike of the new poor law's workhouses was typical of public opinion and so was his break with Brougham, who had introduced the measure. *The Times* allied itself with Peel's Conservatives during their brief government in 1834 and continued in that alignment even after the Whigs came back in for six more years. However, the most characteristic attitude of the decade was widespread disdain for party politics. It has been remarked of Bulwer that "Like so many thoughtful politicians immediately after 1832, he appears to consider parties a thing of the past" (Standish Meacham, Introduction to *England and the English* [Chicago: University of Chicago Press, 1970] xxii). Norman Gash in *Reaction and Reconstruction in English Politics 1832—52* quotes both a remark by Sir John Walsh that " 'No period of our history from the Revolution of 1688 ... was so remarkably distinguished by the absence of party spirit as the reign of George IV' " (118), and a statement by *The Extraordinary Black Book* (1832) that " 'Upon the whole, both Whiggism and Toryism may be considered defunct superstitions' " (229). Gash sees the lack of clear-cut party divisions as not so much the advent of reform as a continuation of the wartime

Coalition mentality, and remarks that "the Duke's essentially coalition Government of 1828 was merely replaced by Grey's coalition Government of 1830" (120). Peel said in a speech of 7 February 1833 that he "'doubted whether the old system of party tactics were applicable to the present state of things'" (*Speeches* II, 612; quoted by Gash, 122n). It is obvious that Peel could credibly have brought forward many of the Reform measures of the 1830s for which the Whigs gained credit.

2 An account of Holland is given by W. J. Carlton in "'Captain Holland' Identified" *Dickensian* 57 no. 334 May 1961: 69—77. The *Monthly*, founded in 1796 by Richard Phillips, the bookseller and publisher of Mary Wollstonecraft, is remembered mainly for its liberalism. During the first thirty years of its existence, the magazine included the encyclopedic array of features routinely offered by monthlies at that time: politics on the Continent, stock trading, obituaries, bankruptcies, book notices, diseases in London, and meteorological summaries. The only customary feature of eighteenth-century magazine literature it declined to offer its readers was poetry. See Geoffrey Carnall, "*The Monthly Magazine*" *Review of English Studies* NS 5 (1954): 158—64, and Kenneth Curry in *British Literary Magazines: The Romantic Age 1788—1836*, ed. A. Sullivan (Westport: Greenwood Press, 1983) 316. After Phillips sold it in 1824, it went in for Toryism, until Holland bought it up in 1833; it then abruptly embraced Radicalism.

In the novel *Godfrey Malvern*, the hero meets the editor of the *Monthly* and says of this magazine which is to give him, like Dickens, his start in literary life, that it is "a work which has so often changed hands, that neither its late respectable proprietors, nor its present talented editor, need fear our mentioning it" (I, 96—97). He also notes that its sales in the 1830s were low and the magazine made only enough to keep the editor. It relied upon the eagerness of new writers to do without payment in order to be published. The editor gives Malvern a book of poems and some plays to review but tells him that the most he could hope to make by writing for the *Monthly* would be ten pounds a month. By December 1833, the month when Dickens's course intersects with the *Monthly*'s, *Bell's New Weekly Messenger* is saying, "The 'Monthly' changes owners as often as a caravanserai changes inmates" (2 8 Dec. 1833: 98). In March 1835, the *United Services Gazette* noted that the editor apologized for the continual changes of cover but found these only slightly less absurd than the inconsistencies of its politics (no. 109 7 Mar. 1835).

3 Robert Mayo, *The English Novel in the Magazines 1740—1815* (Evanston: Northwestern University Press, 1962) 306. A contemporary humorist, John Poole, satirizes the "old-fashioned Magazines" and their amateur contributors: "Together with the charade, the tale interminably 'continued,' the song '*set* by an eminent hand,' the never-failing view of a country church, so scratchy and wiry that it sets one's teeth on edge to look at it; its arithmetical puzzles, queries from ignorant correspondents, and new patterns for ruffles; each succeeding month inflicted

a contribution, by some Constant Reader, or Sincere Admirer, of 'a Biographical Sketch of the late Rev. —,' or 'A life of the late *ingenious* Mr. —' (a favourite epithet in those days;) persons whose very existence was till then a profound secret to all that unfortunate portion of the world not immediately within hearing of those celebrated persons' parish bells" (*Sketches and Recollections* [1835] 152–53).

4 Grant, in his *Great Metropolis* (1836), tells us that Tavistock Street was a street where the nobility went to shop at the turn of the century (I, 14).

5 See Louis James, *Fiction for the Working Man 1830–50* (1963; Harmondsworth: Penguin, 1973) for a description of Renton Nicholson's *The Town* (26).

6 See Duane de Vries, *Dickens' Apprentice Years* (Brighton: Harvester Press, 1976) 22–23.

4 1836–1837 The qualifications of a novelist: *Pickwick Papers* and *Oliver Twist*

1 James Grant says that the *Sun* reviews were written by a journalist named William Deacon (*DNB* 1777–1845), who reviewed for the *Sun* from the early 1830s until his death. Grant comments, "One prominent feature in 'The Sun' is the space it devotes to literature ... They [the notices] often display as intimate an acquaintance with the work reviewed, as if the notices appeared in a quarterly instead of in a daily publication" (*The Great Metropolis* [London: Saunders & Otley, 1836] II, 98). A "W. Deacon" appears in the contributors' lists for early issues of *Bentley's Miscellany*.

2 One notes that *Pickwick*'s contemporary readers were confused on this point. In the fifteenth part, there is a "Notice to Correspondents" (30 June 1837): "We receive every month an immense number of communications, purporting to be 'suggestions' for the Pickwick Papers. We have no doubt that they are forwarded with the kindest intentions; but as it is wholly out of our power to make use of any such hints, and as we really have no time to peruse anonymous letters, we hope the writers will henceforth spare themselves a great deal of unnecessary and useless trouble" (*Pickwick Papers*, ed. J. Kinsley [Oxford: Clarendon Press, 1986] Appendix A, 882). It seems that some readers enthusiastically mistook *Pickwick* for one of those old-fashioned monthly magazines satirized by the *Metropolitan* and John Poole, in which "The Editor's Letter-Box" was a standard feature encouraging amateur contributions.

3 Michael Sadleir, *The Evolution of Publishers' Binding Styles 1770–1900* (London: Constable, 1930) 37.

4 Michael Sadleir, "Aspects of the Victorian Novel" *Publishing History* 5 (1979): 19.

5 *Ibid.*

6 Vizetelly, *Glances Back through Seventy Years*, 2 vols. (London: Kegan Paul, Trench, Trübner & Co. Ltd., 1893) I, 88.

7 *The Author's Printing and Publishing Assistant* (London: Saunders & Otley, 1839) 50.
8 Michael Sadleir, *XIX Century Fiction* (London: Constable, 1951) I, 104.
9 Sadleir, "Aspects of the Victorian Novel" 30. He is quoting from John Carter, *Publisher's Cloth 1820–1900* (New York: R. R. Bowker, 1935) 38.
10 *Author's Printing and Publishing Assistant* 50.
11 G. K. Chesterton, *Charles Dickens* (London: Methuen, 1906) 81.
12 Edward Samuel Morgan, "Brief Retrospect" (1873) in *Publishers' Archives: Richard Bentley & Son 1829–98* (Cambridge: Chadwyck-Healey, 1976).
13 *Ibid.*
14 Kathleen Tillotson, Introduction, *Oliver Twist* (Oxford: Clarendon Press, 1966) xx.
15 See Charles E. Lauterbach and Edward S. Lauterbach, "The Nineteenth Century Three-Volume Novel" *The Papers of the Bibliographical Society of America* 51 (1957): 263–302. Their calculations, from the book text, put the novel's word-count at 160,000; they set this in the context of the average length of the three-volume novel and find *Oliver* coming up short. Dickens still owed Bentley 16,920 words.
16 Tillotson, *Oliver Twist* xxxv.

5 1837–1838 The editor of *Bentley's Miscellany*

1 Royal A. Gettmann, *A Victorian Publisher: A Study of the Bentley Papers* (Cambridge: Cambridge University Press, 1960) 32.
2 Margaret Oliphant, *Annals of a Publishing House: William Blackwood and his Sons* (Edinburgh: Blackwood, 1897) II, 104.
3 Edward Samuel Morgan, "Brief Retrospect" (1873) in *Publishers' Archives: Richard Bentley & Son 1829–98* (Cambridge: Chadwyck-Healey, 1976).
4 Miriam Thrall, *Rebellious "Fraser's"* (New York: Columbia University Press, 1934) 16. Carlyle said of *Blackwood's* and *Fraser's*: "both these are furnished as it were with a kind of theatrical costume, with orchestra and stage-lights" (VII, 71; to John Stuart Mill, 20 Jan. 1834). At this time he preferred *Fraser's* to almost any other magazine, despite his remarks about its poisonous qualities.
5 Gordon N. Ray, *The Uses of Adversity 1811–46* (London: Oxford University Press, 1955) 220.
6 *Ibid.* 222.
7 *Ibid.* 224.
8 The exact reason for Maginn's virulence on this occasion remains obscured by rumours about Letitia E. Landon and Berkeley (Thrall, *Rebellious "Fraser's"* 216–22). Thrall says that the review was written in haste rather than premeditation and was not as slanderous as might seem because the facts about the Berkeley family were public knowledge.

9 See Ray, *Uses of Adversity* 286–87, for Thackeray's description of Dickens's clothes and his opinion that Dickens was definitely not a gentleman.

10 *Conservative* in its modern political sense is thought to have been used first by J. Wilson Croker in the *Quarterly Review* (42 no. 83 Jan. 1830: 276), although the *Wellesley Index* says that the writer of this article is more likely John Fullarton or John Miller. The *OED* gives the following examples (corrected here):

> 1832:   O'Connell, *Parl. Debates* 3s 13: "the fashionable term, the new-fangled phrase now used in polite society to designate the Tory ascendency" (col. 150, 25 May 1832).
>
> 1832:   Macaulay, "Mirabeau" (July 1832) in *Miscellaneous Writings* (1860) II, 78: "he would have died, to use the new cant word, a decided 'Conservative'" (describing political sensibilities of Etienne Dumont, author of book on Mirabeau being reviewed).
>
> 1834:   Marq. Londonderry, in Duke of Buckingham, *Mem. Will. IV & Vict.* (1861) II, 141: "this section of the Reformers coalescing with the Duke's former Government and the ultra Tories, uniting all under the name of Conservatives" (letter to Duke of Buckingham, 18 Nov. 1834).
>
> 1844:   Disraeli, *Coningsby* (1844) I, 220: "'A sound Conservative government,' said Taper musingly. 'I understand: Tory men and Whig measures.'"

11 G. K. Chesterton, *Appreciations and Criticisms of the Works of Charles Dickens* (New York: Dent, 1911) 41. Chesterton contrasts this tendency on Dickens's part to the practice of Shakespeare of "putting comic episodes into a tragedy" (41).

12 See K. J. Fielding's discussion of this in "Charles Whitehead and Charles Dickens" *Review of English Studies* NS 3 no. 10 (1952): 141–54.

13 In 1830 Colburn and Bentley published *Random Records* by George Colman the Younger; *Maxwell* and many other of Hook's novels were published by Bentley in the 1830s.

14 A less successful professional Irishman was Joseph Augustine Wade (1796/1801?–45), called "Augustus Wade" in Bentley's advertisement, a composer, violinist, surgeon, and journalist, who came to London in the 1830s, conducted opera, worked with John Braham and Mark Lemon, but died improvident. He wrote the "Song of the Month" for May and June 1837 and provided innumerable lyrics throughout the *Miscellany*.

15 Dickens perhaps called on Jerrold, but nothing by him seems to have appeared in the *Miscellany* (see *Letters* I, 192–93). No paper by Carleton has been found, nor is there any mention of him in the *Letters*.

16 In his introduction to the novel *Rattlin the Reefer*, Arthur Howse notes the resemblances of *Oliver Twist* to Howard's book, particularly in the portrayal of the hero's childhood and the death of the villain (*Rattlin the Reefer* [London: Oxford University Press, 1971] xi–xiii).

17 S. M. Ellis, *William Harrison Ainsworth and his Friends* (London: John Lane, The Bodley Head, 1911) I, 387n.
18 *Ibid.* I, 161.
19 *Ibid.* I, 383.
20 G. K. Chesterton, *Charles Dickens* (London: Methuen, 1906) 81.

6 1838 The writer of parts

1 See *The Journal of Sir Walter Scott*, ed. W. E. K. Anderson (Oxford: Clarendon Press, 1972) 145; 16 May 1826. The publication of these extracts from Scott's diary in Lockhart's *Life* seems to have touched other people besides Dickens. At the same time as Dickens was resolving to follow Scott's example, Charles Cavendish Fulke Greville writes in his famous *Memoirs*, "*Burghley, January 2nd 1838* – Among other changes of habit, it has occurred to me why should not I begin in the New Year by keeping a regular diary? ... It seems exceedingly ridiculous to say that one strong stimulus proceeds from reading Scott's Diary – which he began very late in life and in consequence of reading Byron's ..." (137–38).
2 Dickens's contributions to the *Examiner* at this time include a review of Thomas Serle's melodrama *Joan of Arc*, Michael Balfe's opera *Joan of Arc*, Joseph Stirling Coyne's melodrama *Valsha*, a ballet *Daughter of the Danube*, and Thomas John Dibdin's opera *The Cabinet* (no. 1557 3 Dec. 1837: 773–74); more comments on Balfe's *Joan of Arc*, and a review of Frederic Lawrance's drama *Pierre Bertrand* (no. 1559 17 Dec. 1837: 805); reviews of the translation by Theodore Hook of Alexander Dumas's *Pascal Bruno* and Nimrod's (Charles James Apperley's) collection of sporting sketches (no. 1565 28 Jan. 1838: 51–52); and the review of William Macready's production of *Lear* (no. 1566 4 Feb. 1838: 69–70).
3 See the *Literary Gazette* 22 no. 1107 7 Apr. 1838: 214.
4 Chesterton, *Appreciations and Criticisms of the Works of Charles Dickens* (New York: Dent, 1911) 30–31. However, Chesterton argues that *Nickleby* represents the first book in which Dickens is not writing simply more sketches. This seems to anticipate a change in Dickens's writing that I would date, instead, from *Dombey and Son*, and some readers would not acknowledge ever took place at all. Certainly, contemporary response in this case does not suggest that Dickens had achieved it in *Nickleby* but quite the reverse. Chesterton in any case contradicts himself. In *Charles Dickens* (London: Methuen, 1906), he had already said: "Dickens's work is not to be reckoned in novels at all. Dickens's work is to be reckoned always by characters, sometimes by groups, oftener by episodes, but never by novels. You cannot discuss whether 'Nicholas Nickleby' is a good novel, or whether 'Our Mutual Friend' is a bad novel. Strictly, there is no such novel as 'Nicholas Nickleby'" (80–81).
5 John Gibson Lockhart, *Memoirs of the Life of Sir Walter Scott, Bart.* (Edinburgh: Robert Cadell, 1837–38) VII, 203. The sequence of

196

publication of the *Life* was: Volume One published 18 March 1837; Two, 1 May 1837; Three, 1 June 1837; Four, 1 July 1837; Five, 2 October 1837; Six, 30 December 1837; Seven, 30 March 1838.

7 1839–1840 The "Man of Feeling": *Nicholas Nickleby* and *Master Humphrey's Clock*

1 The *Atlas*, in a retrospective of the literature of 1838, noted that the number of books had remained steady while that of periodicals had increased. It singled out Dickens by saying that "The unprecedented success of Mr. DICKENS'S tales has encouraged other writers to venture upon the same track of close sketching and humourous delineation," but also remarked that "The department of FICTION has not been so assiduously catered for as it used to be some five or six years ago." In saying this, the *Atlas* distinguished Dickens's work from that of James Morier, D'Israeli (presumably Benjamin), Banim (probably John, rather than Michael), Mrs. Gore, and Bulwer. The other proof of a decline in the taste for fiction in its standard form (which was not Dickens) of the 1820s and 1830s was that Bentley, who had one of the fullest lists, is said to have reduced the prices of all his new novels by 20 percent. Meanwhile, the state of poetry remained indifferent, there was a revival in Shakespeare, and a positive boom in both reprints and travel books. The state of publishing, one would conclude, was not healthy (*Atlas* 14 no. 660 5 Jan. 1839: 9).

2 In fact, Dickens's unselfconscious confounding of life and art comes to seem even mild in the context of his rivals' activities. The same Mrs. Trollope who had written about America and slavery for her readers turned her attention to factory slavery in the Midlands, and the manner in which her publisher, Colburn, packaged her is striking. Colburn advertised *The Life and Adventures of Michael Armstrong, the Factory Boy* as a publication in twenty shilling numbers "printed and embellished uniformly with the 'Pickwick Papers', 'Nicholas Nickleby', &c" (see, for example, the *Examiner* of 3 Feb. 1839). The reviewers noted, without much surprise, what Colburn was doing.

3 A letter to George Cattermole at this time lists Dickens's reading while at Petersham: Leigh Hunt's *Indicator* (a weekly published Oct. 1819–Mar. 1821) and *Companion* (weekly, Jan.–July 1828), *Hood's Own*, *A Legend of Montrose* and *Kenilworth*, and "Goldsmith, Swift, Fielding, Smollett, and the British Essayists" (*Letters* I, 576; [21 Aug. 1839]).

4 Louis Cazamian remarks that Dickens was innovative in being the first to depict the urban lower-middle classes in novels: "No novel had deliberately focused its attention below the line dividing opulent living, ample leisure, and cultivated manners from the steady pursuit of wages and a means of living." Although Wordsworth may have done something of the sort in poetry, "It seemed impossible for a novel to have a hero who was not a gentleman unless it dealt with the fantastic figures

of the Newgate school, like *Paul Clifford*,'' in *The Social Novel in England 1830–1850* (1903; London: Routledge & Kegan Paul, 1973) 156.

5 Henry Mackenzie, *The Man of Feeling* (London: T. Cadell, 1771) 175, 171.

6 *Ibid.* vii.

7 Samuel Johnson, *The Idler and the Adventurer*, eds. W. J. Bate, John M. Bullitt, L. F. Powell, *The Yale Edition of the Works of Samuel Johnson* (New Haven: Yale University Press, 1963) II, 4.

8 We have already seen the resemblances between the *Nickleby* preface and the *Crayon Papers* of 1839. *The Sketch Book of Geoffrey Crayon* (1819–20), which was reprinted a number of times in England from 1821, begins with ''The Author's Account of Himself,'' where Crayon speaks of his ''rambling propensity,'' and the motto on the title-page reminds us that he (like Master Humphrey) is a bachelor: '' 'I have no wife nor children good or bad, to provide for. A mere spectator of other men's fortunes and adventures, and how they play their parts; which, methinks are diversely presented unto me, as from a common theatre or scene.' BURTON.'' The musing sentimentality of Irving here seems very close to the spirit of *Master Humphrey's Clock*.

8 1839–1841 The historical novelist: *Jack Sheppard* and *Barnaby Rudge*

1 Henry Fielding, *The Life of Mr. Jonathan Wild the Great* in *Miscellanies* (London: A. Millar, 1743) III, 4–5. See also, Fielding's preface in the first volume of the *Miscellanies* (3 v).

2 Fielding, *Life of Jonathan Wild* III, 4.

3 Keith Hollingsworth, *The Newgate Novel 1830–47* (Detroit: Wayne State University Press, 1963) 229.

4 Dickens is mentioned in the *Athenaeum*'s review, in passing, as an example of an author who does treat vice correctly: ''If Boz has depicted scenes of hardened vice, and displayed the peculiar phasis of degradation which poverty impresses on the human character under the combinations of a defective civilization, he is guided in his career by a high moral object ...'' (no. 626 26 Oct. 1839: 803).

5 Thomas Carlyle, at a public lecture on 22 May 1840. Printed in *Heroes and Hero-Worship* (1841), *The Works of Thomas Carlyle: Centenary Edition* (London: Chapman & Hall, 1897) V, 202.

6 Recounted in Frederic G. Kitton, *Charles Dickens by Pen and Pencil* (London: Frank T. Sabin, John F. Dexter, 1890) 142.

7 Letter to *Daily News*, 28 Feb. 1846; reprinted in Philip Collins, *Dickens and Crime* (London: Macmillan, 1962) 226.

8 Letter to *Daily News*, 28 Feb. 1846; Collins, *Dickens and Crime* 226.

9 *Ibid.* 244.

10 The page references in this paragraph are to Kathleen Tillotson's Introduction, *Oliver Twist* (Oxford: Clarendon Press).

11 See Lennard Davis, *Factual Fictions* (New York: Columbia University Press, 1983) ch. 10, on criminality.

Conclusion

1 See Thomas Carlyle, *The Collected Letters of Thomas and Jane Welsh Carlyle, Duke-Edinburgh Edition*, eds. C. R. Sanders and K. J. Fielding (Durham: Duke University Press, 1977) V, 272; to John A. Carlyle, 8 May 1831. See also V, 284; to John A. Carlyle, 6 June 1831.
2 Carlyle, *Collected Letters* VI, 395; to James Fraser, 27 May 1833.
3 René Wellek, "What is Literature" in *What is Literature?*, ed. Paul Hernadi (Bloomington: Indiana University Press, 1978) 16–17.
4 *Ibid.* 19.
5 *Ibid.* 21.
6 W. W. Robson, *The Definition of Literature* (Cambridge: Cambridge University Press, 1982) 10.
7 *Ibid.* 12, 13.
8 *Ibid.* 37.
9 Carlyle, *Collected Letters* XII, 348; to John Sterling, 7 Dec. 1840.

Further reading

Eighteenth and nineteenth century

Andrews, Alexander. *The History of British Journalism*. London: Bentley, 1859. 2 vols.

Babbage, Charles. *On the Economy of Machinery and Manufactures*. London: Charles Knight, 1832.

Bentley, Richard. *List of Principal Publications Issued from New Burlington Street 1829–98*. London: Richard Bentley and Son, 1893–1920.

Bourne, H. R. Fox. *English Newspapers*. London: Chatto & Windus, 1887. 2 vols.

[Collier, John Payne.] *An Old Man's Diary, Forty Years Ago*. London: Thomas Richards, 1871–72. 4 vols.

Croal, David. *Early Recollections of a Journalist 1832–59*. Edinburgh: Andrew Elliot, 1898.

Cross, Wilbur L. *The Development of the English Novel*. New York: Macmillan, 1899.

Espinasse, Francis. *Literary Recollections and Sketches*. London: Hodder & Stoughton, 1893.

Forster, John. *The Life and Times of Oliver Goldsmith*. London: Bradbury & Evans, 1848. 2 vols.

Francis, John, comp. *John Francis, Publisher of the Athenaeum*. London: Bentley, 1888. 2 vols.

Froude, James Anthony. *Thomas Carlyle: A History of his Life in London 1834–81*. London: Longmans, Green, 1884. 2 vols.

[Grant, James.] *Random Recollections of the House of Commons 1830–35*. London: Smith, Elder, 1836.

   Random Recollections of the House of Lords 1830–36. London: Smith, Elder, 1836.

Hall, S. C. *A Book of Memories of Great Men and Women of the Age*. London: Virtue, 1871.

   Retrospect of a Long Life 1815–83. London: Richard Bentley & Son, 1883. 2 vols.

Horne, R. H. *Exposition of the False Medium and Barriers Excluding Men of Genius from the Public*. London: Effingham Wilson, 1833.

   A New Spirit of the Age. London: Smith, Elder, 1844. 2 vols.

Hunt, F. Knight. *The Fourth Estate*. London: David Bogue, 1850. 2 vols.

Further reading

Knight, Charles. *The Old Printer and the Modern Press*. London: John Murray, 1854.

Lackington, James. *Memoirs of the Forty-Five First Years of the Life of James Lackington, Bookseller*. London: Hunt & Clarke, 1827.

The London Catalogue of Books 1814–1839. London: Robert Bent, 1839.

The London Catalogue of Books 1814–1846. London: Thomas Hodgson, 1846.

The London Catalogue of Books: Supplement January 1839–January 1844. London: Thomas Hodgson, 1844.

Montgomery, James. *Lectures on Poetry and General Literature*. London: Longman, Rees, Orme, Brown, Green & Longman, 1833.

Porter, G. R. *The Progress of the Nation*. London: Charles Knight, 1836. 3 vols.

Redding, Cyrus. *Fifty Years' Recollections, Literary and Personal*. 2nd ed. London: Charles J. Skeet, 1858. 3 vols.

Rees, Thomas. *Reminiscences of Literary London from 1779 to 1853*. London: Suckling and Galloway, 1896.

Thomson, H. Byerley. *The Choice of a Profession*. London: Chapman & Hall, 1857.

Timperley, C. H. *A Dictionary of Printers and Printing, with the Progress of Literature, Ancient and Modern*. London: H. Johnson, 1839.

Encyclopedia of Literary and Typographical Anecdote. London: H. Bohn, 1842.

Webster, Benjamin, ed. *The Acting National Drama*. London: Chapman & Hall, 1837–47. 13 vols.

Wight, John. *More Mornings at Bow Street*. London: James Robins, 1827.

Twentieth century

Altick, Richard. *The English Common Reader*. Chicago: Univ. of Chicago Press, 1957.

Armstrong, Isobel. *Victorian Scrutinies: Reviews of Poetry 1830–1870*. London: Athlone, 1972.

Barnes, James J. *Free Trade in Books: A Study of the London Book Trade Since 1800*. Oxford: Clarendon Press, 1964.

Bennett, Scott. "John Murray's Family Library and the Cheapening of Books in Early Nineteenth Century Britain" *Studies in Bibliography* 29 (1976): 139–66.

Blakey, Dorothy. *The Minerva Press 1790–1820*. London: Bibliographical Society, 1939.

Brice, Alex W. "Reviewers of Dickens in the Examiner: Fonblanque, Forster, Hunt, and Morley" *Dickens Studies Newsletter* 3 Sept. 1972: 68–80.

Colby, Robert. *Fiction with a Purpose*. Bloomington: Indiana Univ. Press, 1967.

Further reading

Collins, A. S. *The Profession of Letters: A Study of the Relation of Author to Patron, Publisher, and Public, 1780–1832*. London: George Routledge & Sons, 1928.

Collins, Philip. "Dickens and the *Edinburgh Review*" *Review of English Studies* NS 14 no. 54 (1963): 167–72.

    Dickens: The Critical Heritage. New York: Barnes & Noble, 1971.

    "Significance of Dickens's Periodicals" *Review of English Literature* 2 July 1961: 55–64.

Cox, R. G. "The Great Reviews" *Scrutiny* 6 no. 1 June 1937: 2–20; 6 no. 2 Sept. 1937: 155–75.

    "The Reviews and Magazines" in *The Pelican Guide to English Literature: From Dickens to Hardy*, ed. Boris Ford. Harmondsworth: Penguin, 1958: 188–204.

Darton, R. J. Harvey. *Dickens: Positively the First Appearance*. London: Argonaut Press, 1933.

Davis, Lennard J. *Factual Fictions: The Origins of the English Novel*. New York: Columbia Univ. Press, 1983.

Day, Geoffrey. *From Fiction to the Novel*. London: Routledge & Kegan Paul, 1987.

Dexter, W., and J. W. T. Ley. *The Origin of Pickwick*. London: Chapman & Hall, 1936.

Engel, Elliot, and Margaret F. King. *The Victorian Novel Before Victoria: British Fiction during the Reign of William IV 1830–37*. London: Macmillan, 1984.

    "Pickwick's Progress: The Critical Reception of *The Pickwick Papers* from 1836 to 1986" *Dickens Quarterly* 3 no. 1 Mar. 1986: 56–66.

Ferris, Ina. "Story-Telling and the Subversion of Literary Form in Walter Scott's Fiction" *Genre* 18 Spring 1985: 23–35.

Fielding, K. J., and A. W. Brice. "Forster: Critic of Fiction" *Dickensian* 70 no. 734 Sept. 1974: 159–70.

Ford, G. H. *Dickens and his Readers: Aspects of Novel-Criticism Since 1836*. Princeton: Princeton Univ. Press, 1955.

Gash, Norman. *Aristocracy and People: Britain 1815–65*. London: Edward Arnold, 1979.

Greaves, John. *Dickens at Doughty Street*. London: Elm Tree Books, 1975.

Grubb, G. G. "Dickens and the Daily News: The Origin of the Idea" in *Booker Memorial Studies*, ed. H. Shine. Chapel Hill: University of North Carolina Press, 1966. 60–77.

    "Dickens's First Experience as a Parliamentary Reporter" *Dickensian* 36 no. 256 Autumn 1940: 211–18.

Hill, T. W. "Dickens and his 'Ugly Duckling'" *Dickensian* 46 no. 296 Sept. 1950: 190–96.

Jack, Ian. *English Literature 1815–1832*. Oxford: Clarendon Press, 1963.

Jameson, Frederic. *The Political Unconscious: Narrative as a Socially Symbolic Act*. Ithaca: Cornell Univ. Press, 1981.

Further reading

Kincaid, James R., and Albert J. Kuhn, eds. *Victorian Literature and Society: Essays Presented to Richard D. Altick.* Akron: Ohio State Univ. Press, 1983.

Koss, Stephen. *The Rise and Fall of the Political Press in Britain. Volume I: The Nineteenth Century.* London: Hamish Hamilton, 1981.

Landon, Richard, ed. *Book Selling and Book Buying: Aspects of the Nineteenth-Century British and North American Book Trade.* Chicago: American Library Association, 1978.

Lentricchia, Frank. *Criticism and Social Change.* Chicago: Univ. of Chicago Press, 1984.

Levine, George. *The Emergence of Victorian Consciousness: The Spirit of the Age.* New York: Free Press, 1967.

Ley, J. W. T. *The Dickens Circle: A Narrative of the Novelist's Friendships.* London: Chapman & Hall, 1918.

Lounsbury, Thomas R. *The Life and Times of Tennyson 1809–50.* New Haven: Yale Univ. Press, 1915.

Marchand, Leslie A. *The Athenaeum: A Mirror of Victorian Culture.* 1941; New York: Octagon Books, 1971.

Maxted, Ian. *The London Book Trades 1775–1800.* Surrey: Dawson, 1977.

Millgate, Jane. *Walter Scott.* Edinburgh: Edinburgh Univ. Press, 1984.

Morison, Stanley. *The English Newspaper 1622–1932.* Cambridge: Cambridge Univ. Press, 1932.

Olmsted, John Charles. *A Victorian Art of Fiction: Essays on the Novel in British Periodicals 1830–1850.* New York: Garland, 1979.

Patten, Robert L. *Charles Dickens and his Publishers.* Oxford: Clarendon Press, 1978.

  "The Story-Weaver at His Loom: Dickens and the Beginning of *The Old Curiosity Shop*" in *Dickens the Craftsman: Strategies of Presentation,* ed. Robert L. Partlow, Jr. Carbonsdale & Edwardsville: Southern Illinois Univ. Press, 1970.

Pitcher, Edward S. "The Serial Publication and Collecting of Pamphlets 1790–1815" *The Library* 5th series 30 no. 4 Dec. 1975: 323–29.

Raleigh, John Henry. "What Scott Meant to the Victorians" *Victorian Studies* 7 no. 1 Sept. 1963: 7–34.

Rayner, J. L., and G. T. Crook, eds. *The Complete Newgate Calendar.* London: Navarre Society, 1926. 5 vols.

Sadleir, Michael. *Things Past.* London: Constable, 1944.

Schachterle, Lance. "*Oliver Twist* and its Serial Predecessors" *Dickens Studies Annual* 3 (1973): 1–13.

Shattock, Joanne, and Michael Wolff. *The Victorian Periodical Press: Samplings and Soundings.* Leicester: Leicester Univ. Press, 1982.

Smith, Walter E. *Charles Dickens in the Original Cloth.* Los Angeles: Heritage Book Shop, 1982. 2 vols.

Stange, Richard. *The Theory of the Novel in England 1850–70.* New York: Columbia Univ. Press, 1959.

Further reading

Sutherland, J. A. "Henry Colburn, Publisher" *Publishing History* 19 (1986): 59–84.

"John Macrone: Victorian Publisher" *Dickens Studies Annual* 13 (1984): 243–59.

Thomas, William Beach. *The Story of the Spectator 1828–1928*. London: Methuen, 1928.

Tompkins, Jane P., ed. *Reader-Response Criticism: From Formalism to Post-Structuralism*. Baltimore and London: Johns Hopkins Univ. Press, 1980.

Trevelyan, G. M. *British History in the Nineteenth Century and After*. London: Longmans, 1922; 2nd ed. 1937, rpt. 1945.

The Seven Years of William IV: A Reign Cartooned by John Doyle. London: Avalon Press and William Heinemann, 1952.

Vann, J. Don. "The Early Success of *Pickwick*" *Publishing History* 2 (1977): 51–55.

"*Pickwick* in the London Newspapers" *Dickensian* 70 no. 372 Jan. 1974: 49–52.

Vivian, Charles H. "Dickens, the 'True Sun,' and Samuel Laman Blanchard" *Nineteenth-Century Fiction* 4 no. 4   Mar. 1950: 328–30.

Waugh, Arthur. *A Hundred Years of Publishing*. London: Chapman & Hall, 1930.

Weimann, Robert. *Structure and Society in Literary History: Studies in the History and Theory of Historical Criticism*. 1976; Baltimore and London: Johns Hopkins Univ. Press, 1984.

Williams, Ioan. *Sir Walter Scott on Novelists and Fiction*. London: Routledge & Kegan Paul, 1968.

Woodruff, James F. "The Background and Significance of *The Rambler*'s Format" *Publishing History* 4 (1978): 113–33.

Young, G. M. *Early Victorian England 1830–65*. Oxford: Oxford Univ. Press, 1934.

Index

à Beckett, Gilbert 110
Ainsworth, William Harrison 76, 77, 95, 111–13, 116, 146, 153, 155, 157–62, 165, 196
Athenaeum, The 22–24, 27, 36, 67, 98, 111, 155, 198
Atlas, The 61, 63, 90, 125, 197

Barham, the Reverend Richard Harris 110, 112
Barker, Matthew Henry 107
Bayly, Thomas Haynes 110
Beazley, Samuel 107, 109
Bell's Life in London 16, 63, 64, 83, 117, 176
Bell's New Weekly Messenger 35, 47, 75, 83, 90, 117, 118, 119, 131, 192
Bell's Weekly Messenger 147
Bentley, Richard 28, 39, 68, 70–71, 72–73, 76, 77, 81–87, 91, 92–113, 114, 121–22, 177, 188, 194, 195
Bentley's Miscellany x, 49, 69, 72, 74, 75, 81–113, 116, 121, 122, 130, 132, 133, 134, 135, 142, 152–54, 157
Berkeley, Grantley 99–101
Binding technology 66–70, 188, 193
Blackwood's Magazine 30, 32, 65, 102, 153
Blessington, Countess of 3, 106
Book trade 23–42, 66–70, 92–98, 188, 193
Bulwer, Edward Lytton 19, 36–40, 164–65, 181, 184, 187, 190, 191, 197
Byron, Lord George Gordon 1, 22, 37, 38, 68, 95, 97, 98, 189

Carleton, W. H. 107
Carlton Chronicle 76
Carlyle, Thomas 34, 80, 95, 98, 158, 178–79, 181, 187, 189, 198, 199
Chambers's Edinburgh Journal 26, 29, 32, 77

Chamier, Captain 107, 108
Chapman and Hall 67, 68, 69, 70–71, 72, 78–79, 83, 92, 104, 114, 132, 133, 149
Cheap literature 22, 26–35, 67–70
"Christopher North," *see* Wilson, John
Colburn, Henry 20, 28, 39, 68, 92, 107, 108, 144, 188, 195, 197
Coleridge, Samuel Taylor 5, 188, 189
Conolly, Lieutenant Arthur 107–9
Conservatism 5, 98, 183–84, 191, 195
Constable, Archibald 27, 112
Constitutional, The 74
Courier, The 132, 175
Cruikshank, George 63, 82, 93, 107, 110, 116

Dickens, Charles – Works
(Parenthetical references are to original periodical publication, e.g. "MM" = *Monthly Magazine*)
"Astley's" (EC) 52
Barnaby Rudge (MHC) ix, 54, 76, 82, 84, 111, 121–22, 130, 132, 149, 152, 166–70, 172–76, 178, 180–81, 188
Bell's Life in London 55–57
Bell's Weekly Magazine 57
"Black Veil, The" (SB) 51, 62
"Bloomsbury Christening, The" (MM) 46
"Boarding-House, The" (MM) 46–47, 57
"Brokers' and Marine Store Shops" (MC) 52
"Christmas Festivities" (BLL) 56
David Copperfield 1, 8, 9, 150
"Dinner at Poplar Walk, A" (MM) 10, 43, 45–46, 47, 48
Dombey and Son 12, 101
"Early Coaches" (EC) 53
Evening Chronicle, The 52, 54, 55, 58, 64, 143

205

Index

"Fine Old English Gentleman, The" (*Examiner*) 168
"Gin Shops" (EC) 52
"Horatio Sparkins" (MM) 46, 47
"House, The" (EC) 53
Library of Fiction 58, 62, 104
"London Recreations" (EC) 53, 54
Martin Chuzzlewit 12
Master Humphrey's Clock x, 77, 94, 105, 113, 116, 133, 134, 137, 138, 139–51, 152, 166–70, 172–76, 178, 198
Memoirs of Joseph Grimaldi 67, 104, 111, 114, 116
"Miss Evans and 'the Eagle' " (BLL) 55
"Mrs. Joseph Porter, 'over the way' " (MM) 46, 47
"New Year, The" (BLL) 56
Nicholas Nickleby x, 12, 63, 83, 101, 114, 118–20, 122–23, 124, 126, 131–32, 134–39, 143, 152, 153, 154, 175, 176, 181, 196, 197, 198
"Old Bailey, The" (MC) 50–51
Old Curiosity Shop, The (MHC) 148–49, 150–51, 152
Oliver Twist (BM) x, 18, 69, 74–79, 84–90, 92, 100, 103, 105, 110, 111, 115, 116, 119–29, 130, 138, 149, 152, 154, 165, 169, 175, 188, 194, 195, 197
"Omnibuses" (MC) 49, 57
"Our Next Door Neighbours" (SB) 62
"Parish, The" (EC) 53–55
"Parlour, The" (BLL) 56
"Pawnbroker's Shop, The" (EC) 55
Pickwick Papers, The x, 9, 48, 49, 58, 59, 60, 61–71, 72, 73, 74, 75–80, 85, 88, 90, 91, 92, 94, 100, 104, 114, 118, 123, 124, 126, 131, 134, 135, 137, 138, 143, 144, 148, 149, 152, 154, 169, 177, 180, 181, 182, 193
Pic Nic Papers, The 107, 108, 176
"Prisoners' Van, The" (BLL) 56
Scenes and Characters (BLL) 48, 55
"Sentiment" (BWM) 57
"Seven Dials" (BLL) 55
"Shabby-Genteel People" (MC) 51
"Shops and their Tenants" (MC) 49–50, 52
Sketches by Boz 9, 43, 58, 59, 61, 63, 65, 68, 72, 75–76, 78–80, 105, 117, 126, 134, 143, 149

Sketches of London (EC) 52
Sketches of Young Couples 143–44
Sketches of Young Gentlemen 115, 143
"Some Account of an Omnibus Cad" (BLL) 56
Strange Gentleman, The 72
Street Sketches (MC) 47, 48, 50, 51, 52
"Streets at Night, The" (BLL) 57
Sunday under Three Heads 74
"Tuggs's at Ramsgate, The" (MM) 62
Village Coquettes, The 72
"Visit to Newgate, A" (SB) 61
"Watkins Tottle" (MM) 53, 57
Wits' Miscellany, see Bentley's Miscellany

Disraeli, Benjamin 18, 40, 187, 190, 195, 197
Dublin University Magazine 106, 128

Edinburgh Review 22, 27, 33, 40, 97, 112, 123, 126
Eighteenth-century periodicals 77, 133, 139–43, 192, 197
Examiner, The 61, 75, 76, 84, 86, 90, 116, 118, 127, 131, 136, 144, 149, 156–57, 159, 168, 196

"Father Prout" (Francis Mahony) 77, 93, 94, 95, 102, 103, 105–6, 107, 109
Fielding, Henry 21, 39, 70, 79, 88, 89, 90, 98, 118–19, 127, 128, 131, 132, 137, 145, 147, 154–55, 159, 165, 197, 198
Forster, John 13, 75–76, 78–87, 108, 111, 127, 131, 132, 133, 137, 149, 156–57, 159, 168
Fraser's Magazine 11–15, 30–31, 39–42, 65, 93–102, 111, 112, 145–47, 159–64, 181, 184, 194

Galt, John 39, 41, 97, 190
Glascock, Captain 107–8
Godfrey Malvern (Thomas Miller) 1, 3–4, 6–7, 183, 192
Grant, James 11, 44, 184, 193

Hall, Samuel Carter 11, 102
Harley, John 106, 110
Hook, Theodore 46, 93, 105, 106, 107, 190, 195, 196

Irving, Washington 133–34, 147

Index

Jack Sheppard (William Harrison Ainsworth) 69, 110, 112, 153–62, 165, 167–68
Jerdan, William 77, 93, 107, 109, 184, 191
Jerrold, Douglas 107, 109, 195
John Bull 63, 96
Jonathan Wild (Henry Fielding) 154–55, 156, 159, 198

Knowles, James Sheridan 110

Lemon, Mark 110–11, 195
Lewes, George Henry 6–8, 184
Literary Gazette 30, 33, 96, 144, 196
Lockhart, John Gibson 18–21, 41, 67, 87, 95, 96, 186, 190, 196–97
London and Westminster Review 80, 81, 90, 91
Lover, Samuel 77, 93, 103, 106, 107

Mackenzie, Henry 134, 138
Macrone, John 59, 61, 68, 76, 77–79, 80, 86, 105, 111, 116, 177
Maginn, William 11, 41, 93–103, 106, 109, 112, 194
Magnet, The 120
Mahony, Francis, *see* "Father Prout"
Marryat, Captain Frederick 69, 83, 108
Maxwell, William Hamilton 107
Metropolitan Magazine, The 30, 44, 69, 83, 108, 193
Miller, Thomas 3–4, 6, 183
Millingen, John Gideon 107
Monthly Magazine ix, 16, 31, 43–47, 48, 49, 50, 53, 57, 58, 65, 93, 112, 143, 158, 192
Monthly Review 128, 130, 148, 149–50, 157–58
Morning Advertiser, The 8–9, 77, 119, 122, 132, 149, 150
Morning Chronicle, The 7, 10, 11, 12, 16–17, 44, 45, 47–51, 52, 53, 57, 58, 59, 61, 62, 64, 65, 72, 83, 86, 93, 143, 144
Morning Herald, The 12, 63, 147
Morning Post, The 77, 116, 131, 135, 150
Murray, John 18, 28, 34, 68, 92, 93, 95, 186

National Library (Colburn and Bentley) 28, 96, 97, 98
New Monthly 31, 36, 65, 70, 93
Newspaper reporting 8–19, 185
Novel, status of 19–23, 32–42, 92, 96

Observer, The 16, 83, 90, 132, 135
Ollier, Charles 93, 106–7

Party politics 43, 94, 97–98, 102–3, 183–84, 186, 191, 195
Peel, Sir Robert 5, 16, 34, 96, 183–84, 185, 191
Penny Magazine 26, 29
Periodical literature (early-nineteenth-century), rise of 24–41
"Pickwick periodicals" 135, 144, 146, 150, 197
Poetry, state of 6, 23
Publishing, *see* Book Trade

Quarterly Review 19–21, 24, 32, 87–90, 95, 96, 126, 195

Ranthorpe (George Henry Lewes) 6–8, 184
Reform movement 23–24, 33–36, 43, 189, 191–92
Reporting, *see* Newspaper reporting
Reprints, trade in 20, 28–30, 92
Reynolds, John Hamilton 107, 109, 111
Ritchie, Leitch (*Library of Romance*) 67, 70

St. James's Chronicle 74, 153
Saturday Magazine 26, 29
Scott, Sir Walter ix, 9, 18–23, 27–33, 37–41, 66, 79, 97, 98, 112, 114, 121, 128–29, 130, 137–38, 146, 152, 165–67, 175–76, 186, 188, 189, 190, 196, 197
Shipping and Mercantile Gazette, The 135
Skinner, Major 107, 108
Smollett, Tobias 21, 70, 197
Society for the Diffusion of Useful Knowledge 21, 26
Spectator, The (Addison) 133, 139–43, 147
Spectator, The 119, 123, 126–27, 147
Standard Novels (Bentley) 28–30, 66–67, 188
Sun, The 47, 61, 64, 65, 77, 79, 81, 84, 90, 119, 122, 132, 135–36, 138, 146, 147, 153, 171, 193
Sunday Times, The 119, 122, 137, 144, 148, 153

Tablet, The 172–73, 176
Tait's Edinburgh Magazine 29–32, 58, 65

Index

Tatler, The 133, 139–42

Tegg, Thomas 92, 93

Thackeray, William Makepeace 1–8, 15, 41–42, 63, 95, 97, 98, 101–2, 106, 110, 159–64, 166, 183, 184, 185, 194, 195

Times, The 12, 36, 64, 95, 191

Toryism 5, 37–38, 94, 96, 98, 170–71, 175, 187, 191, 195

Town, The 50, 137

True Sun, The 9, 76

United Services Gazette, The 74, 131, 132, 135, 153, 192

Weekly Dispatch, The 82–83, 116, 128

Westminster Review 24–26, 32

Whiggism 5, 94, 100, 191

Wilson, John ("Christopher North") 20, 37, 41, 102, 171